ROY AND ZHORES MEDVEDEV

LOYAL DISSENT IN THE SOVIET UNION

MODERN BIOGRAPHIES

Series Editor
Angela Brintlinger (Ohio State University, US)

Editorial Board
Sara Dickinson (University of Genoa, Italy)
Polly Jones (Oxford University, UK)
Steve Norris (Miami University, US)
Ludmilla Trigos (Independent Scholar, US)
Carol Ueland (Drew University, US)

ROY AND ZHORES MEDVEDEV

LOYAL DISSENT IN THE SOVIET UNION

BARBARA MARTIN

BOSTON
2023

Published with the support of the Swiss National Science Foundation

Library of Congress Cataloging-in-Publication Data

Names: Martin, Barbara, 1986- author.
Title: Roy and Zhores Medvedev: loyal dissent in the Soviet Union / Barbara Martin.
Other titles: Loyal dissent in the Soviet Union
Description: Boston: Academic Studies Press, 2023. | Series: Modern biographies | Includes bibliographical references.
Identifiers: LCCN 2023002672 (print) | LCCN 2023002673 (ebook) | ISBN 9798887191812 (hardback) | ISBN 9798887191829 (paperback) | ISBN 9798887191836 (pdf) | ISBN 9798887191843 (epub)
Subjects: LCSH: Medvedev, Zhores A., 1925-2018. | Medvedev, Roy Aleksandrovich, 1925- | Dissenters--Soviet Union--Biography. | Biologists--Soviet Union--Biography. | Soviet Union--History--1925–1953.
Classification: LCC DK275.A1 M377 2023 (print) | LCC DK275.A1 (ebook) | DDC 907.2/047--dc23/eng/20230131
LC record available at https://lccn.loc.gov/2023002672
LC ebook record available at https://lccn.loc.gov/2023002673

Copyright © Academic Studies Press, 2023

ISBN 9798887191812 (hardback)
ISBN 9798887191829 (paperback)
ISBN 9798887191836 (pdf)
ISBN 9798887191843 (epub)

Book design by PHi Business Solutions (P) Ltd.
Cover design by Ivan Grave
On the cover: Mikhail Gorbachev with Roy and Zhores Medvedev. Gorbachev Foundation Archive, TsMAMLS, F. 333, op. 14, d. 39, l. 7.

Published by Academic Studies Press
1577 Beacon Street
Brookline, MA 02446, USA

press@academicstudiespress.com
www.academicstudiespress.com

This book is subject to a Creative Commons Attribution-NonCommercial 4.0 International Public License (CC BY-NC 4.0). To view a copy of this license, visit https://creativecommons.org/licenses/by-nc/4.0/. Other than as provided by these licenses, no part of this book may be reproduced, transmitted, or displayed by any electronic or mechanical means without permission from the publisher or as permitted by law.

Contents

List of Illustrations   vii
List of Abbreviations   ix
Note on Archives   x

Introduction   1

1   A Youth in Stalin's Shadow   5
2   A Crusade in Soviet Biology   16
3   Stalin Is No More   32
4   Making Sense of Stalinism   47
5   Rebellious Intelligentsia   57
6   A Question of Madness   71
7   New Threats   84
8   Into Exile   97
9   Carving a "Third Way" in the Cold War   107
10   Solzhenitsyn: The End of a Friendship   120
11   Finding and Losing Political Allies   128
12   Under the KGB's Watch   144
13   Andropov's Protection   156
14   The Nuclear Threat   168
15   The Rise and Fall of Gorbachev's Socialist Democracy   179
16   The End of the Soviet Order   195
17   Praising the Strong Rulers   208

Conclusion   221
Index   225

List of Illustrations

1	Aleksandr Medvedev, 1936. OKhDLSM, F. 333, op. 16, d. 19, l. 1.	5
2	Iuliia Reiman. Courtesy of Roy Medvedev.	6
3	Roy and Zhores Medvedev in childhood. OKhDLSM, F. 333, op 9, d. 361, l. 1.	7
4	Zhores Medvedev, 1955. Courtesy of Zhores Medvedev.	18
5	Roy Medvedev's Komsomol ID. 1943. OKhDLSM, F. 333, op. 14, d. 10.	34
6	Roy Medvedev, 1956. OKhDLSM, F. 333, op. 3 d. 16, l. 5.	37
7	Roy Medvedev, 1956. Courtesy of Zhores Medvedev.	40
8	Galina Gaidina, 1960s. OKhDLSM, F. 333, op. 3, d. 22, l. 1.	44
9	Zhores Medvedev, 1966. Courtesy of Zhores Medvedev.	71
10	Zhores Medvedev. London, 1973. OKhDLSM, F. 333, op. 14, d. 39, l.1.	102
11	Zhores Medvedev and Margarita Medvedeva, outside their first London home, early 1970s. Courtesy of Dmitry Medvedev.	105
12	Zhores Medvedev and Margarita Medvedeva on vacation in Southern France, 1970s. Courtesy of Dmitry Medvedev.	105
13	Zhores Medvedev with American colleagues, 1974. Courtesy of Zhores Medvedev.	114
14	Roy Medvedev in his office, 1981. Courtesy of Roy Medvedev.	153
15	Group "Elections-1979" in front of a polling station. Photograph by Vladimir Sychev. OKhDLSM, F. 333, op. 3, d. 23, l. 2.	157
16	Roy Medvedev, 1979. Courtesy of Roy Medvedev.	158
17	Roy Medvedev with Walter Cronkite, 1982. OKhDLSM, F. 333, op 14, d. 39. L. 4.	160
18	Zhores Medvedev in Chernobyl, 1990. Courtesy of Zhores Medvedev.	176
19	Zhores Medvedev, 1987. Courtesy of Zhores Medvedev.	180
20	Roundtable with Roy Medvedev at the V.V. Maiakovskii House of the Writer with Daniil Granin and V. Kavtorin, February 19, 1989. Photograph by F. Lur'e. OKhDLSM, F. 333, op. 9, d. 362, l. 1.	183
21	Roy Medvedev with insignia of People's Deputy, 1989. Courtesy of Zhores Medvedev.	186

22	Zhores Medvedev, London, 1987. OKhDLSM, F. 333, op. 14, d. 39, l. 3.	192
23	Roy Medvedev at the Congress of the SWP, December 1991. OKhDLSM, F. 333, op. 14, d. 39, l. 8.	200
24	Roy and Zhores Medvedev at a demonstration under the SWP banner, 1992. OKhDLSM, F. 333, op. 14, d. 39, l. 5.	201
25	Roy and Zhores Medvedev in London, 2004. OKhDLSM, F. 333, Op. 14, d. 39, l. 9.	206
26	Roy Medvedev in his home office, Nemchinovka, 2002. OKhDLSM, F. 333, op. 3, d. 16, l. 1.	218
27	Roy and Zhores Medvedev in front of Marx's grave, London, 2003. OKhDLSM, F. 333, op. 14, d. 39, l. 6.	223

List of Abbreviations

CIA	Central Intelligence Agency (United States foreign intelligence service)
CPRF	Communist Party of the Russian Federation
CPSU	Communist Party of the Soviet Union
FSB	Federal Security Service (successor of the KGB)
GKChP	State Committee on the State of Emergency
GFR	German Federal Republic
IAG	International Association of Gerontology
KGB	Committee of State Security
MCC	Moscow City Committee
MI-5	Military Intelligence, Section 5 (British Security Service)
NKVD	People's Commissariat of Internal Affairs (predecessor of the KGB)
PCC	Party Control Commission
RSFSR	Russian Soviet Federative Socialist Republic
SWP	Socialist Workers' Party
TASS	Telegraph Agency of the Soviet Union (News Agency)
UNESCO	United Nations Educational, Scientific and Cultural Organization
USSR	Union of Soviet Socialist Republics
VASKhNIL	All-Union Academy of Agricultural Sciences
WHO	World Health Organization

Note on Archives

Most archival documents and photographs used in this book come from Roy and Zhores Medvedevs' Personal Papers at the Central State Archive of Moscow (TsGAM): Department of Conservation of Documents from Personal Collections of Moscow (OKhDLSM), Fond 333.

Introduction

When a group of KGB agents showed up on Roy Medvedev's doorstep in October 1971, the Soviet scholar felt his blood freeze in his veins. In August 1938, when Roy and his twin brother Zhores were twelve, they woke up in the middle of the night to find men in uniforms searching their family's apartment. After going through the children's toys and searching their beds, the NKVD men led away their father Aleksandr Medvedev in handcuffs. This was the last time the twins saw their father, who was swallowed by the grinding machine of Stalin-era repression.

As the KGB men proceeded to seize whole files of newspaper cuttings that Roy Medvedev had carefully collected about the history of Stalinism, his mind was on the alert. He knew that the authorities found his research on the regime's past crimes inconvenient. Two years earlier, he had been excluded from the Communist Party for writing a large manuscript on the origins and consequences of Stalinism. In 1956, General Secretary Nikita Khrushchev had condemned these crimes in his famous "Secret Speech" under the euphemism of Stalin's "personality cult." However, after Leonid Brezhnev came to power in 1964, such historical inquiries were deemed detrimental to the regime if not outright "anti-Soviet." The Medvedev brothers knew to what lengths the authorities were prepared to go to stifle dissent: in 1970, Zhores was forcefully locked up in a psychiatric hospital for his writings criticizing various aspects of Soviet past and present reality, and only broad mobilization from Soviet and foreign intellectuals allowed for his liberation. Now the Medvedev brothers' memoir about this incident was about to appear in print. In addition, Roy expected the publication in the West of his research on Stalinism under the title *Let History Judge*.

The dissident historian decided that he would not let the authorities arrest him. When he was summoned for interrogation a week later, he took the fateful decision of going into hiding. The Soviet Union was the largest state on earth, with wide stretches of uninhabited land, and provided he escaped surveillance in Moscow, he could go off the radar for some time. For five months, Medvedev stayed with friends on the Black Sea, in Leningrad, and in the Baltic region. Neither his wife nor his brother knew his whereabouts.

Eventually, after hearing on Western radio stations that both of his books had come out, he returned to Moscow. In October, Medvedev had asked his wife to send his employer a letter of resignation on his behalf. He was now an independent scholar—a risky status in the land of universal right and obligation to labor in the service of the state. Nevertheless, his fame protected him from repression, and over the years, he was able to publish dozens of historical and political studies in the West. Zhores was less lucky: in 1973, he was allowed to travel to London on scientific leave, only to be stripped of his Soviet citizenship after a few months. From then on, he became his brother's literary representative in the West, and the two brothers closely collaborated on numerous projects.

The Medvedev brothers were not the boldest critics of the regime and were not even anticommunists. Compared with such prominent figures of the dissident movement as Aleksandr Solzhenitsyn or Andrei Sakharov, their views were largely loyal to communism. Paradoxically, precisely this moderate tone allowed them to remain free to publish their works and inform the Western public about the situation in the USSR. Many dissidents were prepared to go to prison to defend their views, but once behind bars, they remained voiceless and could only count on their Western supporters' protests. Martyrdom at the hands of the regime was a necessary stage in a dissident biography, and it was precisely the well-advertised account of Zhores Medvedev's psychiatric ordeal that had turned the Medvedevs into high profile dissidents in the eyes of the West.

Yet later, their conflicts with Solzhenitsyn and Sakharov and decision to adopt a socialist democratic line raised widespread criticism among their fellow dissidents. Accusations of collaboration with the regime were but a step away, and the infamous label stuck to the Medvedevs' image. Roy's successful political career in the Communist Party from 1989 to 1991, and his enthusiastic support of Vladimir Putin since 2000, have further tarnished his reputation and alienated his Western supporters.

These circumstances no doubt explain the lack of interest Western historians have shown in these two controversial figures. While Sakharov's and Solzhenitsyn's fascinating lives have been the subject of numerous biographies, the Medvedevs have remained in a blind spot and have hardly been the object of any academic research since 1991: too socialist and not liberal enough for the West, not consensual enough for Russian historians. Yet their biography offers a remarkable glimpse into the paradoxes of the post-Stalin era, a time when unauthorized publishing of a literary work in the West could land a writer in the camps, and some authors of such works could use their foreign royalties to buy high quality consumer goods from restricted access retail stores. A high-profile dissident could get away with expressing support for a piece of legislation adverse to the Soviet Union's economic interests examined in the US Congress, while others were arrested for raising a banner on Red Square.

As new scholarship on Soviet dissent begins to focus less on the heroic figures of the movement and more on the "grey zones" between loyalty and dissent and the material worlds and cultural practices of the movement, the liminal position of the Medvedev brothers can help us better understand the paradoxes of the times. The key to their success was arguably their very broad social network, which encompassed not only dissidents but also prominent establishment intellectuals, old party veterans who had been through the camps, as well as younger party members working in the Party's Central Committee and with connections at the highest level. This broad range of contacts played a key role in helping the Medvedevs conduct their collaborative historical research by providing them with insider information about Soviet politics, which they made public in the West, and in saving them from repression. What was unusual about the Medvedevs was the hybridity of their DNA: although by their loyalty to the Soviet system they resembled their more conformist peers from the intelligentsia, their outspokenness and fearlessness was characteristic of more oppositional figures.

As this biography was going into print, Roy Medvedev was aged ninety-seven and still professionally active. My personal acquaintance with the Medvedev brothers dates to 2011, when I started research on my PhD dissertation, published in 2019 under the title *Dissident Histories in the Soviet Union*, a central figure of which was Roy Medvedev. Over the years, I have taken about forty hours of interviews with Roy at his country house on the outskirts of Moscow and by phone and had two encounters with Zhores at his London home. I have also done extensive research in their very rich archival fond and read Zhores's huge corpus of memoirs, entitled *A Dangerous Profession*.

These sources reveal a multifaceted portrait of two men who went through perplexing political evolutions, becoming or ceasing to be dissidents depending on the political climate, but who never sought to fit any mold, least of all the mold of "Soviet dissidents" which Western media built for critics of the Soviet regime. Roy Medvedev's support for Vladimir Putin and his benevolent attitude towards other "strong men" in the post-Soviet space are not the least of the paradoxes of a man who first became known for his calls for socialist democracy. This biography attempts to make sense of these two ambivalent figures, by placing their trajectories in their historical context. I have striven to reflect in this work the complexities of their position, to do justice to their ideas without hiding the contradictions of their stance.

Writing the biography of twin brothers is an unusual exercise, but the lives and dissident careers of Roy and Zhores Medvedev were entangled to such a degree that their stories could only be told jointly. While I have sought to give each of them equal attention, in my narrative the focus continually shifts from one to another following a roughly chronological structure.

My gratitude goes to the Swiss National Science Foundation, which has been generously funding my PhD and post-doctoral research and has funded the Open Access publication of this book, but also to Academic Studies Press for encouraging me to write this biography and providing benevolent guidance. By assisting me in turning dozens of hours of interview transcripts into a book manuscript and conducting additional interviews, my husband Oleg Ustinov has also given a new impulse to this research. This book would probably not have seen the light of day without the active assistance of Roy, Zhores, Rita and Dima, who supported this endeavor without ever interfering into the book's content. I thank the staff of the Moscow City Archive for giving me access to the Medvedev brothers' papers before they were properly inventoried and for putting up with my presence all these years. I am also grateful to colleagues who shared with me materials and testimonies about the Medvedev brothers: Gennadii Kuzovkin, Kathleen Smith, Vsevolod Sergeev, Viacheslav Dolinin, and others, and of course peer reviewers whose thoughtful remarks helped me improve this manuscript.

CHAPTER 1

A Youth in Stalin's Shadow

On December 1, 1934, Roy and Zhores Medvedev had just turned nine when politics suddenly entered their lives. Sergei Kirov, the First Secretary of the Leningrad Regional Committee, was killed in what Stalin claimed was a terrorist attack ordered by his political adversaries, Lenin's former comrades Grigorii Zinoviev and Lev Kamenev. Roy and Zhores, who had grown up in Leningrad and whose father was particularly fond of Kirov, followed the events very closely. Aleksandr Medvedev had started his career as a political commissar during the Civil War in Astrakhan by the Caspian Sea, after joining the 11th Army, one of the leaders of which was Kirov. Aleksandr Medvedev was a sacred figure to the twins, the embodiment of the "Red Commissar" veteran of the Civil War, which achieved a cult status in the 1930s. "My father was precisely such a commissar of the 1920s, and I had all the reasons not only to love him, but to be proud of him," remembered Roy.

Aleksandr Medvedev, 1936. OKhDLSM, F. 333, op. 16, d. 19, l. 1.

Born in 1899 into a family of merchants, Aleksandr Romanovich Medvedev had lost both of his parents by age twelve. The eldest sibling of a family of three, he was a brilliant pupil and was offered financial support to finish secondary school. He was more fortunate than his younger sisters: Antonina was placed in a family as a housemaid, while the youngest, Ekaterina, was given away for adoption. In those times of political turmoil, the student corpus was highly politicized, and by the time Aleksandr graduated, he was a convinced communist. In 1918, he joined the ranks of the Communist Party, and when the Civil War spread to his home region, he joined the Red Army as a political worker in 1919. The 11th Army, to which he was attached, marched on the Caucasus, occupied Baku and Tiflis, and helped to install Soviet power. Aleksandr soon thereafter began to teach at the Military Political School in Tiflis.

Iuliia Reiman. Courtesy of Roy Medvedev.

In 1923, Aleksandr Medvedev met Iuliia, a twenty-one-year-old handsome girl with short dark hair and a languid gaze from Tiflis. Iuliia Isaakovna Reiman came from a well-off Jewish family of Swiss origin, and her mother was a renowned midwife. In those post-revolutionary days, as Roy remembered, "bourgeois" conventions were no longer in fashion, and young people simply started living together, without a formal wedding. Iuliia moved into the dormitory of the Military Political School, and on November 14, 1925, she gave birth to two sons. The birth of twins was an unexpected and joyous event, celebrated by

Aleksandr's colleagues and dormitory neighbors, who suggested calling the newborns Romul and Rem, after the twin founders of Rome. After Lenin's death, in 1924, revolutionary names were in fashion within the Communist elite and the intelligentsia, and many children were given names commemorating the founding fathers of Communism, from Vladlen (for Vladimir Lenin) to Oktiabrina. Two versions exist as to the origin of the Medvedev brothers' unusual names. Roy claimed that the twins had been named after French and Indian revolutionaries Manabendra Roy and Jean Jaurès. Zhores, however, recalled that their parents had initially settled for "Roi" and "Reis," supposedly in homage to the Revolution although the exact meaning remains unknown. However, Zhores was ashamed of his funny name, spelled as "Ress" on his birth certificate, which triggered mockery in school. When he applied for his first passport, at age sixteen, he added two letters to his name, turning it into the more common Soviet name "Zhores."

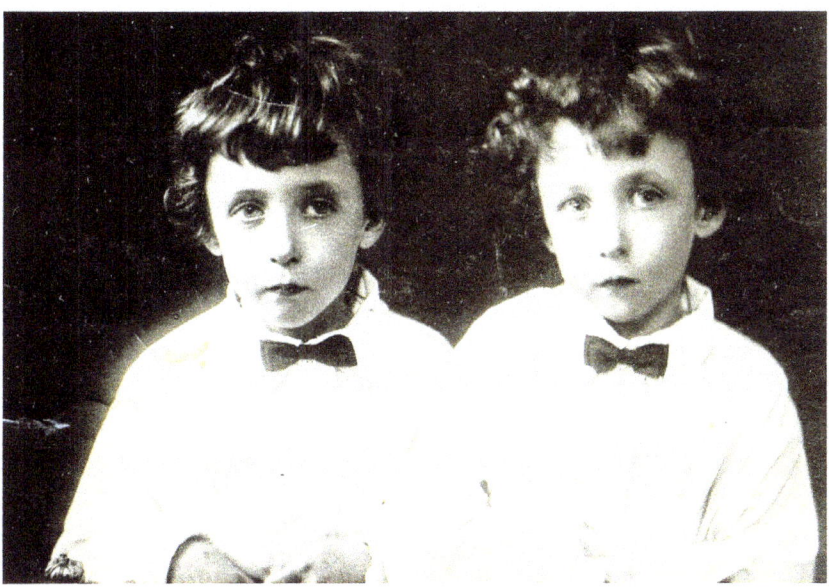

Roy and Zhores Medvedev in childhood. OKhDLSM, F. 333, op 9, d. 361, l. 1.

Theirs was a happy childhood within a loving family, although Roy noted that their mother lacked the skills to raise two boys and entrusted much of their education to a nanny, a kind woman from Byelorussia. Roy believed that from an early age luck had played an important role in his fate. His oldest memory dated back to when he was two-and-a-half-years-old. As the twins were in the countryside with their mother, Roy escaped her attention, went out into the courtyard, and climbed up and tumbled into a large vat of water, kept for fire extinction purposes. However, a man passing by witnessed the scene and jumped to save him from drowning. Luck saved Roy once more when he nearly drowned into the Black Sea, when he was ten, during a summer camp. And later it would save him from the tragic fate of many young men of his age who died on the battlefield.

In 1926, the family moved to Leningrad, where Aleksandr Medvedev was appointed lecturer at the Military-Political Academy. After a few years at the Academy's dormitory on Vasilevskii Island, they enjoyed the rare privilege of living in a separate apartment near the Taurid Garden. And when Iuliia took up studying cello, their aunt Tosia moved in to help raise the twins. Roy and Zhores felt closest to their father, whom they rarely saw but deeply admired. Aleksandr Medvedev was now a professor and vice-head of the department of dialectical and historical materialism at the Military-Political Academy and lectured at Leningrad University. He had the rank of Lieutenant colonel and wore a military uniform, but was also a philosopher, who collected a library of several thousand books and instilled in his sons the love of knowledge. He filled notebooks with texts of his lectures, book summaries, and his own works, in small, neat handwriting. He planned to start publishing after turning forty, waiting for the maturity and wisdom that come with age. Little did he know that he would reach this age in prison.

Kirov's assassination came as a shock to many people, but for Aleksandr Medvedev and his colleagues at the Military-Political Academy, it was a personal tragedy. On December 2, Medvedev took his sons to the Leningrad main square to watch Kirov's funeral procession, amidst hundreds of thousands of grieving Leningraders. A year later, on the first anniversary of Kirov's death, Roy penned a poem commemorating Kirov's memory, which was published by the Communist Youth newspaper *Change* (*Smena*). With his first royalties, the young boy bought a box of chocolate for his mother, but most of all, he wished to earn his father's praise.

Besides Kirov, the figure Aleksandr Medvedev held in highest esteem was Lenin. When Roy and Zhores were ten, their father read them the poem "Vladimir Ilich Lenin," written by the revolutionary poet Vladimir Maiakovskii, with whom Medvedev was on friendly terms. It speaks to Roy's phenomenal memory but also his youth devotion to Lenin that he immediately memorized the six-thousand-word poem. Maiakovskii warned against "processions and mausoleums, the established statute of worship" filling "Lenin's simplicity with luscious unction." Yet not only the founding father of the Soviet regime, but also his successor, Stalin, were becoming the object of quasi-religious worship.

Like most of their peers, Roy and Zhores were raised as children of Stalin's cult. When the family moved to Moscow, in 1936, their father took them to another demonstration on Red Square. Sitting on his fathers' shoulders, Roy saw Stalin for the first time on top of the Mausoleum. He was deeply impressed by this event. By that time, he was keenly interested in politics, read the Party's newspaper *Pravda* and actively discussed the political trials against "enemies of the people" with his classmates. Stalin had accused Lenin's closest friends Lev Kamenev and Grigorii Zinoviev of forming a leftist opposition and plotting Kirov's assassination. Although these accusations were hardly believable, it would be years before the Soviet people uncovered that Stalin had used Kirov's assassination to get rid of his political opponents. Soon, Stalin would turn against another prominent Communist leader, Nikolai Bukharin, a gifted orator who enjoyed popularity at the Military-Political Academy, accused of "rightist deviation." The show trials, staged to demonstrate the accused's guilt through a public confession of their alleged sins, produced a strong impression on Soviet audiences. Few people realized that behind the humiliating admission of guilt of Lenin's former comrades lay the use of torture. Even fewer knew that, in the wake of these trials, hundreds of thousands of alleged political opponents were arrested and sentenced to death or prison. All those who had once raised their voice to express a different opinion, a disagreement with the official line, were now at risk. In retrospect, Roy observed that his father never mentioned Stalin. He likely disapproved of the Soviet leader's action, although he did not share his doubts with his sons.

Indeed, following Kirov's death, the atmosphere had begun to change at the Academy. In 1927, the Academy's teaching staff had protested a military reform that led to the suppression of political commissars, which the Academy had been training. As the Soviet leadership was moving on to a new stage in economic reform, the collectivization of agriculture, which was bound to encounter popular resistance, it could not tolerate any dissent in the army's midst. At the time, however, the Soviet leadership only took mild disciplinary measures against the Academy's protestors, many of whom publicly recanted.

In June 1937, however, the whole country witnessed the trial of first-rank military commanders Marshal Tukhachevskii and others, all of whom were executed for forming an "anti-Soviet Trotskyist military organization." The Academy, which bore the name of Nikolai Tolmachev, a military commissar of the Civil War, was renamed after Lenin and transferred to Moscow. Roy remembered that the family moved in 1936, although the transfer was probably finalized in January 1938. A few months later, the so-called "Byelorussian-Tolmachev army opposition" was singled out for repression for its alleged anti-Soviet activities and betrayal of the motherland. In July 1938, a commission was placed in charge of identifying culprits within the Academy's teaching staff—more than 400 names were included, leading to the dismissal from the army of 187 of them and repression of about 130.

As the pressure mounted, Aleksandr Medvedev grew increasingly nervous. His sons saw him come home late from endless meetings at the Academy; he locked himself in his office at night, worked and smoked a lot but slept little. Eventually, he slid into a nervous breakdown. This was not the only harbinger of the oncoming catastrophe. Roy and Zhores spent the summer of 1938 at an Academy's summer camp. However, shortly before the end of the camp, the boys were publicly shamed for their "bad conduct and lack of discipline" and sent back to Moscow. They came home ashamed and worried about their parents' reaction. However, they soon found out that they had nothing to do with the expulsion: their father had just been dismissed from the Academy and demobilized from the army.

When the secret police showed up on the Medvedevs' doorstep late at night on August 23, 1938, Roy and Zhores woke up to an "unusually loud and insistent knock" on the door, followed by loud voices and a slammed door. The scene would remain etched in their memories forever. Years later, Zhores would write down his memories of the event, hoping that the act of writing would bring him closure. After relapsing into slumber, he woke up again at dawn to the noise of furniture being moved. The police officials then started searching the children's room, overturning mattresses and pillows, digging through toys. Suddenly, Aleksandr Medvedev appeared on the doorstep of the children's room, wearing his uniform, but without his belt or military insignias. He hugged his sons and broke into tears. The boys, who had not yet turned thirteen, understood what was happening without a word and started crying too. Their father kissed them goodbye and left swiftly, never to return.

The following day, the twins found their mother sitting dumbfounded, holding a bottle of wine and muttering about their father's innocence and a slanderous denunciation by his colleagues: "They should set him free soon… We'll now go to the Central Committee right away…" When she emerged from her stupor, she set off, first for the Kremlin, then for the Procuracy, dragging her sons along. After standing in endless lines among other distraught relatives of the repressed, she wrote a petition against her husband's wrongful arrest, which the twins signed as well. In the following weeks, she turned to all possible official bodies, from the People's Commissariat for Internal Affairs (NKVD) to the People's Commissariat for Defense, from the Procuracy to the Supreme Soviet of the USSR. Everywhere the responses would be falsely encouraging. "Don't worry ... The NKVD will solve this... They don't condemn innocents..." At home, Iuliia sometimes broke down in hysteria, insulting not only NKVD head Ezhov, but even Stalin himself. These breakdowns frightened her sons. Two months after her husband's arrest, she started working as a cello player in a cinema to feed her family.

One winter evening upon returning from school, Zhores and Roy found their mother in tears. Their father had just been condemned to eight years of imprisonment during a closed trial. As he told them later in a letter he managed to smuggle out of the camp, he had withstood torture and refused to sign false confessions. It may have been a rather mild sentence for the time, but it seemed a "monstrous injustice" to his family. The accusation against Aleksandr Medvedev linked him to the "rightist" opposition of Nikolai Bukharin. Roy believed that, in his father's case, the accusation of Bukharinist deviation was intended to translate into legible political terms the real ground for repression: participation or tacit support for the 1928 rebellion of the Tolmachev Academy.

A week later, the Medvedevs received an order to vacate the apartment provided by the Academy within two days. Despite Iuliia's protests, the family was thrown onto the street with a heap of furniture and belongings laying in the snow, which were sold on the spot for a cheap price. Iuliia had nowhere to go, and for the first year, she had to leave her sons with relatives in Moscow, while she took up a job in a small town a hundred kilometers north of Moscow. In August 1939, she and the boys moved in with Iuliia's mother and sisters, first in Leningrad, and, after an apartment swap, in Rostov-on-the-Don, in Southern Russia.

In the summer of 1939, Aleksandr Medvedev's first letters began to reach his family. They came from the distant Kolyma region in the Siberian Far East, the deadliest "island" in the Gulag archipelago. Prisoners worked in gold mining, tree felling, and other deadly activities, which rapidly led them to exhaustion. Yet his family never heard about any of this from the heavily censored letters that inmates managed to send their family. In his letters to his sons, Medvedev advised his sons to study hard:

> Precisely now, as you enter teenagerhood, a time of blooming of life, I would like to be by your side—to communicate you my knowledge and experience and, as much as possible, keep you from youthful mistakes. But fate has decided otherwise!...
>
> Most importantly—study, steadfastly, insistently, without limiting yourself to the school program. Make use of this time when your receptivity and memorization skills are particularly strong. Don't spread yourself too thin, be disciplined in your work...

> Learn to think and be organized, work out a strong character and will. Patience, tenacity—this is what you need most. Learn to overcome difficulties, no matter how great they turn out to be.

Although Aleksandr Medvedev advised his sons to learn a trade at a technical school to help their mother financially, the twins knew from a young age that science was their calling.

Roy and Zhores had no idea about the terrible life conditions in the camp and their father's deteriorating health. Years later, Ivan Gavrilov, their father's friend, would tell them how he had met Aleksandr Medvedev in the Kolyma region in 1939, on his way to work in copper mines, where deadly work conditions necessitated a constant influx of new workforce. Medvedev had been evacuated as part of a convoy of prisoners too weak for common work. They suffered from dystrophia, pellagra, scurvy, and severe vitamin deficiency, causing night blindness. The convoy, guarded by German shepherd dogs, walked in temperatures of - 50°C towards a camp nicknamed "the camp of living corpses." The two old friends hugged each other, reflecting with emotion on their fates, but soon enough, they had to part ways. However, they met again when Gavrilov was himself evacuated and sent to a state farm. This time, Medvedev looked healthier; he had been working in the hothouses and taking part in the camp choir and theater group. According to the testimony of another former prisoner who contacted Roy Medvedev in the 1960s, she had met his father after he was transferred to work in the hothouses in 1940, following a hand injury in the copper mines. But he grew weaker over time, until he had to be transferred to the hospital, where he was diagnosed with bone cancer.

In early 1941, Aleksandr Medvedev wrote to his family that he was in the hospital but "recovering," and asked them to send vitamins. Yet this was too little, too late. At the end of March, a money transfer was returned stamped "death of the addressee." In shock, Iuliia initially refused to believe the news, even as more transfers were being returned. Roy and Zhores could not fathom the tragedy that had befallen them. The tragedy of their father's death left a deep imprint on Zhores and Roy Medvedevs' lives. It would take a few more years before they realized the true scale of the political repressions that Stalin had unleashed against his own people and his own party. But when they did, the memory of their father's fate would spur them to denounce Stalin's crimes in front of the tribunal of History.

Losing a father was not the only trial that the Medvedev brothers had to face in their teenage years, however. Rostov-on-the-Don was only a safe haven in peacetime, and when Nazi Germany invaded the Soviet Union on June 22, 1941, the

Wehrmacht forces were able to exploit the combined effect of a surprise attack and the USSR's unpreparedness to make major inroads into Soviet territory. In September 1941, German troops were already close to Rostov, and the city had to be evacuated. Iuliia's last name, Reiman, betrayed her Jewish origins, and she and her family had grounds to fear for their lives. They left for Tbilisi, where some of their relatives still lived. At the end of 1942, Roy and Zhores, who had just turned seventeen, were informed that they would soon be drafted by the Red Army.

The twins had always been an inseparable pair, but at this critical juncture, they made different decisions, which betrayed a certain difference of character. War changed everything, and while for Zhores, it made meaningless such civic rituals as high school examinations, for Roy it gave added urgency to obtaining diplomas that could mean the difference between life and death. Since they were due to be mobilized in February 1943, Roy decided to graduate early, and to do so, he was ready to study twelve to fourteen hours a day for three weeks. In mid-January, he successfully passed his maturity diploma at the Georgian Ministry of Education. Indeed, this move may have saved his life.

By the time Roy and Zhores were conscripted, the German Wehrmacht had lost the advantage, and the war had taken a new turn. Following its victory at Stalingrad, the Red Army was moving south towards Krasnodar. The Medvedev brothers were sent to the Georgian city of Kutaisi for a military training course, where, in Roy's words, they learned "anything but how to fight well." Zhores, one of the few to speak Russian among the new recruits, was hired to help the commander. Given the heavy losses among junior officers, young people with a completed secondary education were in great demand. As a graduate, Roy was sent back to the recruitment office. However, he was not to be recruited for a couple of months, and he asked for an interim assignment to get access to ration cards. He was not sent back to Kutaisi and instead assigned to the Third Artillery Arsenal of the Transcaucasian front, where he ended up working until the end of the war. This was not an idle time for Roy, who read philosophy books in the evenings and made new friends among other sons of "enemies of the people."

Meanwhile, Zhores was about to face the enemy's fire. In mid-May 1943, his regiment was sent to the Taman peninsula. The Red Army was trying to recapture this narrow stretch of land, which controlled access to the straits between the Azov and the Black Seas. On a front of just a hundred kilometers, three Soviet armies counting twenty-one divisions and five brigades faced sixteen German divisions, two tank divisions, and four regiments, assisted by a thousand military planes. After a few days of training in the rear, Zhores and his fellow foot soldiers were sent to the front. They sat in trenches, from which they had to crawl after each artillery attack and run towards the German positions, armed with bayonet rifles, zigzagging among corpses and trying to avoid landmines. By the end of the first day, Zhores's company was left with only thirty soldiers out of one hundred fifty. Undeterred, the Germans launched a counterattack. Over the next few days many soldiers in Zhores's company fell to a sniper's bullets. Among them was a young woman working as signaler, whom Zhores was appointed to replace. He faced the arduous task of restoring the telephone line, which had been cut in several places. In the process, Zhores was shot in the foot. He was taken to the sanitary trench, then transferred to the field hospital, and eventually evacuated to Krasnodar, Baku, and then Tbilisi.

After the fact, Zhores realized that he had been fortunate: many of his peers had been more heavily wounded than he had, yet this injury was serious enough for him to be demobilized. As a result of osteomyelitis, a bone infection, Zhores was hospitalized for three months, and the medical commission registered him as second-grade invalid (loss of a hand or a foot). By December, however, his foot was healed, and he swapped his crutches for a walking stick.

After his recovery, in January 1944, Zhores had the obligation to either find a job, or return to school. Clearly, his preference was to start studying, but this was more easily said than done, in a country that was still at war. He first returned to Rostov, which had been liberated from Nazi occupation. He was entitled to claim back his family's apartment, but he found a city in ruins, and three families whose house had been bombed were now living in the two rooms that once belonged to the Reimans. All their things were gone, and their library, which Roy and Zhores cherished as their father's last relic, had disappeared.

After a six-day journey in a crowded carriage for injured soldiers, Zhores reached Moscow, where he stayed for five days, sleeping at train stations. He successively tried to apply to the Faculty of Biology and the Faculty of Medicine of Moscow State University, and even to the Rostov medical school, but none of these universities, which had only recently returned from evacuation, could offer student accommodation. Ultimately, Zhores settled for the Timiriazev Academy of Agriculture, located in the north of Moscow, where he was offered a place in the dormitory and a job, in expectation of his enrollment for the new academic year. His work consisted of washing mineral salts off quartz sand with the help of concentrated hydrochloric acid, a simple but dangerous task.

Roy was demobilized in late 1945, when the artillery arsenal where he had been working was dismantled. He hoped to study at Moscow State University, but there was no student accommodation, and instead, he enrolled in Leningrad in September 1946. The war had left deep wounds within the country, particularly in Leningrad, which had undergone nine hundred days of a terribly deadly blockade. But by 1946, the university had been restored to its former glory, erasing all traces of wartime damages. Despite his mother's fears, Roy decided to study philosophy, the subject his father had once taught, at the very university where he had lectured. "Fortunately," Roy remembered, "I had learned the rules of sensible caution early on. I strove to learn my father's profession but was not eager to share his fate." In the registration form, he wrote elusively that his father had "died in 1941"—presumably on the front. The truth would come to light later, but in the meantime, Medvedev was spared discrimination.

The death of a father and the experience of war were formative experiences in the Medvedev brothers' lives. Aleksandr Medvedev's arrest had not only put an abrupt end to his sons' childhood but also shattered many of their illusions about the Stalin regime. From an early age, they had been keenly interested in politics, and Roy knew that his interests lay in this field, yet he was also careful, aware of the dire consequences that an incautious word could have. In retrospect, Zhores judged that his direct experience of war had created a difference between him and his brother: he felt bolder; since he had not been killed on the frontline, in such difficult circumstances, he could take political risks. His decision to turn to biology did not signify a lesser political engagement than his brother's. Quite the contrary. In fact, by the late 1940s, biology was about to become one of the most politicized scientific disciplines.

Works Cited

Medvedev, Roy, and Zhores Medvedev. *1925–2010. Iz Vospominanii.* Moscow: Izd. "Prava cheloveka," 2010.

Further Reading

Kolonitskii, B. I. "'Revolutionary Names': Russian Personal Names and Political Consciousness in the 1920s and 1930s." *Revolutionary Russia* 6, no. 2 (December 1, 1993): 210–28.
Main, Steven J. "The Red Army and the Soviet Military and Political Leadership in the Late 1920s: The Case of the 'Inner-Army Opposition of 1928.'" *Europe-Asia Studies* 47, no. 2 (March 1, 1995): 337–55.

CHAPTER 2

A Crusade in Soviet Biology

For a young inquisitive mind such as Zhores Medvedev, science was an open field of exploration. Unlike the humanities, where the weight of official ideology was most strongly felt, biology seemed a realm of objectivity, where only facts mattered. Yet as he soon found out, politics did impinge upon Soviet science in the Stalin era, and being an honest biologist required the same amount of courage as being an honest historian. To find out what happened to Soviet biology, one had to go beyond the scientific controversies to look at the historical context in which one side gained unlimited power over the field.

By April 1945, seven months after Zhores started studying at the Timiriazev Academy in Moscow, the young man had already come up with a new scientific theory, which he was eager to discuss not only with his professors but even with the rising star of Soviet biology, Academician Trofim Lysenko. Questions of aging fascinated Zhores, and he had begun to study the various ways in which plants aged. He formulated a new theory to explain how a plant, which grew new leaves or branches constituted of somatic (regular) cells, could suddenly grow buds and later flowers with male and female reproductive organs. He posited that among somatic cells were potential germ cells and that the aging process led to the replacement of the action of somatic cells by that of germ cells. Eventually, this phenomenon would be explained by the discovery of stem cells, and Zhores's early interest in aging would yield a number of promising discoveries in later years.

Medvedev's decision to send his new theory to Lysenko was bold. An agronomist by training, Lysenko had invented in 1928 a new "miraculous" agricultural technique called "vernalization," (*iarovizatsiia*), which consisted in exposing plants to the cold to induce flowering, a technique believed to improve crop yields. But Lysenko also made broader claims: based on the ideas of early nineteenth century French biologist Jean-Baptiste Lamarck, he claimed that environmentally acquired characteristics (such as those acquired through vernalization) could be inherited. His theory, developed with Izaak Prezent, rejected the concept of heredity discovered by Gregor Mendel and further developed by Thomas Hunt Morgan, who had identified the role of genes on chromosomes as carriers of genetic material in 1915.

Science has always progressed through discussion and rejection of previous paradigms, and Lysenko could well have demonstrated the superiority of his theories experimentally. However, in the Soviet Union, science was also a tool of ideological supremacy over the capitalist West, particularly in the context of the Cold war. Lysenko's success lay not so much in the superiority of his techniques, but rather in the strategic alliance that he formed with Stalin to further them. Classical genetics, represented by the research of an American scientist, Morgan, would thus be declared "bourgeois," non-Marxist, opposed to Darwinism, while Lysenko's own theories would be given a patriotic varnish by connecting them with the research of Ivan Michurin, a Russian agronomist who had developed new methods of selection and hybridization of plants.

In 1935, two years after a terrible famine that had caused the death of millions of peasants on Soviet territory, Lysenko convinced the Soviet leadership to launch a large-scale experimentation of his vernalization process in Soviet agriculture and started actively attacking Soviet geneticists in the press. Several of them were arrested as a result of Lysenko's denunciations. Most prominently, Nikolai Vavilov, pioneer in the field of genetics in the Soviet Union, founder of the Institute of Genetics of the Academy of Sciences in Moscow and initiator of the All-Union Academy of Agricultural Sciences (VASKhNIL) was arrested and died in prison in 1943. Lysenko himself was elected president of VASKhNIL, an institution he would head until 1956 and from 1961 to 1962.

When Zhores Medvedev started studying, at age nineteen, he looked up to Lysenko with admiration. When the academician replied to his letter with an invitation to present his theory, Zhores was elated. However, he was not the only guest that day: after hours of discussion of his agricultural techniques with the thirty visitors who had come from all over the country, Lysenko ended the reception. Needless to say, Medvedev had not been given a chance to present his findings. However, the young man was not discouraged. Piotr Zhukovskii, head of the department of botany at the Timiriazev Academy, had also shown interest in his work and suggested that he verify his theory experimentally once he had learned some more.

Zhores Medvedev, 1955. Courtesy of Zhores Medvedev.

After he became Zhukovskii's *protégé*, Medvedev realized that Lysenko's views were widely debated at the Academy. At the time, classical genetics had not yet been removed from the academic curriculum at the Timiriazev Academy, and the head of the genetics department, Anton Zhebrak, had worked in Morgan's laboratory in the United States. In 1946, Zhukovskii published an article strongly criticizing Lysenko's positions. Lysenko replied with a violent attack in *Pravda*, the Communist Party's official press organ. Zhores Medvedev remembered that he and his fellow students actively discussed Zhukovskii's article, which he found "interesting, logical and brilliant in its form." Shocked by Lysenko's "meaningless and tactless" answer, Medvedev changed his mind regarding the agronomist. "Until then I perceived this debate in the field of genetics as a real scientific debate in which, I thought, both sides deserved respect. By observing the character of the beginning of the discussion in the field of Darwinism, I understood that Lysenko and his followers' most important goal was anything but the clarification of scientific truth."

Indeed, Lysenko was bent on using his political clout to achieve supremacy over his adversaries, and under his influence, the discipline underwent a complete overhaul. On August 1, 1948, *Pravda* published Lysenko's report to the VASKhNIL session, entitled "On the situation in biological science" on its front page. This was a violent onslaught on Mendelian genetics, which

Lysenko branded as a "bourgeois" and "idealistic" science. Zhukovskii, who had tried to oppose Lysenko's theories at the VASKhNIL session, had to recant under pressure. At the time, Zhores Medvedev was interning at the Nikita Botanical Garden near Yalta for a few months. By the time he returned to the Academy in late September, the atmosphere had changed for the worse: Lysenko's partisans had been appointed to key positions, and the academician himself now lectured fifth-year students on "Michurinist genetics." Classical genetics were officially banned, and graduate students were assigned new research themes.

Stalinism demanded blind obedience and loyalty, not intellectual reflection, and the new course seriously impeded scientific research. But in these circumstances, opposing Lysenkoism amounted to professional suicide. Medvedev certainly sided with Zhukovskii, but he could not afford to make his position known. He later recalled writing a couple of articles under Zhukovskii's supervision criticizing "Michurinist" biology, including a critical review of a Lysenkoist work, Ol'ga Lepeshinskaia's book on the origin of cells. Yet they had no chance of making it into print. In the late 1940s, Medvedev also participated in the elaboration of a collective letter by agricultural chemists against Lysenko's interference in this field, which his professor Vsevolod Klechkovskii and others sent to the Central Committee of the Communist Party. However, by the early 1950s, any opposition to Lysenko had been crushed, and anyone who wanted to get published had to pay at least lip service to official views. This certainly explains why, as Valery Soyfer has pointed out in his study on Lysenko, Medvedev praised Lepeshinskaia's book in an article published in 1953. Censorship and the need to get his work published were certainly circumstances explaining such contradictions, far from uncommon at the time.

At this stage, Zhores Medvedev was not yet a dissident. But already then, he developed cunning strategies to avoid confronting the Soviet system head-on without unnecessarily compromising himself. His plans to make a scientific career were seriously affected by the Michurinist turn in Soviet biology. He had no desire to work on a theme imposed from above, and as he was due to graduate from the Timiriazev Academy in 1949, he came up with a plan to defend his PhD (*kandidatskaia*) dissertation ahead of time without getting into graduate school (*aspirantura*). He asked for a transfer to the agrochemistry faculty, which resulted in extending his studies by one year. During this time, he would write his dissertation independently, the final chapter of which could also be defended as a diploma thesis. Aware that his intention to defend his PhD dissertation so early in his career could raise eyebrows, especially coming from a student of Zhukovskii, Medvedev kept his plans secret and decided to present his professors with a *fait accompli*. He planned to defend at the Institute of Plant Physiology of the USSR Academy of Sciences, the director of which he knew well. In March 1950, he defended his diploma thesis and submitted his dissertation to Zhukovskii. His advisor was pleasantly surprised and signed off on it. The defense took place on December 1, 1950.

Medvedev's first professional assignment, in June 1950, was to the laboratory of plant biochemistry of the Nikita Botanical Garden in Crimea. However, his project to study the aging process of plants was disrupted after six months by an official decree reassigning resources to a study of greater strategic significance. In Spring 1951, Medvedev resigned and returned to Moscow, where he was hired by the Timiriazev Academy as a junior researcher.

In Moscow, Zhores was reunited with Margarita Buzina, a former student of the Academy he had grown increasingly fond of since their encounter in 1948. Rita and Zhores shared the same birthday, but Rita was a year younger, and she studied at the agrochemistry faculty, where Zhores transferred in 1948. In the student dormitories, Rita's room stood opposite Zhores's, and she recalled that he would sometimes switch off the music, when Spanish students partied loudly in the evenings, interrupting his studies. Although she liked dancing herself, she was not put off by Zhores's serious demeanor. After graduating, Rita went off to the Caspian Sea region on an expedition of the Academy of Sciences to analyze the results of a reforestation project. When she returned to Moscow, in October 1951, she started working at the Academy. Love matters were not the Medvedev brothers' forte; clearly, they were more at ease perusing books at their desks than dating girls, but there was a kind of quiet harmony between Zhores and Rita, which could be felt until the end of their lives. She remembered that Zhores simply suggested that they be together. A year later they got married and moved into a room in Khimki, north of Moscow, where their first son Aleksandr (Sasha) was born in February 1953.

Roy and Zhores Medvedev had grown up as Stalin's power was consolidating in the USSR, and for a long time, the Soviet leader had seemed almighty and immortal. His death on March 5, 1953 came as a surprise and even as a shock to a large part of the Soviet population, which felt orphaned and helpless. Zhores, however, remembered reacting to Stalin's death "without emotions, even with some relief." In addition to killing his father, Stalin-era repression had left Soviet biology in shambles. Several scientists of Zhores's acquaintance had been arrested, among them the geneticist Vladimir Efroimson, who would, like Zhores, write an anti-Lysenko work that was broadly circulated among Soviet scientists. Meanwhile, Lysenko's supporters made brilliant careers based on spurious scientific claims. "Michurinist" theories had appeared in many fields, while previously acknowledged scientific evidence was turned down and whole research fields castigated as "bourgeois" or "idealistic."

Stalin's death put an end to the recent wave of antisemitic repression and was followed by the first amnesty of Gulag prisoners on short sentences. In the field of biology, however, the new Soviet leader, Nikita Khrushchev, followed a line of continuity and confirmed the priority of "Michurinist" biology. Lysenko and his followers maintained their monopoly over leading positions in several scientific fields. Yet new winds were blowing: Khrushchev's "Secret Speech" at the 20th Party Congress in February 1956, denouncing Stalin's crimes, signaled the beginning of a policy of de-Stalinization. Although it would be implemented in a haphazard fashion, with frequent ideological zigzags, de-Stalinization led to the rehabilitation (sometimes posthumously) of many victims of political repression, among them prominent geneticists arrested in 1937–1941. This allowed Soviet scientists to cite the work of these authors without being censored. Lysenko's ideas encountered increasing criticism in the field of botany, where they contradicted existing evidence on the evolution of species. In 1955, three hundred prominent Soviet scientists sent an open letter to the Presidium of the Central Committee of the Party, criticizing Lysenko's scientific views. As the signatories pointed out: "The heavy consequences of T.D. Lysenko's monopoly position in science have not been eliminated yet, as a result of which Soviet biology and agronomy as a whole have been lagging behind the development of world science." Despite Khrushchev's active support of Lysenko, the letter did have an impact, and the agronomist was removed from the presidency of VASKhNIL.

Indeed, beyond ideological labels, the Soviet leadership did have an interest in achieving real supremacy in science, as the Soviet successes in the atomic and cosmic fields showed. After years of isolation, Soviet biology could finally attempt to catch up with recent Western discoveries in the genetic field. In summer 1953, James Dewey Watson and Francis Crick identified the DNA structure. This paved the way for the identification of a direct connection between DNA and protein synthesis, which was confirmed with the cracking of the genetic code, in 1966. These scientific breakthroughs had a decisive impact on Medvedev's research on the role of protein synthesis in the aging process. Although the lack of equipment still caused Soviet scientists to lag considerably behind their Western peers in the experimental field, Medvedev's research took a decisive turn in May 1954, when he was granted access to radioactive phosphorus to conduct experiments. His promotion to the position of senior researcher not only allowed him to move from Khimki to Moscow but also to supervise a small team composed of two PhD students and a few interns.

In 1955, Medvedev successfully elaborated a new method of autoradiography of plant leaves to investigate the localization of the synthesis of proteins and nucleic acids—a discovery which he patented.

Stalin's death also led to a greater opening of the USSR towards the West, including a simplification of scientific and cultural exchanges. From 1956 onward, Medvedev started receiving letters from Western colleagues who requested offprints of his articles, and he began corresponding with them. In 1957, he was invited to a conference on the use of radioisotopes in scientific research organized by UNESCO in Paris. Research in this field was only beginning in the USSR, and Medvedev's discovery made him a good candidate to join the Soviet delegation in Paris. For the first time, he experienced the cumbersome administrative process that Soviet scientists had to go through to travel abroad. But this first encounter with the West was an eye opener in many respects: Medvedev made the acquaintance of many British and American colleagues. Upon returning to Moscow, he decided to take English courses, which he attended three evenings a week for the next two years.

The more Medvedev read Western scientific literature, the more he encountered contradictions with Lysenko's theories, which offered no explanation for mechanisms of heredity. And yet there were no works in the Soviet Union in the field of biochemical genetics or molecular biology or even textbooks on genetics. Medvedev started publishing articles popularizing genetic analysis of biochemical problems in the field of protein synthesis, and in 1958–1959 wrote a book synthesizing and analyzing new discoveries in the field of protein synthesis and ontogenesis (processes of development and aging). However, publishing such a work in the USSR was not an easy task, even though Medvedev did not try to argue against Lysenko's conceptions and simply did not mention them.

Medvedev made a first attempt to submit his manuscript to the "Higher School" publishing house in late 1959. Although preliminary reviews were positive and preorders were made for ten-thousand copies, the full review, issued with a thirteen-month delay, was a "death sentence" for the book, in Medvedev's words. The reviewer demanded the rewriting of the central chapter on the biochemical bases of heredity in a "balanced" way, presenting both the "Michurinist" and "Mendelian-Morganist" conceptions of heredity. Ultimately, in 1961, the manuscript was rejected under a spurious pretext.

Ever since Medvedev started his scientific career, he faced impediments of a political nature. To do good science, he had to go beyond the narrow frame dictated by "Michurinist" biology, but in publishing his results, he faced obstacles, which had nothing to do with science. Yet he was not someone who would be intimidated by such challenges, quite the contrary. He reacted to this pressure in two ways: one the one hand, by turning to the West as an outlet for his scientific output, and on the other hand, by setting on a crusade to discredit Lysenko's scientific authority.

Medvedev's scientific network had been developing steadily since his participation in the Paris conference in 1957. In March 1960, he received an invitation to the International Congress of Gerontology in San Francisco from Nathan Shock, President of the American Gerontological Association. Although he was eventually denied permission to travel abroad, Medvedev managed to send the abstract of his presentation in a handwritten letter, bypassing Soviet preliminary review. He was keen on sharing his new theory of molecular aspects of aging with the scientific community and decided to send his paper for publication, regardless of whether he could attend the conference. With the assistance of Chester Bliss, cofounder of the International Biometric Society, he successfully smuggled the manuscript to the West, and it was published in the Congress's proceedings.

This first experiment had shown Medvedev that, with a little help from committed Western colleagues, manuscripts could easily cross the Iron Curtain. Although publication abroad is a common practice in the scientific field, doing so outside official channels, circumventing preliminary censorship, was a dangerous game. In the literary field, Soviet authors who published their works in the West without authorization were subjected to ostracism, sometimes even prosecution. In the 1960s–1970s, two practices allowed Soviet writers and their readers to bypass censorship. *Samizdat*—meaning "self-published"—was the underground reproduction of uncensored texts on typewriters, and their circulation among circles of readers within the Soviet Union. The other practice, labelled *tamizdat*—*tam* meaning "over there"—consisted in smuggling manuscripts to the West for publication. Boris Pasternak, who had been awarded the Nobel Prize for his work *Doctor Zhivago*, first published the novel in Italy in 1957. He was, however, coerced by the Soviet authorities into declining the Prize.

Admittedly, genetics was a less sensitive field than literature, and Medvedev thought that sharing his work with Western colleagues was worth the risk. Once again, he showed his ability to "hack the system" by exploiting its cracks to achieve his goals. During the fifth International Biochemical Congress, organized in 1961 in Moscow, Medvedev was tasked with chaperoning foreign visitors. As he was showing the Timiriazev Academy to Richard Synge, a British biochemist he had met in 1957, Medvedev told him about his difficulties in publishing his book. His visitor offered to take the manuscript to Britain and to arrange for its publication in Edinburgh. It would take four years for Synge's wife to translate the six-hundred-page work, which Medvedev regularly updated to stay abreast of new research on the subject, but it eventually came out in 1966.

Meanwhile, the Soviet publication of Medvedev's book had experienced additional misadventures. In 1963, the biologist made a second attempt to publish it through "Medgiz," the state publisher of medical research, which was more independent politically. Discussion of genetics was no longer taboo, and Medvedev had compromised to include some discussion of Michurinist views in his chapter on heredity. Yet Lysenko's supporters retained key positions in Soviet science and despite the manuscript's good reviews, they had the publication stopped at the last minute. According to Medvedev, the Secretary of Agriculture in the Central Committee, a supporter of Lysenko, had characterized the book as "ideological diversion" and demanded the destruction of the whole print run. He only succeeded in delaying the publication by a few months, though: a commission appointed by the Central Committee Secretariat identified fifteen pages containing criticism of Lysenko and had them replaced by the usual practice of cutting and pasting a new text.

By that time, Zhores Medvedev's name was widely known among scientists, in connection with the circulation of a polemical text that the researcher had started writing in 1961. Entitled "Biological science and the personality cult," the manuscript provided the first historical overview of the Lysenko phenomenon. Other Soviet scientists, such as A.A. Liubishchev and Vladimir Efroimson, had criticized Lysenko's theories from a scientific point of view, and their works were circulating in samizdat. Medvedev's approach was different: "I decided that it would be more effective to show that Lysenko actually built his career on repressions against geneticists, that the discussion of the 1930s was not so harmless, and that Soviet genetics lost many scientists through the system of repressions."

Since Khrushchev had made the denunciation of Stalin-era repression a hallmark of his politics, Medvedev deemed that to be the most effective strategy. Indeed, in 1961 the Soviet leader had staged a wholesale attack against Stalin and Stalinism at the 22nd Congress of the CPSU. Stalin's body was removed from the Red Square Mausoleum, and the glorious city of Stalingrad was renamed Volgograd. But by far not all elements of his legacy had disappeared, and the First Secretary's support for Lysenko was not the least of these contradictions.

Without access to archival material, Medvedev had to rely on information he could scrape together from publicly available sources in libraries. By tracing articles published by Lysenko and his supporters in the 1930s, he was able to connect them with arrests of geneticists that seemed to result from denunciations against them in the press. He identified two waves of political repression caused by Lysenko and his disciples. During the first wave, in 1937, Lysenko had used the general climate of terror to strike deadly blows at his opponents, reducing the scientific debate to political denunciations, which translated into arrests of such prominent figures as Nikolai Vavilov. The second wave, which Medvedev had witnessed, starting in 1948, occurred in the context of the Cold War, and was characterized by growing anti-Western sentiments. In the more pacific postwar atmosphere, the weapon used against Lysenko's opponents was simply dismissal: Medvedev estimated that over three thousand academics had thus lost their positions in 1948. In addition, those arrested in the 1930s who had survived their first Gulag camp terms were re-arrested.

Medvedev produced a first version of his manuscript, about sixty pages long. Colleagues from the Timiriazev Academy and the Academy of Sciences who read it suggested additional material. Particularly helpful was Liubishchev's and Efroimson's assistance but also feedback from Anton Zhebrak, Nikolai Maisurian (Dean of the Faculty of Agronomy of the Timiriazev Academy), and Fatikh Bakhteev, who was Vavilov's disciple and had witnessed his arrest. Piotr Zhukovskii, who had been appointed head of the All-Union Institute of Plant Industry (VIR), not only read the manuscript but also arranged for Medvedev to work two weeks at the archives of this institute founded by Vavilov, where he found stenographic records of official discussions from the 1930s. He was also in contact with Iurii Vavilov, the geneticist's son, who had endeavored to collect material on his father's life.

Zhores Medvedev had come up with a research method that would inspire his brother, and that proved most productive in the conditions of the 1960s: witnesses of the Stalin era were still alive and could share their testimony, regardless of any access to archives. Circulating the manuscript among scientists was a peer-review process that minimized factual errors and allowed the corpus of sources to grow significantly.

By February 1962, Medvedev had already prepared a third version of his manuscript and sent it to the literary journals *Neva* and *Novyi mir* and to the newspaper *Komsomol'skaia pravda*. All three editorial committees were enthusiastic about the manuscript and wanted to publish shorter versions of it, ranging from twenty-five to one hundred pages. Lysenko was still a powerful figure, and censorship would not have allowed any publication attacking him or his theories. The journal *Neva* thus ordered an article coauthored with a geneticist from Leningrad, Valentin Kirpichnikov, who had worked with Vavilov. It came out in March 1963. In July 1962, *Komsomol'skaia Pravda* also showed interest in publishing an article, and decided to send a copy of it along with Medvedev's manuscript to twenty-five reviewers, among whom were several prominent academicians (Boris Astaurov, Vladimir Engelgardt) and some progressive party officials (Len Karpinskii, Fedor Burlatskii and Aleksandr Bovin). However, in July 1962, Khrushchev visited Lysenko's experimental farm and the Soviet media unanimously reproduced his speech in support of Lysenko. The editor of *Komsomol'skaia Pravda* was soon dismissed by a decision of the Central Committee of the CPSU and accused of spreading calumnious materials.

This initiative, however, had an unexpected effect. The reviewers not only read Medvedev's manuscript but shared it with colleagues, starting a process of spontaneous samizdat reproduction, which could no longer be stopped. Never before had a nonliterary work circulated so broadly in samizdat. Many scientists wrote to Medvedev, offering their comments and additional materials, and in two years, the manuscript had doubled in size. Judging by the letters he received, Medvedev's work had reached not only the science-cities around Moscow, Kyiv, and Riga but also Ufa and Sverdlovsk in the Urals, Novosibirsk and Khabarovsk in Eastern Siberia, and Tashkent in Central Asia. "I later met people from the most various regions and groups—scientists and even party workers—and was surprised that almost everyone I met had read the manuscript," remembered Medvedev. Thousands of copies were then in circulation, according to his estimates, and each reached more than one reader.

Samizdat was a double-edged sword: the popularity of Medvedev's manuscript showed that he enjoyed the support of a large part of the scientific community, but it could also get him into trouble. Whether to avert repression or in the genuine hope of convincing the Soviet leadership to change its course, Zhores Medvedev repeatedly tried to draw the authorities' attention to the issues raised in his manuscript. In February–March 1962, he sent detailed memoranda to the Central Committee departments of Agriculture and Science and to the USSR Academy of Sciences about the repression of Soviet biologists who had opposed Lysenko's views. Disappointed by the lack of response, he complained in a December 1962 letter to the first deputy of the Party Control Commission about the "obviously mistaken, nonobjective, dilettante, and servile line" of the Central Committee departments, who were directly responsible for a situation "harmful to the political prestige of our country and weakening to a certain extent the economic situation of the Soviet Union." The thirty-five-page memorandum, containing copies of letters by Nikolai Vavilov, ended with the regret that all press organs remained closed to scientific criticism of Lysenko's views and with a call to open a discussion of genetic issues and of the situation in Soviet biology. Medvedev added that his call was supported by many Soviet scientists "out of patriotic considerations." He concluded: "Soviet biology must become an instrument of knowledge, must serve the Soviet people, it must become a true science."

It did not take long until Medvedev had to suffer the consequences of his opposition to Khrushchev's *protégé*. In July 1962, Klechkovskii, his superior, was summoned to a meeting of the Timiriazev Academy's party committee to discuss Medvedev's "anti-party, anti-scientific, anti-Soviet and calumnious" manuscript. When Klechkovskii attempted to defend the author, he received a strict reprimand. Although Medvedev retained his position, he felt he was becoming a burden to the Academy, which was at the time struggling for its survival, and he decided to resign.

These were still politically mild times, the peak of a period known as "the Thaw" after the Stalinist winter, and measures taken against dissenting scientists were still soft. As a qualified specialist, Medvedev was confident he could find a new position in the research institutes which were being opened at the time in various science-cities. These were technopoles concentrating a large number of research and development institutions in strategic fields, some of them secret and closed to non-residents. He settled for the Institute of Medical Radiobiology of the Academy of Medical Sciences in Obninsk. About one hundred kilometers southwest of Moscow, the city was known for its nuclear power plant, the first one inaugurated worldwide, in 1954. It also hosted a closed Institute of Physics and Power Engineering, which produced reactors for atomic submarines, and a center of monitoring of radioactive isotopes in the atmosphere. The Institute of Medical Radiobiology, founded in 1958, was intended to become the largest center of its kind in Europe, employing two thousand researchers. Not only could Medvedev be hired without too many bureaucratic hurdles, but he was invited to create his own laboratory of molecular radiobiology to study radiation-induced aging. It would take three years for the laboratory to be fully functional. Rita also started working on her husband's team, first on a voluntary basis, then as a junior researcher. Their younger son Dmitrii (Dima), born in late 1956, was now six, and he, like his brother, grew up without seeing much of his parents.

Medvedev's direct superior, also recently hired, would be Nikolai Timofeev-Resovskii, a geneticist and radiobiologist of worldwide renown. He had worked in Germany from 1925 to 1945. After the Red Army conquered Berlin, in 1945, he was arrested by the Soviet authorities and sent to the Gulag. After his liberation in 1955, he became head of the department of radiobiology at the Urals branch of the Academy of Sciences in Sverdlovsk and created an informal summer school of genetics which kept the discipline alive during the dark ages. His nomination in Obninsk, however, was delayed until 1964, as it had to be approved by the Central Committee and KGB, who were unwilling to see a scientist of Timofeev-Resovskii's reputation settle close to Moscow.

The threat of repression did not abate after Medvedev's move to Obninsk. His and Kirpichinkov's article in *Neva*, which for the first time linked the 1948 VASKhNIL session to Stalinism, raised more than a few eyebrows. In April 1963, Medvedev heard that Lysenko's supporters had made moves to introduce a condemnation of this article into the speech of Leonid Il'ichev, Central Committee Secretary in charge of Ideology, at the forthcoming June 1963 Plenum. Medvedev wrote him a letter to try to avert this outcome. Although the Soviet leader did not raise the subject, Zhores Medvedev's name cropped up in the speech of Nikolai Egorychev, First Secretary of the Moscow City Committee. He denounced Medvedev's manuscript for its "incorrect" treatment of the development of Soviet biology, for "besmirching" Michurinist science and praising "bourgeois research." Egorychev's attack was a bad omen, but worse was yet to come. On August 18, 1963, the newspaper *Sel'skaia Zhizn'* ("Village Life") published a large article by M.A. Ol'shanskii, President of VASKhNIL, entitled "Against falsification in biological science," which accused Medvedev and his coauthor of "slandering Michurinist science" and "kowtowing to foreign science." An editorial in *Pravda* further branded them as "misanthropes," "slanderers," and "idealists" and called the article "incorrect and harmful to our science." *Neva* published a statement of recantation. Medvedev and Kirpichinkov anticipated measures of repression, but neither was arrested or dismissed.

Lysenko knew he was steadily losing ground, and this made his attacks all the fiercer. In June 1964, he sustained a defeat when he tried to get two of his supporters elected to the Academy of Sciences. Several prominent academicians spoke up against the nomination of Nikolai Nuzhdin: Vladimir Engelgardt, founder of molecular biology in the Soviet Union; Nobel Prize Laureate Igor' Tamm; and the future dissident and father of the Soviet hydrogen bomb Andrei Sakharov. As a result of their interventions, 114 out of 137 academicians rejected Nuzhdin's candidacy—a defeat unheard of for a candidate supported by the Soviet leadership. This incident exasperated Ol'shanskii, the president of VASKhNIL, who informed Khrushchev and demanded that Lysenko be defended against slander being spread against him by the likes of Medvedev and Sakharov. Khrushchev was infuriated.

On August 29, 1964, as Zhores Medvedev was returning from a vacation in Crimea, he bought the latest issue of *Sel'skaia Zhizn'* and discovered with awe a new assault of Ol'shanskii on Lysenko's detractors, entitled "Against disinformation and slander." The article attacked Medvedev's manuscript on Lysenko, calling it "full of dirty inventions about our biological science," and accused it of having influenced "some ill-informed and overly naïve people," such as Andrei

Sakharov. He concluded that Medvedev should be prosecuted for "spreading calumny." The threat of arrest was now very real. Shortly thereafter, Medvedev was summoned by his Institute's party committee.

Yet an unexpected event soon reshuffled the cards. On October 13, 1964, Khrushchev was ousted from power by his Presidium colleagues, and replaced by Leonid Brezhnev. They had resented Khrushchev's unpredictable leadership, which had had dire consequences for Soviet agriculture, among other fields. It took three days for the new Party leadership to announce Khrushchev's "voluntary" resignation in the media, but on the day of the coup, orders were already given to reverse the official course in relation to genetics. The journal *Sel'skaia Zhizn'* immediately ordered an article on practical and theoretical successes of genetics from Iosif Rapoport, a famous specialist. Several new publications, but also new nominations to key positions, confirmed the ideological U-turn. In February 1965, Lysenko himself was removed from his position of director of the Institute of Genetics, which was dissolved and founded anew under the name of "Institute of General Genetics."

These transformations created positive conditions for the publication of Zhores Medvedev's essay "Biological Science and the Personality Cult." In 1965, Medvedev was in contact with the publisher "Nauka," and he asked colleagues and friends among biologists, biochemists and other scientists to vouch for the publication. Among them were prominent physicists (Igor' Tamm, Andrei Sakharov, Mikhail Leontovich), geneticists (Boris Astaurov and Daniil Lebedev), and other renowned scientists. They all argued for the timeliness of the publication, which would help create clarity in the minds of Soviet readers. In his letter, Leontovich emphasized the "incredible confusion of representations" he had witnessed in the past few months, not only among agronomists and teachers but even among many higher education instructors, who were still under the influence of "the strong hypnosis of 1948." Recent publications on genetics were too specialized for this public, while materials published in the press were too general. The style of Medvedev's book was accessible to these professionals and could "play a very important role in the enlightenment of this important cohort."

Despite these solid recommendations, "Nauka" did not proceed further with the publication for reasons that remain unclear. The changing political climate probably made such a publication risky for the publisher: starting from 1966, the new Soviet leadership proceeded to roll back Khrushchev's policy of de-Stalinization. Brezhnev may have ended Lysenko's sway over Soviet science, but his major concern was to restore stability, and this entailed a return to a more conservative course in the historical field. The small stream of literary and historical works revealing Stalin-era crimes, which had appeared in the early 1960s, dried up. Works accused of "blackening" the Soviet past disappeared from bookstore shelves and libraries. The editor-in-chief of "Nauka" was blamed in 1967 for authorizing the publication of a book by historian Aleksandr Nekrich that denounced Stalin's strategic mistakes in preparing the Soviet Union for the 1941 German invasion. In a climate of uncertainty, the publisher may have anticipated difficulties with the publication of Medvedev's book and backed off.

Despite ominous signs of tightening of the ideological screws, Medvedev made another attempt to publish his book, with the support of the scientific community. In 1966, two academicians, Vladimir Engelgardt and Boris Astaurov, irritated by the persistence of Lysenko's influence in Soviet sciences, wrote a report to Mstislav Keldysh, the President of the USSR Academy of Sciences, to propose the publication of Medvedev's book by the Academy's publishing house. Keldysh received the proposal favorably and appointed a commission to examine this request. Despite an auspicious report, in January 1967, requesting that Medvedev write an "optimistic" concluding section on recent changes in the field of biology, this new attempt was equally unsuccessful. It turned out that the commission's recommendation was not enough to exempt the manuscript from censorship.

By the mid-1960s, Zhores Medvedev had become a well-known figure in Soviet science, not so much for his research in the field of aging, but more so for the bold challenge that he posed to Lysenko's supremacy in Soviet biology. For a young scientist in his late twenties, it was a daring endeavor, and it had earned him the support and respect of the country's most famous names. Soon, he would become well-known worldwide for his dissenting behavior.

Stalin's shadow had hung over Roy and Zhores's childhood and youth, robbing them of the presence of a beloved father and directly impacting their professional orientation and careers. His death and the denunciation of his crimes by his successors had a strong effect on them. While Zhores felt compelled to denounce Stalin's *protégé* Lysenko to rehabilitate the field of genetics, Roy had even broader ambitions: to identify the roots of the "disease" of Stalinism, purge Soviet society of its remnants, and thus rehabilitate the socialist idea as a whole. Before he came to this ambitious project, however, Roy first experienced the complex social fabric of late Stalinism hands-on and participated in Khrushchev's reforms in the field of education.

Works Cited

Martin, Barbara, "Pis'ma sovetskikh uchenykh v izdatel'stvo 'Nauka' v poddezhku izdaniia ocherka Zh.A. Medvedeva 'Biologicheskaia nauka i kul't lichnosti'," *Istoriko-biologicheskie issledovaniia*, vol. 11 no. 2 (2019), 20–40.

Medvedev, Zhores. *Opasnaia professiia*. Moscow: Vremia, 2019.

———. *The Rise and Fall of T.D. Lysenko*. New York: Columbia University Press, 1969.

Soyfer, Valery. *Lysenko and the Tragedy of Soviet Science*. New Brunswick, New Jersey: Rutgers University Press, 1994.

Zhimulev, I.F., Dubinina L.G., "K 50-letiiu 'pis'ma trekhsot'," *Vestnik VOGiS* (2005), Vol. 9 (1), 12–33.

Further Reading

Bergman, Jay. "The Nuzhdin Affair." In *Meeting the Demands of Reason: The Life and Thought of Andrei Sakharov*, 105–118. Ithaca: Cornell University Press, 2009.

Roll-Hansen, Nils, *The Lysenko Effect: The Politics of Science*. Amherst: Humanity Books, 2005.

Smith, Kathleen E. "July: Intellectual Heat." In *Moscow 1956. The Silenced Spring*. Cambridge, Massachusetts: Harvard University Press, 2017.

CHAPTER 3

Stalin Is No More

Roy had always been fascinated by philosophy. In Tbilisi, his closest friend was Roland Simongulian, who, like Roy, had lost his father to political repression and dreamed of becoming a philosopher. Together, they could spend hours discussing philosophical questions. With a few classmates, they also organized a discussion circle. Simongulian would later teach Marxist-Leninist philosophy at the Academy of Social Sciences in Moscow. He and another childhood mate, Norair Ter-Akopian, a future Marxist historian, would remain Roy's faithful friends until the end of their lives and resist any official pressure to break ties with him. As Roy remembered, in the 1970s, Roland was once summoned to the local party committee: "Roland Grigor'evich, do you know that Roy Medvedev is an anti-Soviet element? We recommend that you stop talking to him." But Simongulian only laughed and replied: "We are from the Caucasus and childhood friends. It is not our custom to abandon friends. If I avoid contacts with Roy, all my acquaintances from Georgia and Armenia will shun me. Do you want me to become an outcast?"

By the time Roy graduated from high school, he had already read some of the classic works by Marx, Engels, Hegel, and Kant. He was particularly curious about the concepts of necessity, chance, and freedom, and in tenth grade he wrote his first essay on the categories of dialectical materialism. He was no less interested in natural sciences philosophy, which he had first discovered through Engels's *Dialectics of Nature*: "I was, and I remain fascinated by the exceptional intelligence of the foundations of the universe (*mirozdanie*)," from atoms to elementary particles, remembered Roy. His philosophical musings, however, were of a purely materialistic nature: "It gave the impression that all those primary elements had been created by some kind of Higher intelligence. But it could not be, for the universe exists eternally. This eternity excludes a Creator, there just isn't any need for it." A few months before he started studying, Roy wrote two essays: on gravitation forces, and on electricity's capacity to travel at lightspeed through thousands of kilometers of wires.

Like his brother, Roy was a scholar at heart, endowed with a passion for resolving complex scientific tasks. Yet his interest in politics, which had been present since childhood, oriented him towards the field of "historical materialism," sociopolitical analysis, rather than the more theoretic study of "dialectical materialism." He remembered his five years of study at Leningrad State University as "the best of his life." Roy was so absorbed in his studies, spending entire days at the library and skipping classes with boring lecturers, that he barely took notice of the world outside. He was thrilled by the academic freedom he enjoyed and his access to the library's rich collections, which had not yet been purged of all "forbidden" authors. "For me the striving for knowledge, curiosity was foremost. I wanted to know how the world, the human being function, how society functions, how people live in other countries. I was interested most of all in three sciences: philosophy, history, and physics. Then in university I also became interested in pedagogy."

Roy left a diary of those years of early adulthood, from 1949 to 1955. The diary entries reflect his deep engagement with books, passionate discovery of the Marxist classics, and progress on his budding research projects, only occasionally broken off by scant remarks on girls or his Komsomol activities. Such diaries were not uncommon at the time: they were even encouraged by the regime, to the extent that they promoted self-improvement and conscious action and did not hamper inclusion in the socialist collective. Medvedev's diary was typical of the time, with its emphasis on careful planning of work with precise milestones to reach and its occasional remarks of self-criticism. On May 29, 1949, as Roy was finishing his third year, he started his diary with a list of research topics for the future. These showed that from early on, his focus was on sociopolitical dynamics, both within the capitalist and communist camps and in their struggle with each other. The socialist camp was getting stronger: the countries liberated by the USSR from Nazi occupation had become "popular democracies," after communist parties backed by Moscow had seized power. Roy studied with students from Bulgaria, Albania, Czechoslovakia, Yugoslavia, later China. He was greatly interested in the establishment of people's democracies; however, as he confessed later, it was difficult to get an idea of the dynamics at play in the socialist camp, when political leaders who were put on a pedestal one day could be vilified the next day. Roy also planned to study the national liberation movements of India and China, as well as questions of natural sciences and philosophy.

By the time Roy started his senior year, in fall 1949, the Communist party had seized power in China, and he decided to write his graduation thesis on the Chinese revolutionary movement. Roy's ideas were very orthodox, buttressed by the reading of Soviet and Chinese primary sources translated by his university's Department of Oriental Studies. His graduation thesis received high praise, and he even considered publishing it. At the time, he looked up to Mao with greater esteem and respect than to Stalin. Mao's writings were "marked by originality and independence of thought," in sharp contrast with Soviet literature on the Communist movement. He also approved of Mao's revolutionary tactics and his plans for creating a new society in China. In 1958, however, the failure of Mao's "Great Leap Forward" would put an end to Medvedev's support of the Chinese leader, whose failed grand social experiments reminded him of Khrushchev's. As for the Cultural Revolution, he remembered, it "elicited in all my friends not simply disillusionment but disgust." This fascination with China would nevertheless remain constant until the end of his life.

Membership in the Communist youth (Komsomol) was nearly obligatory for students, and represented a precious experience in politics, which could take up considerable time for the most involved students. Unlike Zhores, who never joined the Komsomol, Roy had from early on an interest in political and ideological activities. Being a good orator, he was immediately elected to the Komsomol committee, and became Komsomol secretary of his faculty in his third year. He supplemented his meager scholarship by lecturing on current domestic and international politics for the scientific society "Knowledge" (*Znanie*) at collective and state farms in the countryside. During the summer, he

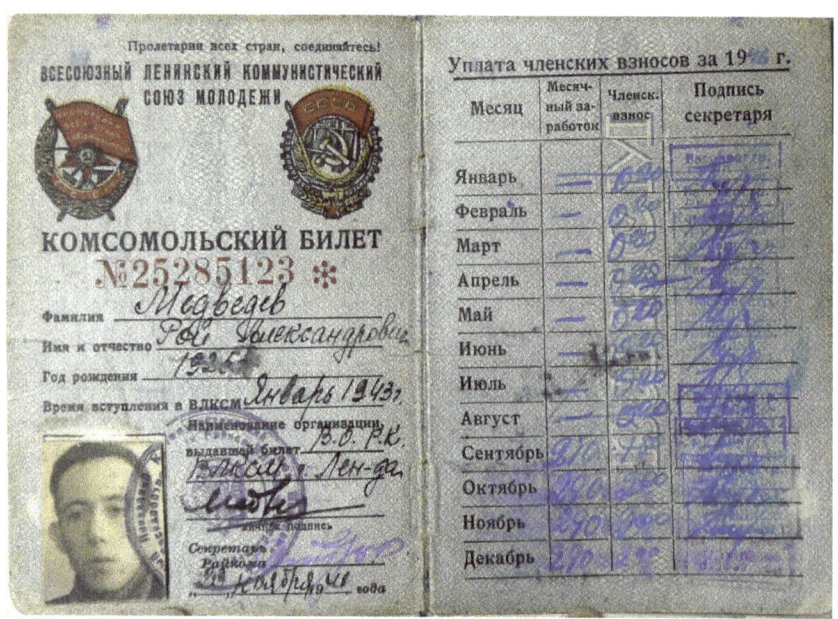

Roy Medvedev's Komsomol ID. 1943. OKhDLSM, F. 333, op. 14, d. 10.

also volunteered with fellow students on construction projects managed by the Komsomol. In 1950, his team worked on the construction site of a hydropower plant. The experience was disappointing, however. In addition to disagreements with the team's leaders, heavy rains made the living conditions very precarious. Hundreds of students sleeping under tents and lacking drinking water made for a poor workforce: every day forty to sixty of them were sick, and the morale was particularly low after one of the students accidentally drowned.

Medvedev could have made a promising career in the Komsomol, if not for the repressive climate of the late Stalin years and his independence of thought. His application to the party was not accepted: his father's arrest and conviction were easily discovered. His diaries also reveal conflicts with the Komsomol cell leadership, starting from April 1949. In Spring 1950, he was temporarily suspended from his activity as "dormitory agitator," despite having recently been nominated for an award in this function and banned from lecturing on the topic of his research. Entries from August 1953 referred to past mistakes he hoped would be forgotten in the future, which he explained by his "political immaturity" and "carelessness." Although Medvedev generally kept a low profile throughout the period, he was bold enough to send a written protest to the First Secretary of the Komsomol Regional Committee in October 1950 when he disagreed with the election of the secretary of his district committee. However, these did not seem to have triggered repression and his "mistakes" did not figure on his Komsomol membership card, which only listed a minor blame for unpaid dues in 1946.

These numerous activities took up a lot of time, and Roy was concerned about the difficulty of maintaining a balance between the imperatives of good comradeship and his ambitious research plan, which demanded great work discipline. A diary entry from June 2, 1949 reflected his predicament. He had set himself "great goals," which demanded "enormous work, a lot of time," and he was unwilling to postpone the start of these projects. However, neglecting daily tasks and duties, on the pretext of more important affairs, could only raise hostility. Still, he felt that scholarly work was his true vocation, much more so than pragmatic party work. Medvedev's confidence in his ability to reach great results was occasionally broken off by moments of doubt or self-critique. In January 1951, he stated that not having fought on the frontline was "the most important mistake that I made in my life."

The late Stalin years were marked by repressive campaigns throughout the country and in Leningrad in particular, with the campaign against "anti-Cosmopolitanism" that targeted Jews, and the "Leningrad Affair," leading to a purge in the Leningrad party organization and among the city's public figures.

At Leningrad University, several professors were arrested, and a former rector, Aleksandr Voznesenskii, was executed. Eight students in Medvedev's faculty were also prosecuted for participating in an anti-Stalinist philosophical circle. Medvedev, however, remained wary of such groups, participating only in debates on Eastern Europe and China, but not discussing Soviet history: "I remembered my father's fate and was careful."

Medvedev was aware from early on that his future was uncertain and that everything hinged on the political situation. In university, when he failed to criticize Hegel after Stalin had denounced German philosophy as "idealistic" he received for the first time a lower grade (four instead of five). Although he graduated from university with honors, his unfavorable family background made his admission into a graduate program unlikely, and he ultimately decided against applying. At the time, students were automatically assigned after graduation to a work position, which they were required to accept for the first three years. Scaling down his ambitions, Medvedev hoped to become a technical college history teacher in the North Caucasus region, but his assignment, after his graduation in 1951, turned out to be even more modest: he was sent to a school in the village of Krasnyi Ural, in the Sverdlovsk region (now Ekaterinburg region). Yet this did not come as a blow. As his diary entry of July 29 showed, he looked beyond the current political context, which made free scholarly work impossible, aiming for intellectual achievements that held permanent value:

> I have nothing to complain about. Many were assigned better positions. But if one considers the conditions for scholarly work, schoolteacher is also a very good position for a philosopher. I don't occupy an official position in my field. Therefore, I am deprived of the possibility of writing (as I would do no worse than others) conjunctural articles and works, which only have a scientific lifespan of a few years, and which others are assigned to write. But I don't want to write such works. My goal and dream is to write something worthwhile, enduring, important for science.

Roy arrived in the Urals in early August. He was perfectly content with the room he was assigned, in a village with all commodities of modern life: electricity, running water and even a cinema. The village of Krasnyi Ural, near Nizhnii Tagil, was a workers' settlements located near a mine where gold, platinum and diamonds were extracted. Roy considered that the six years he worked as a teacher gave him a solid knowledge about the country, the life of the Soviet people far from the large metropoles, its needs and life conditions. He observed the various social groups around him, from Old Believers, a schismatic branch of the Russian Orthodox Church, to kulaks, prosperous peasants deported to the region during collectivization. While the Old Believers' "fanaticism" put him off, he was interested in the life of kulaks, who were once sent into internal exile but had been progressively released from their fetters, while their sons had earned their freedom on the battlefield during the war.

Medvedev taught students from the eighth to the tenth grade not only history but also logic, psychology and German. In addition, he gave lectures to the local population on philosophy and international affairs and enjoyed authority among his colleagues and students. In the Urals, Roy Medvedev stood out among his colleagues. While alcoholism was ubiquitous in the region and social drinking was an unbendable rule, the young teacher never shared a drink with his colleagues, eliciting suspicion. One day, the school director told him: "Roy Aleksandrovich, you are a young, healthy man. I was told that you drink a lot of vodka, but on your own. You sit in your room and drink. This is not the custom here. You have to drink with us." When Roy replied that he never drank vodka and did not like alcohol, the director did not believe his words. Over time, however, Roy's colleagues got used to this awkward young man, who preferred cross-country skiing and books to vodka and girls.

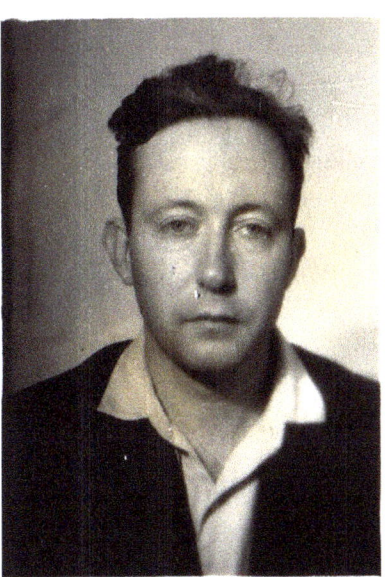

Roy Medvedev, 1956. OKhDLSM, F. 333, op. 3 d. 16, l. 5.

In his teaching, Medvedev relied on his natural authority and refrained from any punishment, even when he faced difficult pupils. He carefully prepared his courses and followed the method once taught by his father: "to teach so as to make the subject interesting and understandable to my students. I never repeated the textbook." He also bought microfilms, which he projected to his students to illustrate his lectures. Sometimes, he would meet his pupils' parents. Despite his alcohol abstinence, he was received warmly. His rule was simple: "Not to tell the parents anything negative about their children." He always found positive formulations, such as: "He does not study as well as he could."

This work assignment may have been imposed, but over time, Medvedev grew fond of it, and his research interests shifted to the field of pedagogy. With the idea of starting a PhD within three or four years and becoming an "official" scholar, he decided to concentrate on concrete pedagogical research, rather than more abstract philosophical themes, which required ten or fifteen years of study. In May 1953, Roy was appointed director of the local evening school for working youth: this entailed administrative duties, in addition to his previous teaching activities and his various research projects.

In addition, Roy continued his work on China and started a new project on Poland. He became a regular reader at the Sverdlovsk library, and the list of materials that he went through during the first two years of his stay suggests that he read an average of six hundred journal issues and between two hundred and two hundred fifty books a year, in addition to polishing his German, watching films, and occasionally going to the theater and museums. During the summer, Roy travelled to Leningrad and Moscow, studying at libraries, and visiting his brother and friends. When a day went by without reading a hundred pages or advancing his research projects, he felt like he had wasted his time. In September 1952, he was also elected secretary of the Komsomol cell. Although he thought about joining the Communist Party, he feared that his application would be rejected. His strategy was to pursue his independent research, hoping that his future scholarly publications would help support his application. In August 1953, he judged his research accomplished enough to start publishing journal articles. In the following years, he sent policy recommendations to ministries and articles to journals, receiving a few positive replies.

As a history teacher, Roy was constrained by the official narrative, particularly concerning Stalin's historical role, for he knew that he was under constant watch, no matter how far from Moscow his school was. Once, as he was teaching the history of the Civil War and was describing Stalin as a "great military commander" in the defense of Tsaritsyn, the director came in to listen to his lecture, but he found nothing to criticize in Medvedev's faithful rendition of the *History of the*

Civil War. "Of course, I did not have the full freedom to think, speak, behave as I wanted. But neither did I have the desire at the time to discuss with anyone the figure of the 'leader and teacher', because I had no idea about the scale and character of the terror that Stalin had organized in our country." He did know about his father's fate, and realized that this was not an isolated case, following his encounter with Ivan Gavrilov, his father's friend who had since been re-arrested. But it would take several years before the whole truth was unveiled.

On March 4, 1953, Roy's diary mentioned laconically "Stalin is severely ill." It was clear that the situation was serious. Roy knew that the press had only published information about Lenin's condition when he was already terminally ill. That evening, Roy met with some war veterans of his acquaintance to discuss the situation. One of the officers, in shock, asked: "Roy Aleksandrovich, who will we die for now? For Viacheslav Molotov? I don't want to die for Molotov!" Stalin had been more than a leader, he had been the "Father of nations," someone who seemed irreplaceable. Roy, however, felt neither fear nor regret. The next day, he wrote in his diary: "Stalin has died." The top of the next page had been torn from the diary and was followed by innocent remarks on the weather. The tyrant had died, but fear had yet to recede. At school, the director pronounced a speech in front of a mourning audience, but some sons and daughters of exiled kulaks silently rejoiced. Roy remembered that one girl was arrested for failing to display the required measure of grief.

The repressive machine was still functioning by inertia, yet times were changing, and the new rulers had already begun to reconsider the repressive measures of the Stalin era. In March 1953, following the amnesty of Gulag prisoners serving short sentences, a state of emergency was declared in the village, because recently released criminals were hiding in the woods. In April, it was announced that the Jewish "Kremlin doctors" whom the paranoid Stalin had prosecuted in January were in fact innocent. This was the first time that such a high-profile case was overturned. In June 1953, Lavrentii Beria, head of the political police from 1938 to 1945 and then Deputy Prime Minister, was arrested. He was executed a few months later.

In 1954, Ivan Gavrilov was released from the Gulag, and Roy and Zhores applied once again for the revision of their father's case. Every month, Zhores would go to the Military College of the USSR Supreme Court to find out about the state of their inquiry. Finally, in September 1956, he received a confirmation that Aleksandr Medvedev's case had been overturned "for lack of elements of crime." All attempts to obtain the restitution of his confiscated manuscripts, however, remained vain: they had been destroyed, along with millions of personal documents. Roy's hope to get inspiration from his father's unpublished philosophical works were to remain unfulfilled. When Zhores went to the Military-Political Academy to receive the compensation they were due, amounting to two months of salary, the cashier declared bluntly "You're very lucky, comrade Medvedev, they doubled the professors' salaries last year!" Aleksandr Medvedev's rehabilitation gave his widow the right to a pension, and she could apply for an apartment in Moscow. Instead, she asked for one in Tbilisi, where she lived. However, by the time her request was being examined, in 1961, another tragedy befell the family: Iuliia Isaakovna had died from carbon monoxide intoxication.

After his father's rehabilitation in September 1956, Roy decided to join the Communist party. Far from incriminating the party for Stalin's crimes, he now felt confident that past abuses would be overcome, and he was convinced that Communism had nothing to do with Stalinism. Indeed, after the 20th Party Congress, the new Soviet leadership seemed to have radically turned the page of Stalinism.

Roy Medvedev, 1956. Courtesy of Zhores Medvedev.

In March 1956, Roy Medvedev was a school director in the Leningrad region, when he and his school's teaching staff were summoned to a neighboring factory for a reading of Khrushchev's Secret Speech. The audience listened to this four-hour lecture frozen in horror and dispersed without a word. Medvedev was far from suspecting the real scale of the phenomenon. But the Secret Speech shattered any illusions he still entertained about Stalin's role in the Great Terror of 1937–1938. As he remembered:

> Before, I thought that Stalin knew nothing about torture in prison, hunger and the unbearable life conditions in the camps. I believed in my father's innocence, but I also believed in Stalin's innocence. I thought he had been deceived. The 20th Congress destroyed my previous trust in Stalin. I was oblivious to the conflicts between Lenin and Stalin. I knew nothing of Stalin's shameful behavior and responsibility in the first defeats of the war. I did not know he had encouraged his own personality cult.

Throughout the country, work collectives and party cells organized such lectures, raising widespread confusion in Soviet citizens' minds. If the man who had reigned over the country for three decades was guilty of unprecedented crimes, what did this imply about the nature of the Soviet system? This political cataclysm, the impact of which the authorities would try in vain to mitigate in the coming years, sent shockwaves from which the regime would never fully recover.

Beyond Stalin, hundreds of thousands of Soviet citizens had been involved in the terror: in addition to secret police officials, investigators, and camp wardens were all those who had benefited from the purges and denounced a colleague, an inconvenient neighbor, or a love rival. The temptation of revenge was strong for those who knew the identity of their persecutors. Aleksandr Medvedev's rehabilitation was a relief to his sons, who had always known that he was innocent. In some letters smuggled from the Gulag to evade censorship, he revealed to his family that he had refused to sign any confession of guilt, despite torture. He also wrote to the Central Committee of the Party and other official bodies, asking for a revision of his case, and denouncing the interrogators who had used torture. He gave the name of those who had calumniously denounced him: his colleagues Chagin, Pruchanskii and Vasiukov. During his studies in Leningrad, Roy came across Boris Chagin, who was then head of the department of dialectical and historical materialism—although he rarely appeared at the university. Pruchanskii also occasionally lectured at the university and produced on Roy the impression of "an absolutely miserable man." As for Vasiukov, he had been arrested and disappeared in the years of terror; perhaps his testimonies against Aleksandr Medvedev had been given under torture.

Roy had no doubt that Chagin had worked in the Academy as an NKVD informer. By the late 1940s, Chagin's past denunciations were no secret at the university where he worked. After several of his victims had been rehabilitated in 1939–1940, he was excluded from the party, but later reinstated. "I felt only contempt for this person, but no hatred or revenge thirst," remembered Roy. As for Zhores, he seems to have shared Roy's disdain, emphasizing that Chagin had reached a prominent position less through his scientific achievements than due to his unswerving political loyalty. In 1963, as Zhores was reading the newspaper *Izvestiia*, he saw that Chagin was running for a seat in the USSR Academy of Philosophy and Law, of which he was a corresponding member. Chagin's publications showed a pattern of political opportunism and revealed that the philosopher's career had been built on eliminating his competitors and participating in all the shameful ideological campaigns of the postwar years. However, he enjoyed little esteem among his colleagues, and his three attempts to be elected to the Academy failed.

For both Roy and Zhores, their father remained the most important figure in their lives. They both named their firstborn Aleksandr. And the research on Stalinism that they undertook in the 1960s was closely related to their firsthand experience of Stalinist repression. Indeed, they lived in a society where former Gulag prisoners and the sons of Terror victims had to live side by side with their denouncers and persecutors, some of whom occupied the highest position in the political and scientific hierarchies. The only weapon against them was to ensure that their crimes would not be forgotten.

The onset of de-Stalinization coincided with a new period in Roy's life. In 1954, after finishing his mandatory three-year-period of employment in the Urals, he decided to move to a warmer region and to apply for a PhD program. His heart wavered between pedagogy and philosophy; he considered studying both simultaneously, but eventually settled for the former. The field of education required less political conformism than philosophy, and he no longer dreamed of teaching at university. He opted for a correspondence PhD program at the Moscow State Pedagogical Institute.

While Roy was equally at ease teaching eight-year-olds and high school students, as a scholar he was interested in innovation, experimentation in the pedagogic field. His research focused on polytechnic education: the incorporation of productive labor into the school curriculum. Since the 19th Party Congress, in 1952, the introduction of polytechnic education had been designated an important axis of school reform. As the Soviet economy experienced an acute shortage in the workforce after the war, Soviet schools were called on to train a new generation of qualified workers. In 1954, "labor" classes were introduced into school curricula, from manual labor in primary school to hands-on internships in factories or collective farms in the senior grades. Schools were equipped with workshops and applied components were introduced into scientific disciplines.

Early experiments failed to yield convincing results, however, and a new reform was introduced in 1958: the school curriculum was lengthened by one year to make room for polytechnic education, and the connection between schools and local economic and political actors was strengthened.

Medvedev was in the center of this process, both as a teacher and school director and as a future specialist in pedagogy. In 1954, he applied for positions of school director both in the Leningrad region and in the Moscow periphery. Although Moscow was a more practical choice, Leningrad was where his heart was attached. For the past few months, he had been dating Svetlana, a seventeen-year-old pupil from his school. She was planning to move to Leningrad to pursue her studies. Therefore, his preference was for a position in a region halfway between the two metropoles, ideally in the Kalinin (Tver') region. Eventually, he was appointed director of a secondary school in the village of Kliuchevoe, in the Vyborg region, near the Gulf of Finland, 130 kilometers northwest of Leningrad. He judged this position most advantageous to conduct pedagogical experiments: he wrote in his diary that his goal was "to transform our school, unnoticeably for educators and students, into a kind of pedagogical laboratory." He would, on the one hand, apply methods tried out at "advanced schools," and, on the other, assess these methods and experiment with new ones. He liked the idea of teaching not only theoretical knowledge, but also professional skills: at his school, students cut firewood, worked on a vegetable garden plot and in a carpenter workshop. Based on these experiments, Medvedev developed concrete policy proposals in the field of education, which he started submitting to the press and policy makers: during a trip to Moscow, in early 1955, he had contacts with editors at *Pravda* and *Izvestiia* as well as officials in the Central Committee and the State Planning Committee. They expressed interest in his research and gave him useful comments.

Roy's relationship with Svetlana ended in late 1954: although he had asked her to marry him, she had turned down his proposal. In summer 1956, however, at a gathering of his school friends from Tbilisi in Moscow he made the acquaintance of Galina Gaidina. The young woman, aged twenty-eight, came from Vladikavkaz, in North Ossetia, a city of the North Caucasus Roy knew well. Galina shared Roy's interest in scientific research, had a PhD in medicine and worked at the Institute of Endocrinology of the Academy of Medical Sciences in Moscow. After the party, Roy walked her home; they began to exchange letters, and in the winter, Galina visited him in Leningrad. After walking for hours around the city and going to the theater, Roy invited her to stay with him in Karelia and go skiing, a sport they both loved. When Roy presented the young woman to his colleagues, he introduced her as his wife, to their great joy. And indeed, soon they got married. Roy remembered fondly the three weddings they organized for friends and relatives in Moscow, Leningrad, and at Roy's school. By then, Roy was over thirty, and he clearly felt that the time had come to get married. In retrospect, he judged his family "exemplary," although he and his wife clearly lived separate lives, each engrossed in their scientific research, while a nanny, who almost became part of the family, raised their son.

Galina Gaidina, 1960s. OKhDLSM, F. 333, op. 3, d. 22, l. 1.

Indeed, starting from 1957, Roy's career took a new turn, as he moved to Moscow. He had been studying for his PhD on a distance learning program for three years and decided to study one more year full time at the Moscow State Pedagogical Institute. He defended his dissertation in March 1959 under the title "Productive labor of senior school students in industry and the problem of productive specialization." In summer 1958, thanks to the contacts he had gained in the educational field, he was recommended for a position of school director. It would have given him access to accommodation and the precious registration stamp necessary to live in the Soviet capital. The question of accommodation was a crucial one for the young couple, who could not afford to rent a room in Moscow: Galina shared a room with an elderly lady, taking care of her in exchange for free housing. However, the district party committee rejected

Medvedev's application: he was considered too young for such a responsible and difficult position. Instead, he was offered a position of vice-director for education affairs, but it did not entail free accommodation and Medvedev had to turn down the offer.

In October 1958, Medvedev was hired as editor of the journal *Polytechnic Education*. A year later, he was promoted vice-editor-in-chief of "Uchpedgiz," the state publishing house for pedagogical literature. The family's material situation also improved: in 1959, Medvedev received a room in a communal apartment in the city center. He and Galina lived there with their newly born son Aleksandr until they were able to buy a cooperative apartment on Dybenko Street, in a northwestern suburb of Moscow, with funds loaned by Galina's family. This career rise was made possible by Roy's new party full membership, a prerequisite for such responsible positions. Yet Medvedev no doubt joined the party out of idealistic, rather than opportunistic considerations. Making a career was not his top priority: although he enjoyed his job, it left little time for independent research, and when disagreements with the new editor-in-chief arose, he resigned.

Until then, Roy Medvedev had a nearly flawless record. But his independence of thought did not escape the party authorities' attention. The first flaw in his party record dates to this period: Medvedev was blamed for his "unconscientious editing" of a geography reader, which presented life in capitalist Britain in an excessively positive light. The party functionary who summoned Medvedev asked him: "Comrade Medvedev, what's wrong with your publishing house, do you consider that Communism has already been built in England? I read the section on Britain, London, palaces, green meadows… and I enjoy it so much, as if people there lived better than in the Soviet Union. As if there were no unemployment, no hunger, no homeless people, and no evils of capitalism…" After this conversation, Medvedev had no choice but to abide by orders from "above," and "homeless and unemployed people appeared in London, and everything that is appropriate for the worst capitalist country." In 1969, this trivial episode would be mentioned in a report of the Central Committee to emphasize that Medvedev had long been a hidden opponent of the regime.

Nevertheless, in October 1961 Medvedev was hired as a senior researcher by the Institute of Production Education of the Academy of Pedagogical Sciences. He enjoyed the freedom this position granted him: as a prodigiously productive researcher, he could process in three or four hours the daily workload entailed by his position and spend the rest of his day working on parallel research projects. In the early 1960s, he published around fifty articles and two books: *Professional Education of School Students on Industrial Plants* (1960), which was also published in the German Democratic Republic and in Bulgaria, and *Questions of Organization of Professional Education of School Students* (1963).

Roy Medvedev's professional career started more modestly than his brother's. Despite being a brilliant student, his background as the son of an "enemy of the people" stood in the way of his career advancement. To get a PhD in philosophy and work in the ideological sphere, he would have needed strong credentials, and most of all membership in the party. But Medvedev was unwilling to fulfill blindly political orders, to compromise with his conscience for immediate political gains. He believed that the merits of his scholarly work, which, already then, he preferred to conduct independently, would speak for themselves. At the same time, his research in the field of education was closely connected with his socialist beliefs: the concept of polytechnic education was based on the idea that manual and intellectual skills could be acquired jointly for a more complete education, further bridging the gap between social classes. In this, Roy's views differed from that of another future dissident, Andrei Sakharov, who in 1958 advocated for special schools for talented young specialists.

Stalin's death opened new possibilities for sons of former "enemies of the people," who wished to make a career. Eventually Roy did join the party and became a recognized scholar in his field. Yet his interests were much broader than the prescribed framework in which he was constrained to work, and he felt compelled to make a greater contribution to society through his research by investigating the darkest pages of the Soviet past.

Works Cited

Medvedev, Roy, and Zhores Medvedev. *1925–2010. Iz Vospominanii*. Moscow: Izd. "Prava cheloveka," 2010.

Further Reading

Fürst, Juliane, *Stalin's Last Generation: Soviet Post-War Youth and the Emergence of Mature Socialism*. Oxford: Oxford University Press, 2010.
Jochen Hellbeck, *Revolution on My Mind: Writing a Diary under Stalin*. Cambridge, Massachusetts: Harvard University Press, 2006.
Polly Jones, "From the Secret Speech to the Burial of Stalin. Real and Ideal Responses to De-Stalinization." In *The Dilemmas of De-Stalinization: Negotiating Cultural and Social Change in the Khrushchev Era*, edited by Polly Jones, 41–63. London: Routledge, 2009.
Tromly, Benjamin. *Making the Soviet Intelligentsia: Universities and Intellectual Life under Stalin and Khrushchev*. Cambridge: Cambridge University Press, 2014.

CHAPTER 4

Making Sense of Stalinism

The period of relaxed censorship in Soviet literature that followed Stalin's demise has been poetically labelled "the Thaw," in reference to a 1954 novel by Il'ia Ehrenburg. Admittedly, what characterized the following decade was less a steady process of liberalization than an alternation of thaws and freezes, which fostered both hopes and frustration. Nevertheless, for the "sixtiers" generation, born and raised in the Stalin era, to which Roy and Zhores Medvedev belonged, a wind of change was blowing. Taking advantage of new opportunities, a whole generation of Soviet intellectuals sought to use its influence in the field of arts, literature, history, or science to denounce past crimes and help reform the regime. As the Medvedev brothers both became engaged in underground research projects, they made the acquaintance of like-minded writers and scientists, who contributed to their research and assisted them in various ways.

In 1962, Roy Medvedev was at a colleague's birthday party when the discussion touched upon the question of Stalin's crimes, a subject then ubiquitous. Someone asked: "But how could all these horrible things happen?" Roy, who had been giving some thoughts to the question and had even started writing down his preliminary hypotheses, launched into an hour-long speech on the topic, to the bemusement of his colleagues. "Roy, why don't you write all this down?" was their reaction. He smiled: "Indeed, why not!" This conversation gave new impulse to a research project he had recently started. His goal was not only to reconstruct the history of Stalin-era political repression but, more broadly, to engage in a philosophical reflection on the origins and nature of Stalinism.

Since he was seventeen, Roy had considered writing a study on the merits and flaws of Soviet society. After the 20th Party Congress and his father's rehabilitation, he felt more acutely than ever the necessity of shedding light on the causes of the tragedy that had befallen his country for thirty years. As a Communist, he felt a duty to help the Party understand the origins of its self-inflicted catastrophe and draw the necessary lessons. But the material for such research was missing, and Khrushchev's policy of de-Stalinization was far from consistent.

Although hundreds of thousands of prisoners had been liberated from the Gulag and rehabilitated, the Secret speech remained unpublished, and those historians who had tried to investigate the dark pages of the past learned the hard way that some topics remained taboo. There was no guarantee that the party would welcome such research as Medvedev wished to undertake.

The year 1961 constituted in this regard a watershed and, as it seemed at the time, a point of no return to the past. At the 22nd Party Congress, Khrushchev renewed his denunciation of Stalin's crimes, this time openly: the fiery anti-Stalinist speeches uttered at the Congress filled the newspapers, and the news that Stalin's body had been removed from the Red Square Mausoleum, where it previously lay alongside Lenin's, stunned Soviet citizens. At Roy's workplace, a party meeting was convened after the Congress, and Roy spoke eloquently about the need to condemn Stalin's crimes. In the literary and historical fields, a relaxation of censorship opened new possibilities. The Thaw was at its peak after the 22nd Party Congress. In November 1962, the literary journal *Novyi mir* published *One Day in the Life of Ivan Denisovich*, a novella by Aleksandr Solzhenitsyn, which described the life of a Gulag prisoner. It was an immediate success with the public and made the author famous nationwide.

Soviet newspapers also started publishing commemorative articles about rehabilitated victims of Stalin-era repression. Taken together, these articles from the central and regional press, which Roy began to collect systematically, gave an idea of the scale of repression and its wide geographic scope. By systematizing this information, Roy produced in a year a first, ninety-page long, manuscript. By 1964, it was four hundred pages long. This version had a heavy emphasis on the years 1937–1938, the height of Stalin's "Great Terror," and contained an analysis of the reasons for mass repression, the conditions which had facilitated Stalin's abuses of power, and the consequences of his "personality cult."

An important impulse for Roy's research was also the example of his brother. He had witnessed the circulation of Zhores's manuscript on Lysenko and taken note of the materials he had been able to gather from numerous scientists as a result. This was precisely what Roy needed to reconstruct events of the recent past, as archives were still inaccessible. He knew Ivan Gavrilov, his father's friend, who introduced him to other Old Bolsheviks. These veterans of the Revolution and the Civil War, who had occupied prominent positions in the political apparatus, had often been arrested during the Great Terror. They had experienced Stalinist repression firsthand and could best of all inform him on the inner workings of the party and its repressive machine, the NKVD. They also trusted him, a fellow party member and the son of a repressed Communist.

Among them was Aleksei Snegov, a veteran of the Civil War who had met Lenin, Stalin, and many Bolshevik leaders after the Revolution. Arrested in 1937, he had survived monstrous torture and spent fifteen years in the Kolyma Gulag camps. After Stalin's death, however, he had reminded Khrushchev of their acquaintance and testified at Beria's trial, opening the Soviet leader's eyes on the horrors of the Stalin era. His testimony and that of another former prisoner, Ol'ga Shatunovskaia, were crucial in convincing Khrushchev to denounce Stalin at the 20th Congress. After his liberation, Snegov also played an active role in the release of unjustly convicted Gulag prisoners, following his appointment to the position of deputy director of the political Department of the Gulag administration. Several hundred thousand prisoners were thus freed from the camps in the years 1954–1956. After retiring, in 1961, Snegov spoke relentlessly in public about the evils of Stalinism, even after the official ideological line changed in 1965 and positive appraisals of Stalin reappeared in the press. Snegov was eager to help Medvedev, sharing his own memories about the Stalin era and connecting him with other witnesses. His outspokenness and the assistance he provided to several dissident historians, however, nearly caused his exclusion from the party in the late 1960s.

Another important witness for Medvedev's research was Suren Gazarian, whose Gulag memoirs were the first Medvedev read. A veteran of the Revolution and Civil War, he had risen to the position of head of the economic section of the NKVD in the Transcaucasian region (Georgia, Armenia and Azerbaijan). Arrested in 1937, he was released after the war, and after Stalin's death he testified at the trial of Beria's henchmen in the Caucasus. Gazarian tried to publish his memoirs in the 1960s, but the end of de-Stalinization in 1964 prevented the publication. Medvedev was happy to use the rich information contained in this work, and the two men became friends.

Medvedev's research methods were not common at the time: they corresponded to what we would now call oral history. Oral testimonies have both advantages and drawbacks: while they allow the researcher to get insider information that would not have been reflected in official documents, they can also contain unverified hearsay or deformation caused by faulty human memory. Yet, to conduct the research that Medvedev wanted to undertake, there was no alternative to personal testimonies, whether oral or written: archives were closed, and when he turned to such official institutions as the Institute of Marxism-Leninism, he was denied any assistance.

Medvedev did receive help from individual professional historians, however, most of them employed by the Institute of History of the USSR Academy of Sciences. They shared his views on Stalinism and had tried to push back the boundaries of censorship in their research field, but in the late 1960s they increasingly faced censorship and repression. As professional historians, they were certainly better-skilled than he was, Medvedev reasoned, but none of them was ready to undertake the kind of work that he had taken upon himself.

Judged from today's point of view, Medvedev's research may appear excessively tame and ideologically biased. His 1964 manuscript, entitled "In Front of the Tribunal of History," was written at a time when Medvedev could still hope to see it published in the Soviet Union. Starting his research at the height of de-Stalinization, Medvedev felt he could count on the party's endorsement. In the introduction, he cited as a guideline for his research a quote by Khrushchev:

> Our duty... is to carefully and thoroughly investigate such affairs as those connected with abuse of power. Time will pass, we will die, but while we are working, we can, and we must clarify many [things] and tell the party and the people the truth... We have to do it, so that such phenomena may never be repeated.

The bulk of his work was dedicated to the sensitive question of the causes of Stalinism and conditions that had facilitated Stalin's abuse of power, as well as the consequences of Stalin's "personality cult" for the Soviet system. In his conclusion, he underscored the necessity for the party to tell the people the truth: "... only an open and honest self-critique of our party can bring forth the movement which will sweep away from our path all these consequences and will make the return of new cults and a new arbitrary rule impossible."

Medvedev, however, was constrained both by the political framework of the Secret Speech, and by the sources he used. Concentrating particularly on the years 1937–1938 and terror against the Communist party apparatus, his work said little about the impact of repression on the broader population and left aside such key pages as the collectivization of agriculture or industrialization. His judgment on Stalin's political opponents within the party, still unrehabilitated, remained very orthodox. Yet he denounced the use of torture to extract "heartfelt confessions" during the show trials of the 1930s, which he called "a monstrous spectacle, a scary show that obviously had to be rehearsed many times before being shown to the public." Most of Stalin's victims, he emphasized, had never taken part in any opposition, and had been unjustly repressed. Among them were "the best people of our party and state. It was the most dreadful act in the tragedy of the 1930s."

The grandiloquent formulas, quotes from Marxist classics and Khrushchev's speeches testify to Medvedev's ambition to see his work in print in the Soviet

Union. By speaking the party's language, he hoped to make his research acceptable to the Soviet leadership. But his design was still bold, and even at this early stage he went beyond the mere critique of Stalin-era crimes. He also denounced the concentration in the Soviet leader's hands of "immense power and decisive influence in all spheres of the life of society," from foreign policy to economics, and from science to arts. This definition certainly equally applied to Stalin and Khrushchev, as did Medvedev's critique of the reign of "bureaucratism."

Medvedev made no secret of his work, and although he was not afforded the assistance he hoped from the Party, word of his research began to spread to the higher spheres of power. In September 1964, the director of the State Publisher Politizdat called him:

- Roy Aleksandrovich, you are writing a book on Stalin, may I have a look at it?
- No, you can't have a look, because you're a publisher, you publish finished manuscripts, and this is still work in progress. I'm not yet ready to show it to a publisher.
- Can we just read it? Central Committee Secretary Leonid Il'ichev is requesting it.
- You're welcome to.

A year later, however, the manuscript was returned with a rejection letter. The accompanying review testified to the authorities' interest in his work but overall critical judgment. "R. Medvedev's manuscript is entitled 'In Front of the Tribunal of History'. But a judgment can only be just, authentic, when each word of accusation is buttressed by facts, evidence. Very important historical and political problems cannot be solved superficially, groundlessly, as the author does in several places."

Apart from Leonid Il'ichev, the Central Committee Secretary in charge of ideology, Medvedev's research aroused the curiosity of two other secretaries: Iurii Andropov and Boris Ponomarev. They had heard of Medvedev's research through his acquaintances in the Central Committee: Iurii Krasin, a professor of philosophy at Moscow State University whom Roy had befriended during their studies in Leningrad, and Georgii Shakhnazarov, whom he had met as he worked in publishing. The Central Committee departments headed by Andropov and Ponomarev had a liberal reputation, and some of the young consultants in these teams, including Shakhnazarov, would go on to make brilliant careers during Perestroika. Among the consultants Medvedev knew were also Aleksandr Bovin, who, as Brezhnev's speechwriter, would play a role in Zhores Medvedev's liberation from the psychiatric hospital in 1970; Fedor Burlatskii, who also had a doctorate in philosophy; and China specialist Lev Deliusin. Georgii Arbatov, who started working as a consultant in Andropov's team at the time, called it "one of the most outstanding oases of creative thought." What united them was "anti-Stalinism and their support for democratic reforms, a more liberal policy in culture, and, of course, a desire for better relations with the West."

Medvedev agreed to share his manuscript with Andropov, and once he had read it, the Soviet leader came by during one of Medvedev's visits to Shakhnazarov's office for a short informal introduction. He called Medvedev's research "interesting" and asked to keep the manuscript. As for Ponomarev, he transmitted his request anonymously through his aide, refusing to meet the author, and Medvedev turned it down. Medvedev's account of Andropov's measured approval of his work constitutes an important element in his own narrative about his unusual dissident career. The historian believed his work had produced a favorable impression on Andropov in 1964, and that once at the head of the KGB, and later as General Secretary of the Party, he had protected Medvedev from arrest. While there is no direct evidence of such support, these early contacts certainly show the affinity between Medvedev's position in 1964 and that of some inner-party reformers within the Soviet apparatus.

However, 1964 marked a watershed in the official attitude towards Stalin. While Medvedev's hopes to see his research in print in the Soviet Union may have been bold under Khrushchev, they became outright unrealistic a year later. In October 1964, Khrushchev was ousted from power, and his policy of de-Stalinization was one of the first to be discarded. Brezhnev, whose position on the subject was probably middle-of-the-road, was surrounded by influential neo-Stalinist advisors who lobbied the Soviet leadership throughout the late 1960s to exclude anti-Stalinist works from print and rehabilitate Stalin's legacy. Although Stalin was never officially rehabilitated through a party resolution, criticism of his legacy was now deemed undesirable. Over the years 1966 to 1970, a growing number of publications praising Stalin's achievements—particularly his wartime leadership—appeared in print, while anti-Stalinist works were accused of "blackening" Soviet history and censored.

Meanwhile, Medvedev continued to enlarge his work. His friendships with writers, dissidents, and Old Bolsheviks allowed him to gather ever more material, and every six months he would produce a new version of his manuscript. Some of the new testimonies he gathered led to a radicalization of his interpretation. A key witness in this regard was Mikhail Iakubovich, a Menshevik whom Medvedev met in 1966. After over two decades in the Gulag, this old man was still living in internal exile in Kazakhstan, but occasionally visited friends in the capital. The Russian Social-Democratic Labor Party had split in 1903 into a Menshevik and a Bolshevik branch, but after the February 1917 Revolution, some Mensheviks, such as Iakubovich, decided to collaborate with the Bolsheviks. During the 1920s, he held leadership positions in the Soviet economy, but in 1930 he was arrested in the framework of a fabricated affair, the "All Union Bureau of Mensheviks." After suffering monstrous torture and surviving a suicide attempt, he agreed to play the role he was assigned in a "show trial." In the 1930s, Stalin staged such trials against prominent political rivals to both discredit and eliminate them. The accused all dutifully recognized their guilt, even as they were accused of the most fantastic crimes. How these once proud leaders of the Communist party could fall so low mystified the public and seemed to vindicate Stalin's repressions. Iakubovich's account showed for the first time the story of a show trial "behind the scene," and Roy chose to reproduce his testimony in full in his book.

Medvedev was also interested in other stories Iakubovich had to tell: the old Menshevik had met not only Stalin, but also his political opponents within the party: Trotskii, Kamenev, and Zinoviev. He had even penned several essays about these figures, which displayed them in a more nuanced light than official history books. Through these writings, Medvedev discovered a new picture of the early Soviet years: as he stated in *Let History Judge*, "no problem of Party history was as blatantly falsified for twenty to thirty years as the struggle with the oppositions." Even after denouncing Stalin's crimes, Khrushchev had shied away from rehabilitating the tyrant's political opponents, although they had once been Lenin's closest allies. Now Medvedev realized that Stalin had cunningly maneuvered to neutralize his opponents: thanks to a tactical alliance with the "right wing" of the party, he had eliminated the "leftist" opposition of Zinoviev and Kamenev, united with Trotskii. Then he had turned against the "rightist" opposition of Nikolai Bukharin. Increasingly, Medvedev's view on Soviet history departed from the official course, and successive versions of his manuscript reflected this shift.

By 1965, Zhores Medvedev's name was widely known in the Moscow literary and scientific intelligentsia, and word of his twin brother's research was also spreading. When he submitted his manuscript on Lysenko for publication in the journal *Novyi mir*, Zhores mentioned that his brother researched the history of Stalinism, and the editors expressed the wish to meet him. *Novyi mir* was what Russians call a "thick journal": a monthly journal combining literary and sociopolitical orientations, emphasizing literary critique, and with a distinct identity. Under Tvardovskii's editorship during the Thaw, *Novyi mir* had become the favorite literary journal of the liberal intelligentsia. Medvedev remembered buying the journal every month in the 1960s and reading it "almost always from cover to cover." He valued not only the high literary quality of the works published but also "the social, political and moral platform of the journal and its editorial team," combining anti-Stalinism and a faith in democratic socialism. In fall 1966, Roy finally brought the newest version of his manuscript to *Novyi mir*. After taking turns reading it, the editors transmitted it to the editor-in-chief, Aleksandr Tvardovskii, who called the author to express the wish to meet him. Roy was elated.

As soon as they met in late 1966, the two of them hit it off. Tvardovskii, who had managed to convince Khrushchev to let him publish Aleksandr Solzhenitsyn's Gulag novella *One Day in the Life of Ivan Denisovich*, shared Roy Medvedev's conviction that the party had to denounce Stalin's crimes and his faith in democratic socialism. In his diary, the editor expressed his deep admiration for Medvedev's work, praising both its thoroughness and the author's political loyalty: "What a truly epic, huge, audacious and noble work one person has undertaken, in order to collect everything that is available, and build a comprehensive, convincing, and deeply party-minded account of the history of the Stalin era." In the following years, they met regularly, exchanging samizdat and restricted access documents that Tvardovskii received. In May 1968, Tvardovskii also read with interest Medvedev's work of political philosophy entitled *On Socialist Democracy*.

Tvardovskii was not the first famous writer and editor Medvedev had befriended. Before him, he had met Konstantin Simonov, recipient of six Stalin prizes and former editor-in-chief of *Novyi mir*. As a wartime correspondent and author of popular works about the war, Simonov had personally known Stalin. In the 1960s, Simonov had come to reconsider Stalin's historical role and his own participation in several shameful ideological campaigns. Again, it was after reading and meeting Zhores Medvedev in 1963 that Simonov heard about Roy's research. The historian remembered giving Simonov his manuscript to read in late 1964 or early 1965. When they met again, Roy was disappointed by Simonov's failure to comment on his work or to tell him about his encounters with Stalin. Instead, however, the writer offered to grant Medvedev access to his personal archive, which contained unpublished manuscripts about the Stalin era that the writer had received from their authors and interviews with military staff that Simonov had collected for his own works. In 1965–1966, Medvedev visited Simonov's house four or five times to work with these documents, which provided him with valuable information.

In 1963, Roy Medvedev met Evgeniia Ginzburg, author of Gulag memoirs which were then circulating in samizdat and were later published in the West under the title *Into the Whirlwind*. She gathered at her apartment a circle of fellow writers and rehabilitated Gulag inmates. Among them was Natal'ia Stoliarova, a former prisoner who was the secretary of Il'ia Ehrenburg. She read Medvedev's manuscript and offered to show it to her boss. Like Simonov, Ehrenburg had been a popular wartime correspondent and writer and had personally known Stalin. In early 1966, he invited Medvedev to meet him. Unlike Simonov, who asked a lot of questions but said little, Ehrenburg pronounced a long monologue, which Medvedev found highly interesting, although he disagreed with many of the writer's judgments on Stalin. In his memoirs published in the 1960s, Ehrenburg displayed his continued admiration for the Soviet ruler, even as he condemned Stalin-era political repressions. He had also witnessed the trial of his childhood friend Nikolai Bukharin, Stalin's opponent, executed in 1938. Another time, Medvedev was invited for dinner along with Evgeniia Ginzburg and Nadezhda Mandel'shtam, widow of a famous poet who had died on his way to a Gulag camp in 1938. A secular Jew and compiler, along with Vasilii Grossman, of the unpublished "Black Book" of the Holocaust on Soviet and Polish territory, Ehrenburg spoke about his controversial silence in the face of Stalin-era anti-Semitic repressions in the early 1950s, which had earned him widespread criticism.

Another author published by *Novyi mir* whom Medvedev met in the 1960s was Iurii Trifonov. His novel *The Impatient Ones* (1976), telling the story of the assassination of Czar Aleksandr II, earned him a Nobel Prize nomination in 1981. He was also the author of a cycle of urban prose that culminated in the popular novel *The House on the Embankment* (1976). It played out in the house where Trifonov had grown up, the scene of countless arrests in the 1930s. Trifonov was the Medvedev brothers' age and had also lost his father to Stalinist repression—a story he told in his novel *Fireglow*. Over the years, Medvedev became a regular guest at Trifonov's apartment and his dacha in the "writers' village" in Krasnaia Pakhra, where Tvardovskii and other friends of Medvedev's also had their summer quarters. In exchange for samizdat material, Trifonov gave Medvedev access to his rich library and collection of old journals.

Roy Medvedev not only managed to attract witnesses and supporters for his project, but he also coalesced around him a small community of like-minded intellectuals, who aspired, like him, to a democratization of the Soviet system and opposed Stalin's rehabilitation. They would become readers of his samizdat journal, later published in the West under the title *Political Diary*. But by 1965, the Thaw was already coming to an end, and the research on the crimes of the Stalin era that the Medvedev brothers had undertook was becoming undesirable. Slowly, they began to drift towards what would be called the Soviet dissident movement: a coalition of independent minds, who called for political change and the respect of human rights in the USSR.

Works Cited

Arbatov, Georgi. *The System: An Insider's Life in Soviet Politics*. New York: Times Books, 1992.
Medvedev, Roy, and Zhores Medvedev. *1925–2010. Iz Vospominanii*. Moscow: Izd. "Prava cheloveka," 2010.
Medvedev, Roy. *Let History Judge: The Origins and Consequences of Stalinism*. Revised and Expanded ed. Oxford: Oxford University Press, 1989.
———. *Neizvestnyi Andropov. Politicheskaia Biografiia Iuriia Andropova*. Moscow: "Prava cheloveka," 1999.

Further Reading

Cohen, Stephen F. *The Victims Return: Survivors of the Gulag After Stalin*. Exeter, New Hampshire: PublishingWorks, 2010.
Heer, Nancy Whittier. *Politics and History in the Soviet Union*. Cambridge, Massachusetts: MIT Press, 1973.
Jones, Polly. *Myth, Memory, Trauma: Rethinking the Stalinist Past in the Soviet Union (1953–1970)*. New Haven: Yale University Press, 2013.
Markwick, Roger D. *Rewriting History in Soviet Russia: The Politics of Revisionist Historiography, 1956–1974*. Basingstoke: Palgrave, 2001.
Martin, Barbara, *Dissident Histories in the Soviet Union. From De-Stalinization to Perestroika*. London: Bloomsbury Academic, 2019.
Rubenstein, Joshua. *Tangled Loyalties: The Life and Times of Ilya Ehrenburg*. New York: BasicBooks, 1996.
Slusser, Robert M. "History and the Democratic Opposition." In *Dissent in the USSR: Politics, Ideology and People*, 329–53. Baltimore: Johns Hopkins University Press, 1975.

CHAPTER 5

Rebellious Intelligentsia

―――――

Under Stalin's ruthless rule, any hint of opposition was most severely punished. With the onset of the Thaw, however, a cautious expression of dissenting views, whether in the official press, using Aesopian language, or in alternative outlets through samizdat and tamizdat, became possible. Khrushchev's own rhetoric of a "return to socialist legality" implied the possibility—indeed the necessity—of criticizing past excesses and crimes. Yet the Soviet leadership remained deeply ambivalent about any criticism of its failings, both past and present. The risk of discrediting the regime as a whole was too strong to allow dissenting views into the open, and publication in samizdat and tamizdat increasingly came under fire as well. When the excesses of a Soviet ruler's actions became too obvious, as was the case with Khrushchev in the early 1960s, his colleagues overthrew him. But there were no institutional mechanisms to take into account feedback from below. Starting from the nineteenth century, the intelligentsia had been a force of opposition to the state's authority in Russia, and, although Soviet rulers had succeeded, through material incentives and prestigious positions, in creating a caste of loyal intellectuals, a liberal fringe of the intelligentsia remained highly critical of the lack of democracy.

While Khrushchev's rule had inspired hopes of a democratization of the regime, his ouster aroused widespread fears within the liberal intelligentsia. When Roy Medvedev found out about Khrushchev's removal, which had been approved by the Central Committee of the Party during a Plenum on October 14, 1964, he sat down to compile information he was receiving from various unofficial channels and write down his own reflections. In these uncertain times, the official media was not to be trusted, and he decided to circulate a monthly news bulletin among writers, scientists and old Bolsheviks of his acquaintance. What began as a kind of "political diary"—as the periodical would be called after publication in the West—soon turned into a full-fledged samizdat journal of over a hundred pages, which Roy Medvedev almost single-handedly wrote and edited for about seven years. It offered a digest of Soviet press and samizdat, summaries of foreign publications, and philosophical, historical and economic analyses of past and current political events, as well as preliminary versions of chapters of Medvedev's research on Stalinism, socialist democracy and Soviet agriculture.

In the 1970s, a broad variety of samizdat periodicals appeared in Soviet informal circles, covering fields ranging from poetry and philosophy to religion and historical explorations. What could not be expressed publicly was discussed in Soviet kitchens, but also home seminars, and many of these circles typed their own samizdat journals. They offered uncensored outlets for creative writing and essays, independent research, and information. Some of these periodicals had a very limited circulation, while others crossed the Iron Curtain, and their content was broadcast on Radio Liberty. Most well-known was *The Chronicle of Current Events*, published with interruptions between 1968 and 1982, which aimed at providing objective and nonpartisan information about political repression in the USSR. *Political Diary* was one of the first, and for a time the longest-lived samizdat publication in the USSR. Unlike traditional samizdat, however, its circulation was carefully monitored and limited to a circle of forty to sixty readers. The journal appeared anonymously, and its title page only bore the issue's month. Medvedev produced five to eight copies, then left them at a few trusted friends' places, who were instructed not to let the copies circulate. As Medvedev remembered, given the political context, "wide distribution would immediately leave the magazine open to attacks by the authorities." This approach restricted the journal's political influence, but also allowed for its continued existence.

The journal also differed from others in its political orientation, which was socialist and democratic. Medvedev's ambition was to foster a productive discussion with his readers, who were carefully selected to "include only those people who themselves wanted to do creative political work and develop Marxist theory, as well as certain writers and other prominent representatives of the intelligentsia." Medvedev stated that *Political Diary* was "*not* a non-party" publication. This equivocal formulation reflected the journal's ambiguous position between the official and unofficial realms: while many of its readers were party members of a reformist outlook, only outside the party could they find the necessary space of freedom to discuss such sensitive questions as Stalin's crimes, socialist democracy, or debates within the world communist movement.

Although Medvedev played a leading role in the publication, he also benefitted from the assistance of many helpers, who collected information for *Political Diary*, discussed and prepared materials for publication, but also typed and safeguarded issues of the journal. He received numerous documents from Evgenii Frolov, a former editor of the party journal *Kommunist*, as well as several Old

Bolsheviks of his acquaintance, such as Suren Gazarian. Among his helpers and information providers were dissident physicists Valerii Pavlinchuk and Valentin Turchin, and writers and editors who shared Medvedev's interest in the Stalin era, such as Aleksandr Tvardovskii.

Although Khrushchev had been ousted from power primarily for his "voluntaristic" management of the Soviet economy and agriculture and his incautious moves in foreign policy, which had led the USSR to the brink of a nuclear war in 1962, the Brezhnev leadership was also hostile to his de-Stalinization policy. Whether Brezhnev was prepared to fully reverse the course of the 20th and 22nd Party Congresses and officially rehabilitate Stalin was unclear, but in the weeks leading up to the 23rd Party Congress, in February–March 1966, fears ran high in the anti-Stalinist intelligentsia. In January 1966, an open letter to the Soviet leadership, signed by twenty-five prominent intellectuals, started circulating. It called on the Soviet leadership to renounce plans to rehabilitate Stalin. "We have yet to learn of a single fact, a single argument, which would allow us to think that the condemnation of Stalin's cult was in any way unjustified" wrote the signatories. They warned that "our people will not understand and will not accept any departure—even partial—from the decisions on (Stalin's) personality cult." The petition was signed by famous scientists, writers, and artists. Shortly after the first letter began to circulate, a second letter signed by an additional thirteen intellectuals reached the Soviet leadership. Roy Medvedev helped collect signatures for the second letter: he convinced writers Il'ia Ehrenburg and Vladimir Dudintsev, chemist Ivan Kuniants and film director Grigorii Chukhrai to sign it. He had less success with Simonov, who preferred to write an individual letter.

While writing letters to the authorities was a common practice throughout the Soviet era, in the 1960s, organized protest such as collective petitions—many of which circulated in samizdat and could even be broadcast on Western radios—was often punished by dismissal or exclusion from the party or professional unions. Nevertheless, when the signatories were prominent enough, as in the case of this petition, such open letters could influence the Soviet leadership. The KGB was alarmed by the letter's uncontrolled circulation in the country and abroad. According to Roy Medvedev, however, the authorities had, if not initiated, then at least condoned the letter, which emerged from "the depths of the party apparatus" in response to the lobbying of military leaders to obtain Stalin's rehabilitation at the Congress. Medvedev was a strong believer in the existence of "healthy forces" within the apparatus, which were still struggling for influence after Khrushchev's fall. The existence of rival factions explained Brezhnev's ultimate compromise position: although no official rehabilitation of

Stalin was ever undertaken, anti-Stalinist works ceased to appear and dissenting voices were silenced.

Over the following years, *Political Diary* published numerous open letters protesting neo-Stalinist publications in the Soviet press. Medvedev also closely followed political trials against dissidents, which became a common occurrence after 1966. The tightening of the screws was also visible on the literary scene. In September 1965, Iulii Daniel' and Andrei Siniavskii, two writers who had published literary works under pseudonyms in the West, were arrested. Their trial, in February 1966, sent a strong signal that tamizdat publication would not be tolerated. It was also the first indictment of writers for the political content of their works in the post-Stalin era. For the community of liberal intellectuals who had welcomed the literary "Thaw" of the early 1960s, this was an ominous signal of retreat from previously won positions.

In December 1965, on Constitution Day, an unsanctioned demonstration in favor of "*glasnost*" (transparency), attended by over a hundred people, called for a fair and public trial for the two writers. The initiator of the demonstration, mathematician Aleksandr Esenin-Vol'pin, staked on a strategy of "legal obedience" and called upon the Soviet authorities to respect their own legislation. This demonstration has traditionally been considered as the founding moment of the Soviet human rights movement. The mobilization around the Daniel' and Siniavskii trial grew apace in the following months. In the February 1966 issue of *Political Diary*, Medvedev commented on the trial, reproducing stenographic minutes and letters of protest circulating in samizdat. His commentary revealed his opposition to the regime's repressive policies, not only on the grounds that they violated Soviet law, but also for the harm they inflicted on the Soviet Union's international image. "Generally speaking, the recent trial has provided our enemies with considerably more material for anti-Soviet purposes than all of Siniavskii and Daniel's writings taken together."

Medvedev's commentary betrayed a certain uneasiness in reaction to political trials of the late 1960s, which he condemned, while not fully subscribing to the defendants' methods of protests. The position Medvedev usually privileged was that of a participant observer and analyst. In *Political Diary*, and later in *On Socialist Democracy*, he analyzed the existence of various currents, both within the Communist Party and within Soviet dissent. He identified three main groups within the Party: the reformist, democratic wing, which he supported; the conservative-moderate centrists, to which Brezhnev belonged; and the neo-Stalinists. The task of the reformist faction was "to elaborate a positive Socialist and Communist platform," but also "to rethink unequivocally many events of the past, to reject obsolete dogmas and develop

Marxism-Leninism in conformity with the conditions of the second half of the twentieth century." While the conservatives opposed such reform, ignoring the flaws of a system, the foundations of which were rotting, the Stalinists pushed for a radical return to the old order—a perspective Medvedev found unacceptable. Nor could he agree with those dissidents who found fault with the Communist system at large. His approach was reformist, not revolutionary:

> Without ignoring the defects and flaws in the construction of society's building, we have to extract and change, rapidly enough but with utmost care, the rotting parts of the foundations, to be replaced with something more stable and durable. This work has to be consistent and progressive; here it is vain to hope for a sudden and decisive turn of events. It is precisely this painstaking and difficult work that represents, in my opinion, the main task of this democratic current within our party.

Attempts to reform the socialist system were central to the "Prague Spring" that unfolded in Czechoslovakia in 1968. In *Political Diary*, Medvedev expressed his full support for the Czechoslovak Communist Party's democratization course. Dissidents and liberal intellectuals widely shared his enthusiasm for the Prague Spring. Medvedev obtained documents from the Czechoslovak embassy and read translations from Czech circulated in Moscow circles. His disappointment was all the stronger when Soviet tanks crushed this peaceful experiment. Official claims of impending NATO takeover in Czechoslovakia were absurd, he reasoned, and the real motive for intervention was "fear of democratization and freedom of speech," which could spill over into the USSR.

The Soviet intervention came as a shock to all Soviet democrats. However, very few summoned the courage to protest. Roy remembered that his friend, the film director Mikhail Romm, wrote a very convincing protest letter, but neither he, nor anyone of their acquaintance dared to sign it. Medvedev expressed his protest in his samizdat journal, but judged any public protest vain, because the authorities were behaving "irrationally," arresting or firing anyone who raised a banner or signed a letter. What he could do, however, was to avoid taking part in war propaganda. From 1964 to 1967, he had been secretary of his Institute's party committee, and in 1967–1969 he led a discussion circle on politics, but he refused to convene a meeting to approve the intervention, as collectives throughout the country were prompted to do. Medvedev was not alone in displaying caution. The wave of repression following the intervention caused many dissenting intellectuals to scale down their activism. Only a minority remained committed to the struggle for human rights.

Roy Medvedev's caution contrasted with the audacity of seven dissidents who raised their banners in solidarity with the Czechoslovak people on Red Square in August 1968, only to be immediately arrested. As they stood trial for this act of bravery in October 1968, Medvedev expressed his admiration in *Political Diary*. He noted the formation, since 1966, of a "kind of political movement" which, "from a struggle against concrete forms of abuse of power" was progressively turning into "a political opposition to the regime." He commended the democratic orientation of the movement, which made it less vulnerable to attacks, but was put off by the worldviews and moral make-up of some of its participants, which included some very "suspicious" personalities, in his view. This attitude of suspicion towards certain dissidents would remain a defining feature of Medvedev's relationship to the human rights movement, even as he came to be closely associated with it.

The reading and reproduction of samizdat had created a broad network of dissenters who shared a longing for greater freedom, but whose political orientations were most varied, ranging from nationalist and religious—particularly in the Soviet republics forcibly integrated into the USSR—to social-democratic and liberal views. To express their grievances, however, they relied on the same set of practices: petitions to the authorities, and later to international organizations and governments, demonstrations, hunger strikes. What gave added weight to their protest was the attention that the Western press began to give them, starting from the late 1960s: the word *dissident*, a neologism in Russian, was coined to designate this group of dissenters, who were prepared to face trial to defend their freedom. And indeed, in the 1960s the regime enacted a number of laws specifically targeting dissent: Article 70, punishing "anti-Soviet agitation and propaganda," and Article 190(1) against "the dissemination of deliberately false fabrications, defaming the Soviet state and social system."

Although neither of them was ever convicted, and their caution later evaded accusations of collusion with the regime, the Medvedev brothers came down in history as dissidents, and this was due in no small part to their association in the 1960s with famous intellectuals who would form the backbone of the dissident movement: Aleksandr Solzhenitsyn and Andrei Sakharov.

In August 1964, as Zhores Medvedev was returning from his vacation in Crimea, he bought *Sel'skaia Zhizn'*, the only newspaper left at the airport. He was shocked to discover the attack launched against him and Andrei Sakharov by Ol'shanskii, the director of VASKhNIL. In the following days, he expected to receive numerous letters of support from fellow scientists, but his mailbox remained empty, and his telephone stood silent. Just a decade after Stalin's death fear remained a powerful weapon: intellectuals with prestigious positions knew that defending a dissenting peer could threaten their livelihood—or at the least their ability to publish or travel abroad.

On September 5, however, Zhores received a letter from Riazan, a provincial city east of Moscow where he had no acquaintance. Couched in small handwriting, the letter was signed by none other than Solzhenitsyn. The writer had recently read Medvedev's manuscript and assured him: "In many years I literally don't remember any book that would have gripped and moved me like yours... I know that many readers are also moved by it, no matter how far they may be from biology. No one can remain indifferent to its further fate." In November, they met at the *Novyi mir* office, where Solzhenitsyn was discussing the publication of his new novel *The First Circle*, and the writer encouraged the editorial board to publish Medvedev's essay on Lysenko. Their first encounter was cordial. "Thinking about Solzhenitsyn, I expected to see a sick and somber man, but my interlocutor was tall, full of energy, joyful, outwardly healthy and very welcoming," remembered Zhores. Medvedev also "produced the most positive impression" on Solzhenitsyn. It turned out that they had a common friend: Zhores's superior Nikolai Timofeev-Resovskii, who had met Solzhenitsyn in 1945 in a Moscow prison. Through Medvedev, the two former cellmates were soon reunited.

Solzhenitsyn's literary fate in the USSR was closely connected with Khrushchev's de-Stalinization policy, and after 1964, the prospect of publishing his novels grew ever dimmer. In Riazan, the writer's living conditions were precarious, and local authorities were bent on preventing his move to a new flat. In these circumstances, in Spring 1965, Medvedev and Timofeev-Resovskii offered to help Solzhenitsyn move to Obninsk, where his wife Natal'ia Reshetovskaia, a chemist, could be appointed to work at Medvedev's Institute. Solzhenitsyn agreed with this plan and even acquired in the neighboring countryside a garden plot with a small wooden house, where he would write in peace several new works in the following years, among them parts of *The Gulag Archipelago*.

Despite the eagerness displayed by Zhores's colleagues and superiors, Solzhenitsyn's move to Obninsk ran into difficulties early on. This had to do, as Zhores remembered, with Reshetovskaia's aspiration to a senior position, appointment to which, unlike junior vacancies, had to be approved by the Presidium of the Academy of Medical Sciences. What may have been a formality in most cases was a serious obstacle after Solzhenitsyn came under close KGB surveillance, following the confiscation of his literary archive in a house search in September 1965. In October 1965, the Presidium of the Academy of Medical

Sciences rejected Reshetovskaia's appointment, arguing that she lacked the necessary qualifications. When the Institute's director protested, the position opening was cancelled. Clearly, orders had been sent to prevent Solzhenitsyn's move to Obninsk. Eventually, he was offered a new apartment in Riazan.

In her memoirs, Reshetovskaia spoke uncharitably about Zhores's "frenetic activity" on her behalf, judging that Medvedev's actions were only motivated by the aspiration to pose as "Solzhenitsyn's friend." She remembered his unprompted visits at their dacha, although "he could not fail to see that we were far from always happy about his visits." While Reshetovskaia's words reflected her own bitterness about Zhores siding with Solzhenitsyn following their divorce, it could be that Zhores's admiration for Solzhenitsyn blinded him to the unrequited nature of his friendship. Later, Medvedev would characterize his friendship with Solzhenitsyn as "a business-oriented friendship of two samizdat authors, who strove to unite their various forces and possibilities for a common goal." While for Solzhenitsyn, the collaboration may have been indeed instrumental to his objectives, Zhores's emotional involvement is indisputable, although he downplayed it after they fell out.

In May 1967, Solzhenitsyn showed Zhores an open letter he was about to send to the Fourth Congress of the Writers' Union, denouncing repression and censorship in the literary field. The letter, which then circulated widely in samizdat and was published abroad, sent the authorities a strong signal that Solzhenitsyn would not react silently to his exclusion from print. The same year, he released his novel *The Cancer Ward* into samizdat, and in 1968, it appeared in the West, followed shortly thereafter by *The First Circle*. Solzhenitsyn had arranged for the book's translation and publication through Olga Andreyeva Carlisle, granddaughter of the famous Russian writer Leonid Andreev.

A report of the KGB to the Central Committee dated July 31, 1967 showed that Zhores Medvedev's association with Solzhenitsyn was a source of concern to the authorities. They noted that Medvedev and Valerii Pavlinchuk, a physicist from Obninsk, had begun to reproduce and circulate *The First Circle*, identified as "a politically harmful work," and intended on passing copies to the Moscow dissident Piotr Iakir. This note showed the extent to which the KGB could distort collected evidence about dissident activities, to exaggerate the threat they represented. Although Zhores had read *The First Circle* in 1965, he denied having circulated it (or any other work) in samizdat. His hunch was that the KGB's note was based on false information obtained through Iakir's tapped conversations.

Zhores remembered microfilming a manuscript of *The First Circle*, an episode Solzhenitsyn confirms in his memoirs, but the biologist dated these events to September 1968, around the time the book first appeared in the West. According to Medvedev's account, following the Czechoslovak invasion, Solzhenitsyn showed up on his doorstep and asked him to microfilm "Circle-96," an uncensored, nine-hundred-page version of *The First Circle* which he had just "restored" to its initial format. Zhores owned a microfilming installation, on which he used special fine-grained photographic film from his Institute to produce microfilms of manuscripts, and he was happy to oblige. Zhores was useful to Solzhenitsyn in other ways: he introduced him to foreign correspondents Per Hegge, a Norwegian journalist who was the first to interview Solzhenitsyn for the Western media, Robert Kaiser from the *Washington Post* and Hedrick Smith from the *New York Times*. In 1972, with the writer's authorization, Zhores Medvedev published in the West *Ten Years after Ivan Denisovich*, a memoir dedicated to Solzhenitsyn's literary career in the Soviet Union. Like many of Solzhenitsyn's committed helpers, the biologist did his utmost to help the great author. And when Zhores announced that he was leaving for a one-year stay in London, Solzhenitsyn welcomed the opportunity to have him solve several professional and personal issues on his behalf in the West.

However, Solzhenitsyn's brief encounter with Roy Medvedev showed that the writer was chiefly interested in receiving assistance, rather than collaborating with others. When Solzhenitsyn asked to read Roy's manuscript, the historian requested in exchange access to the letters Solzhenitsyn had received from former Gulag prisoners after the publication of *Ivan Denisovich*. But the writer replied: "There isn't anything interesting there, only details on daily life, canteen, toilets. It's not even interesting to me." Roy could guess that Solzhenitsyn was lying—he had heard that the letters contained manuscripts. Indeed, as he later found out, these letters had provided the basis for a book Solzhenitsyn was secretly writing, *The Gulag Archipelago*. "This produced a bad impression on me, I was ready to bring him everything I had, but he would not share anything himself."

In his memoirs, Solzhenitsyn expressed his gratefulness for everything Zhores had done for him and others, from helping him reunite with Timofeev-Resovskii and organize his move to Obninsk to procuring rare medication in the West for his friends' daughter who suffered from leukemia. In return, Solzhenitsyn protested Zhores's forced committal to a psychiatric hospital in 1970. Once the need for a mutually advantageous collaboration evaporated, however, the differences in worldviews came to the fore, and Solzhenitsyn demonstratively broke his ties with the Medvedevs in 1974.

While Zhores associated with the author of *The Gulag Archipelago*, his brother befriended the dissident physicist Andrei Sakharov. Academician Sakharov had received the highest honors of the Soviet state for his contribution to the invention of the Soviet hydrogen bomb, yet until the 1970s he worked at a secret facility of the Soviet atomic project in Arzamas and his name remained unknown to the Soviet public. Sakharov was not content to enjoy the privileges attached to his position, however. Over the years, he became increasingly concerned with radioactive fallouts resulting from nuclear weapon testing and sought to use his influence to convince Khrushchev to ban atmospheric testing. In the 1960s, he turned his attention to two burning questions: the Lysenko polemics and the struggle against Stalin's rehabilitation.

In June 1964, when Lysenko's supporter Nikolai Nuzhdin sought election to the Academy of Sciences, Sakharov played a decisive role in preventing it—an episode which earned him criticism (alongside Zhores Medvedev) from Ol'shanskii in *Sel'skaia Zhizn'*. Sakharov's encounter with the Medvedev brothers resulted from this episode. In his memoirs, the academician wrote that Zhores Medvedev had visited him of his own initiative a few days after his intervention against Nuzhdin. Zhores dated the encounter to a few months later, in September 1964, after Ol'shanskii's attack. Boris Astaurov, a prominent biologist and friend of Zhores, transmitted him Sakharov's invitation. During his first visit, Zhores brought Sakharov his manuscript on Lysenko. "He told me that his intervention [against Nuzhdin] had strongly displeased Khrushchev. Sometimes, he would point his finger at the ceiling—a common sign to show that conversations in the apartment could be monitored by the KGB. Therefore, the conversation was restrained." When they met again a month later, the situation in Soviet biology had radically changed, following Khrushchev's ouster.

At the time, Zhores Medvedev was unaware of the nature of Sakharov's work, and refrained from asking any personal questions. Only a year later, when the physicist signed the "letter of the 25" against Stalin's rehabilitation, did his name begin to circulate in Moscow intelligentsia circles. Roy Medvedev heard from Ernst Henri, the petition's initiator, that the academician had not only readily signed it, but even offered his help in finding additional signatories. It was also through Henri that Sakharov first heard about Roy Medvedev's research on Stalinism, and that he asked to meet the author. The meeting eventually took place in early 1967, at Sakharov's apartment. In his memoirs, Sakharov described their encounter as follows:

> In 1966, I made a new acquaintance, which turned out to be important. Zhores Medvedev's brother, Roy, whom I did not know before, visited me in my Moscow apartment . . . Roy Medvedev left me a few chapters of his manuscript. Then he came many more times and brought new chapters in exchange for the previous ones. During each visit he also informed me

> of many public rumors, including about dissidents and their persecution... For me, all of this was very important and interesting, opened up a lot, from which I was fully isolated. Even if these stories were not fully objective, at first what mattered was to escape the closed world in which I found myself. Medvedev's book on Stalin was highly interesting to me. I did not know [Robert] Conquest's book "The Great Terror" then, and generally I knew too little about many Stalin-era crimes.

Roy confirmed that they met repeatedly over the following months, often at Roy's apartment. Sakharov read with great interest samizdat material Medvedev lent him, from *The First Circle* and Evgeniia Ginzburg's and Varlam Shalamov's writings about the Gulag to open letters by human rights activists and stenographic records of political trials. In 1968, Sakharov also became a reader of *Political Diary*. In the March 1967 issue of his journal, Roy had published a dialogue between Ernst Henri and Sakharov on "world science and world politics," which the two authors had once hoped to publish in the Soviet press, and which Henri had shared with Medvedev. When *Political Diary* appeared anonymously in the West in 1972, Sakharov did not recognize that the news bulletin was Medvedev's and was dismayed to find his text in print.

In Spring 1968, Sakharov started working on his famous essay *Reflections on Progress, Peaceful Coexistence and Intellectual Freedom*. His reading of *Political Diary*, which featured extensive coverage of the Prague Spring and excerpts of Medvedev's work of political philosophy *On Socialist Democracy*, likely contributed to the maturation of Sakharov's ideas. Roy was an important interlocutor for Sakharov at this stage and remembered that Sakharov had shown him his text for the first time in April 1968. "There were both deep thoughts and naïve, in my view, reflections, but the whole work appealed by its freshness of thought, originality and sincerity." Medvedev considered Sakharov's advocacy against Stalinism and for democratic socialism to be of crucial importance, given the author's prominence. He made a few critical remarks, and, on Sakharov's request, circulated the essay among historians and writers of his acquaintance to gather their reactions, as he had done for his own work. Sakharov also entrusted him with the retyping of his essay, bringing him new additions as he reworked it. Yet, in the process, an earlier version of the text, which had been circulating in samizdat, was published in the Western media.

On July 10, Sakharov called Roy to ask him to turn on the BBC: they were broadcasting his essay! The physicist did not conceal his joy. The text instantly became a worldwide bestseller, selling millions of copies. The fame that

Sakharov acquired overnight radically changed his position, both in relation to the authorities and in the world of Soviet dissent. In the following years, he became increasingly involved in human rights activism, and his relationship with Roy progressively soured. In his memoirs, Sakharov recognized that "the concrete information contained in Medvedev's book largely influenced the acceleration of the evolution of my views in these crucial years for me" but he insisted that "already then I could not agree with the conceptions of the book." Yet these words seem to have had more to do with later disagreements between the two men than with Sakharov's views in 1968. Indeed, the depiction of the evils of Stalinism in Sakharov's 1968 *Reflections* owed a lot to his reading of Roy's manuscript. In his essay, he commended the book, which remained unfortunately unpublished, as "a profound analysis of the origin and development of Stalinism" and emphasized that it was "written from a socialist, Marxist point of view."

In his *Reflections*, Sakharov insisted that his own views were "profoundly socialist" and rejected the label of "Westernizer" that Medvedev allegedly applied him, thus minimizing their worldview differences. These remarks may have been triggered by the publication in *Political Diary* in December 1967 of a long analytical article entitled "On some sociopolitical currents in our country," in which Medvedev described the existence of an influential "Westernist" current within the anti-Stalinist intelligentsia, whose views were close to that of the "Western radical (leftist) intelligentsia." Despite their support of socialism, they admired the functioning of Western democracies and hoped for pluralism in the Soviet Union rather than the "recovery" of the Communist party. One can see how this depiction could apply to Sakharov, and the wedge between his and Roy Medvedev's views would grow larger over the years. By 1972, the scientist declared to *Newsweek* that he no longer considered himself a socialist, and a year later, as he and Solzhenitsyn became number one opponents of the Soviet regime, the Medvedev brothers would make their disagreement with Sakharov's positions on détente and emigration public.

Roy's friendship with Sakharov predictably drew the KGB's attention. Sakharov's mention of Medvedev's work on Stalinism in his *Reflections* was a source of concern to the Soviet leadership. In a confidential letter addressed on August 19, 1968 to Howland Sargeant, President of the Radio Liberty Committee, CIA agent Robert L. Tuck noted: "Sakharov's reference to a one-thousand-page indictment of Stalin by Medvedev, a military historian, is particularly interesting, since it too has been circulating in manuscript form and is considered absolute dynamite to the system." Andropov's first report on Roy Medvedev as new KGB head noted that Sakharov had provided the historian with data about the repression of physicists for his research. Clearly relying on transcripts from monitored conversations, Andropov commented on the two friends' conversations on the situation in Czechoslovakia and noted that Roy Medvedev had circulated Sakharov's essay among his friends. "Medvedev approves on the whole of Sakharov's article, because it calls, in his opinion, for a democratization of spiritual life, but at the same time he notes its utopian character. Medvedev expresses his concern for Sakharov's fate and considers that he 'is wrong to use his authority to put pressure on the government.'" Whether this analysis reflected Medvedev's position at the time is hard to tell: measured risk-taking combined with a degree of caution had always been the historian's strategy of action, and the academician's sudden fame in the West could rightly preoccupy him. Indeed, as a result of the publication, Sakharov was deprived access to secret work and fired from his job at Arzamas.

The dissident movement was constituted of personalities who varied greatly in their degree of caution, moral values, and political views. Through their samizdat and tamizdat publications, Roy and Zhores Medvedev came to be associated with a movement with which they only partly identified. While the Medvedevs' views were closer to those of in-system reformers and establishment intellectuals, they were prepared to expose themselves to repression to defend those views. And it was precisely the Medvedev brothers' determination and the fame that it earned them that led to their labelling as dissidents in the West.

Works Cited

Medvedev, Roy, and Zhores Medvedev. *Nobelevskie laureaty Rossii*. Moscow: Vremia, 2015.
[Medvedev, Roy.] *Politicheskii Dnevnik. 1964–1970*. Amsterdam: Fond imeni Gertsena, 1972.
Medvedev, Roy. *Politicheskii Dnevnik II. 1965–1970*. Amsterdam: Fond imeni Gertsena, 1975.
Medvedev, Roy. "How Political Diary was created." In *An End to Silence: Uncensored Opinion in the Soviet Union, from Roy Medvedev's Underground Magazine Political Diary*, edited by Stephen F. Cohen, 17–21. New York: W.W. Norton, 1982.
Reshetovskaia, Natal'ia. *V spore so vremenem, Vospominaniia*. Moscow: APN, 1975.
Sakharov, Andrei. *Progress, Coexistence, and Intellectual Freedom*. New York: W.W. Norton, 1968.
Sakharov, Andrei. *Vospominaniia*. New York: Izd. im. Chekhova, 1990.
Sakharov, Andrei. *Vospominaniia 1921–1971: Tak slozhilas' zhizn'*. Moscow: KoLibri, Azbuka-Attikus, 2016.
Saraskina, Liudmila. *Aleksandr Solzhenitsyn*. Moscow: "Molodaia Gvardiia," 2008.
Solzhenitsyn, Aleksandr Isaevich. *The Oak and the Calf*. Collins/Fontana, 1980.
Solzhenitsyn, Aleksandr Isaevich. *Le grain tombé entre les meules: Esquisses d'exil. Première partie*. Paris: Fayard, 1998.

Further Reading

Alexeyeva, Liudmilla. *Soviet Dissent: Contemporary Movements for National, Religious, and Human Rights.* Middletown, Connecticut: Wesleyan University Press, 1985.

Bergman, Jay. *Meeting the Demands of Reason: The Life and Thought of Andrei Sakharov.* Ithaca: Cornell University Press, 2009.

Gorbanevskaia, Natal'ia E., and Alexander Lieven. *Red Square at Noon.* Harmondsworth Penguin, 1973.

Martin, Barbara. "Roy Medvedev's Political Diary: An Experiment in Free Socialist Press." *Jahrbücher für Geschichte Osteuropas* 67, no. 4 (April 2020): 601–26.

Scammell, Michael. *Solzhenitsyn: A Biography.* London: Hutchinson, 1985.

Shatz, Marshall S. *Soviet Dissent in Historical Perspective.* Cambridge: Cambridge University Press, 1980.

Zubok, Vladislav Martinovich. *Zhivago's Children: The Last Russian Intelligentsia.* Cambridge, Massachusetts: Belknap Press of Harvard University Press, 2009.

CHAPTER 6

A Question of Madness

By the mid-1960s, Zhores Medvedev had become a prominent biologist, recognized by his Western peers, and he could rely on a broad network of contacts abroad. Yet in the Soviet authorities' eyes, he increasingly appeared as an "unreliable" element, and this had dire consequences for his scientific career, the most immediate being the impossibility to travel to the West. When he applied for an exit visa to attend the Seventh Congress of Gerontology in Vienna in July 1966, to which he had been invited to serve as European chairman of a symposium in biology, Medvedev was notified that the Soviet delegation had already been formed and that his name was not included. After requesting a personal invitation from the Congress's organizers, he found out that the Academy of Medical Sciences had turned down the invitation on his behalf, on the pretext that Medvedev was "extremely busy with a number of projects."

Zhores Medvedev, 1966. Courtesy of Zhores Medvedev.

This was but one of several unsuccessful attempts that Zhores Medvedev undertook to travel abroad in the 1960s to attend conferences or give invited lectures, and which he recounted in a book entitled *National Frontiers and International Scientific Co-operation*, published in London in 1971. In the aftermath of Khrushchev's ouster, the need to catch up with Western science in the field of genetics, molecular biology and other disciplines was acutely felt. Scientific exchanges were a good way for Soviet researchers to familiarize themselves with the newest techniques and develop their own research agenda. Yet the barriers imposed by the Soviet authorities on scientific collaboration remained overwhelming, particularly for Soviet researchers who had run afoul of the regime. As Medvedev found out through his multiple appeals to higher instances and countless rejections, the system prioritized political loyalty over scientific prestige. Travelling to the capitalist West was a privilege of which few Soviet citizens could avail themselves, and the prerequisite was flawless political reliability, and often, the promise to provide the KGB with information on fellow travelers or foreign colleagues.

When Zhores Medvedev received an invitation from Bernhard Strehler, a prominent American gerontologist, to spend a year as a visiting researcher in his laboratory in Baltimore, starting from January 1966, his institute initially welcomed the invitation. After a few months, the International Section of the Academy of Sciences requested Medvedev's "exit dossier," a character reference and medical report for a trip of six to eight months. For his dossier to be approved, however, he needed more than recommendations. During a formal interview by a high-ranking official at his workplace, Medvedev received an offer to "co-operate" with the KGB during his visit to the United States. As the author of a widely known dissident work, he would certainly draw the attention of American intelligence, with whom he was to "flirt": "It was quite a simple business, therefore, and consisted of not refusing to engage in any conversations which someone or other might start in the USA." The biologist realized that his refusal to collaborate would ruin his chances and agreed to report any conversation with non-scientific bodies. His interlocutor, however, also wished to know Medvedev's opinion of Solzhenitsyn, which he asked him to put in writing—a request Medvedev evaded. At the next meeting, however, the official requested that he provide the KGB with a list of his close friends and relatives of potential interest to the CIA, with information about them and their possession of state or military secrets. Such collaboration was inacceptable to Medvedev, and he notified Strehler and his Institute's Party committee that his visit to the United States was postponed.

The failure of this project also threatened another related plan. In 1965, the Ciba Foundation, a well-known pharmaceutical firm, had invited him as a keynote speaker for its annual lecture on ageing in Sheffield in September 1966. Previous speakers included famous scientists, and Medvedev realized that such an invitation "rarely comes twice in a lifetime" and could not be declined. He decided to "mobilize all his forces, all possible means, to carry out his mission and go to the highest level." The Academy of Medical Sciences understood that such an invitation was an honor for Soviet science at large, and was supportive of this visit, which could be combined with Medvedev's planned trip to the United States, thus making a second "exit dossier" unnecessary.

However, when his American visit became impossible, Medvedev realized that he would have to take his case to higher levels if he was to secure the authorization to travel abroad. With the active support of Dr Wolstenholme, his interlocutor at the Ciba Foundation, he repeatedly appealed to various levels of the Ministry of Health and had meetings with two officials of the ministry and another high ranking official, who blamed him for his attempts to circumvent standard procedures. The invitation was "too great an honor" for him, as one of them argued, and he had to turn it down. Vladimir Engelgardt and Mikhail Shemiakin, two Soviet academicians who were members of the Ciba Foundation's Scientific Advisory Panel, tried in vain to intercede, warning about the negative impact of this affair on Soviet scientific contacts abroad. Finally, Medvedev sought a meeting with the International Section for Capitalist Countries of the Central Committee of the CPSU, but the Deputy Secretary's promise to arrange for his visit remained unfulfilled. Ultimately, Medvedev was summoned by his Institute's Special Section, severely scolded, and asked to provide a memorandum of explanation for his behavior.

Chances of flying to England to give his lecture in person had now evaporated, but with the help of a British biochemist, Medvedev managed to send the text of his lecture, which Bernard Strehler agreed to deliver on his behalf.

> And so came the day of 6 September, a day which should have been a day of triumph for any scientist. Early in the morning, I set my watch to British time. My lecture was to take place at the evening session. The morning was given over to two sessions on problems of the ageing of plants. I was listed as the chairman of one of them. In Obninsk, however, a sterner task awaited me.
>
> In the autumn, all city organizations take part for a couple of months in the potato harvest. It just happened that the turn of our section, that of Radiobiology and Genetics which comprised four laboratories, to go potato picking came exactly on September 6 and 7. That morning, with my colleagues from

our laboratory, I travelled twenty-five kilometres by bus, out to the state farm. In Sheffield they were just getting ready for the first morning session, someone else was in the Chairman's seat instead of me, while we were carrying baskets and starting to sort the potatoes, moving back and forth along the furrows.

When the evening came, Medvedev invited a few friends over to celebrate and read them out a statement he had sent to Sheffield, in which he expressed the regret that all the efforts invested to arrange Medvedev's trip to Sheffield had failed and complained about "the stupidity of the whole arrangement system here based on the law of counteraction much more than the laws of co-operation." Later, Medvedev received several accounts of the symposium and a tape of the lecture, which was soon published. The English translation of his book *Protein Synthesis and the Problems of Ontogenesis* had been released just in time for the symposium. Two years later, Medvedev published in the Soviet Union a new monograph, *Molecular-Genetic Mechanisms of Development*, which was also translated into English and published in New York in 1970 through legal channels, without his participation.

Through these experiences, Medvedev gained unique insights into the functioning of the Soviet bureaucratic machine regarding scientific exchanges. Far from discouraging him from exchanging with his Western colleagues, these difficulties convinced him that the West was the only outlet for his works, including his research on Lysenko.

Medvedev was not the only scientist to be ostracized: his colleague Timofeev-Resovskii continued to suffer the same fate, despite enjoying international renown. Since moving to Obninsk in 1964, the scientist had done considerable work to set up a new center for research on radiation and theoretical and medical genetics and trained a new generation of geneticists through countless lectures and an annual summer school attended by hundreds of young scientists. In 1965, Timofeev-Resovskii received news that he was one of twenty laureates of a Mendel medal, which would be awarded at a symposium organized for the one hundredth anniversary of Gregor Mendel's discovery on heredity, in Brno, Czechoslovakia. Although the procedure to travel to socialist countries was less strict than for capitalist countries, Timofeev-Resovskii's "exit dossier" was blocked by the regional party organization in Kaluga and he was not authorized to travel.

Medvedev, however, had decided to travel to Brno as a tourist, which did not entail any complex procedures. At the symposium, he made the acquaintance of Michael Lerner, an American geneticist who wanted to transmit some materials to Timofeev-Resovskii on behalf of Theodosius Dobzhansky, a famous geneticist living in the United States. Lerner took the opportunity to speak to Medvedev about his manuscript on Lysenko, which he had read in a copy that had crossed the Iron Curtain. Dobzhansky had been asked to review it for possible publication in the United States, and Lerner wanted to obtain Medvedev's approval. At the time, however, Medvedev was still hopeful that a Soviet version of the book would come out, and he declined the offer. A publication abroad could put him in a difficult position in the USSR, and his work would have to be updated first.

Nevertheless, after exhausting all possibilities of publication in the Soviet Union, Medvedev reconsidered Lerner's offer. He felt that the victims of this tragic history deserved more than a simple judicial rehabilitation. The world had to know about their "struggle against pseudo-science," about their scientific accomplishments and their role in the development of Soviet and world science. "Therefore, I took the decision to publish the book in English without any hesitation," remembered Medvedev. During a symposium in memory of Vavilov, organized in 1967 by the All-Union Society of Geneticists on the eightieth anniversary of his birth, Medvedev transmitted his manuscript to a Swedish scientist, Ake Karl Gustafsson, who sent it on to Lerner. The book was published by Columbia University Press in 1969 under the title *The Rise and Fall of T.D. Lysenko*.

A month before the publication, on February 11, 1969, Zhores was summoned to the office of his Institute's director and interrogated by several party officials. Their main concern was not his manuscript on Lysenko, but the correspondence that Zhores, who spoke English, had undertaken on his brother's behalf to arrange for the publication of Roy's research on Stalinism in the West. The officials showed him letters intercepted by postal censorship sent to two Western scholars who served as intermediaries with publishers. The next day, the biologist was dismissed from his job for "unsuitability to the position." Around the same time his superior Timofeev-Resovskii was also fired for political reasons, and both laboratories were disbanded.

By dismissing Zhores Medvedev from his position in Obninsk, the Soviet authorities were using a classical "prophylactic" measure of repression that the KGB had developed in relation to dissidents. Before taking this measure, the authorities usually confronted the dissenter, giving him the opportunity to repent before striking the decisive blow. During the three-hour talk Zhores had with the director of his institute and S.N. Kopylov, a local party official, he understood that the KGB had read his letters, and this provided the impulse for writing a new manuscript on the KGB's violation of the privacy of correspondence.

In the following days, Kopylov gave a series of talks in Obninsk entitled "The ideological level of the scientific worker." In them, he offered a justification for the interception of Medvedev's correspondence: his letters had been opened because they contained stamps banned from export, but the examination had revealed that they contained "ideological diversion." Kopylov added new fantastic details with each lecture: Zhores Medvedev had sent his brother's manuscript abroad, he was trying to rehabilitate Stalin.... Zhores believed that the goal of this campaign was to nip in the bud any movement of solidarity within the scientific community, which was likely, given the biologist's popularity. He reacted by sending letters to several of his colleagues, in which he denied the accusations made against him and argued that the goal of this defamation campaign was to defend the violation of postal secrecy and to isolate him by insisting on his connections with "foreigners." However, five of the seven letters were intercepted, his colleagues were summoned for interrogation, and the only one who had indeed received the letter hurried to demonstratively blame Medvedev's action.

Medvedev's next step was to try to appeal his dismissal in a letter to the President of the Academy of Medical Sciences Academician V.D. Timakov, who until recently had supported his work on Lysenko. He asked to be reinstated, even in the lower-ranking position of "senior researcher"—to no avail. On May 22, the Academy of Medical Sciences confirmed that the dismissal of an employee for "unsuitability" could be justified not only on the basis of their "qualifications and work capability, but also their moral profile, behavior in the collective, and lifestyle."

Initially, Zhores was not preoccupied by his unemployment: Rita continued her work in another laboratory, and their savings and Western book royalties were enough to live on modestly. In March 1970, he received a first payment from Columbia university, which he could spend in special "Beriozka" retail stores, where deficit goods were sold in exchange for foreign currency. There were some distressing signals, though: after his dismissal, several of his articles and book chapters currently in press were urgently excluded from publication. And when he offered his services to do translation work, the publishers turned his offer down. Nor would his former employer give him the character references necessary to find another position, despite his repeated requests. In a letter to the Ministry of Health on December 23, 1969, Medvedev complained about the situation and concluded: "If there is an 'order' not to allow me to conduct scientific work, then I request that an application be filed to grant me a two-year passport to travel abroad." He had received several invitations from American and English colleagues, and "given the current situation and the violation of all basic laws" in relation to him, he felt entitled to "take advantage of the possibilities" offered by these invitations. Three years later, the authorities would indeed allow him to travel to the West, but not before Medvedev had turned from a minor annoyance into a thorn in the Soviet regime's side.

The advantage of the situation was that he now had more time to write non-scientific works. In 1968, he had started writing *National Frontiers and International Scientific Co-operation*, which focused on the hindrances placed by the Soviet authorities on the cooperation of Soviet scientists with their Western colleagues. The first part of the manuscript recounted the difficulties Medvedev and Timofeev-Resovskii had faced in the 1960s in trying to travel abroad for conferences or lectures or to receive scientific awards, while the second and third parts offered more general reflections on scientific exchanges and legal aspects restricting these contacts between East and West.

In late 1969, Medvedev turned to a new topic: his manuscript entitled *Secrecy of Correspondence is Guaranteed by Law* dealt with the issue of postal censorship in the USSR, another question Medvedev knew firsthand. As he realized that his registered letters to the West regularly went missing, he started studying in detail the speed of delivery of letters, depending on various parameters. He also began to systematically claim compensations foreseen by international postal agreements. While Medvedev studied the question from a theoretical point of view, another dissident took upon himself the practical task of claiming the right to correspondence in court. Boris Zuckerman, a physicist and human rights activists, and a member of Sakharov's Human Rights Committee, had undertaken to send a large number of registered parcels to the West, declaring high values, to claim compensation in court when they did not arrive. Medvedev believed that their combined actions led to a change in Soviet practices: since the country responsible for the loss of the registered letter was obliged to pay a compensation, it became unprofitable for the Soviet authorities to pursue past practices of confiscation of correspondence. Over time, his letters, though still subjected to perlustration, were eventually sent to their intended recipient.

At the beginning of 1970, Medvedev sent *National Frontiers* to the West with the help of John Ziman, a British physicist from Bristol University, who also edited the manuscript for publication. The publisher, Macmillan, sent one of its editors to Moscow in April or May 1970 to fetch *Secrecy of Correspondence* and they appeared under one cover in 1971 under the title *The Medvedev Papers*. Meanwhile, however, in March 1970, a manuscript copy of *National Frontiers* was seized during a house search in the apartment of a friend's colleague.

For a scientist, being unemployed means a loss of livelihood and deprivation of the possibility to conduct experimental work. A year after his dismissal, Zhores continued to conduct theoretical research in his field, but he had grounds to worry about his scientific future. In the USSR, where the state was the sole employer, and work was an obligation, the authorities often used the weapon of (un)employment to put pressure on dissenters. Indeed, it was hinted to Zhores that he could be reinstated at his former workplace if he repented his "sins," but he refused to do so. Now the threat of being accused of "parasitism," a criminal offence punishable by years of camp, was real. Iosif Brodskii, a highly talented poet and future Nobel Prize laureate who did not belong to the Soviet Writer's Union, had been condemned under this article of the penal code in 1964. To avoid such accusations, Medvedev had applied for a position at the Institute of Medical Genetics in Moscow in 1969. As a highly qualified specialist, he was entitled to work in his field of specialization, but despite being the only qualified candidate, he could not be hired unless his application was approved by the authorities.

The Soviet regime's reaction to Medvedev's pleas, however, took an unexpected turn. On April 9, 1970, he was summoned to the office of the Chairman of the Obninsk City Soviet, to discuss not his work situation, but the case of his elder son. Sasha was seventeen and about to graduate from high school, but his reckless behavior and friendship with criminal elements worried his parents, who had sought the help of a psychiatrist. Two years earlier, he had run away from home during the summer and been caught by the police. A few years later, he would end up behind bars for a criminal offense. Was this behavior connected, as his parents later came to believe, with an attempt by the KGB to put pressure on Zhores? The KGB often used relatives, especially children, to put pressure on dissidents, for example by expelling them from university, as happened to Sakharov's stepdaughter in 1972. Or was Sasha simply an unstable teenager trying to catch the attention of absentee parents? We may never know, but the KGB certainly instrumentalized a difficult family situation to put Zhores under pressure.

Following several insistent summonses to discuss his son's case with a psychiatrist, Medvedev began to suspect that it was a trap intended for none other than him. Psychiatric repression against dissidents was commonplace, especially when the authorities could give a semblance of truth to their diagnosis based on an existing psychiatric record. In the 1960s, Soviet psychiatrist Andrei Snezhnevskii had come up with the concept of "sluggish schizophrenia" to characterize a slowly progressing disease with almost indetectable deviations from the norm—a bogus diagnosis mostly used in the case of dissidents. New legal instructions governing forced psychiatric incarceration were labelled in deliberately vague terms, giving psychiatrists considerable leeway to abide by the KGB's instructions and formulate whatever diagnosis was expected of them.

In early May, Zhores answered a request from Y. Kiriushin, his son's psychiatrist, and came to the Obninsk psychiatric clinic for an appointment. After the talk, he was led into a waiting room while the doctor talked to his son. Soon he realized that the door was locked from the outside. Although he managed to escape, this was a clear signal of what to expect. On May 29, a Friday evening, Kiriushin rang again, asking for an urgent meeting. Soon thereafter, a small bus drove up to their house and the psychiatrist, accompanied by policemen, burst into their apartment. He asked Zhores to follow them for examination, promising that he would be released by Monday. Ignoring Medvedev's protests, Kiriushin began to interrogate him about his book on Lysenko, implying that his obsession with long past events was a symptom of mental illness. Kiriushin's cursory acquaintance with Medvedev's manuscript on scientific cooperation, which did not circulate in samizdat, showed that he was on a KGB assignment. Shortly thereafter, former colleagues of Zhores's informed by Rita came over and joined the conversation, insisting that the biologist was perfectly sane and that there were no grounds whatsoever to commit him. When it became clear that Medvedev would not be persuaded to follow them, the police removed him by force and carted him off to the Kaluga psychiatric hospital.

Meanwhile, Roy was informed about the situation, and began to organize his brother's defense. By Saturday evening, Western radio stations were broadcasting news reports about Zhores Medvedev's incarceration. It was clear that the dissident would not be released by Monday. Although the psychiatrists uncovered no significant mental illness, Medvedev was kept under observation, and the USSR Minister of Health sent a new commission on June 5, tasked with issuing a new diagnosis. According to Zhores, the plan was to transfer him to the infamous Serbskii Institute of Forensic Psychiatry in Moscow, where many dissidents were incarcerated. For this, however, the KGB needed substantial incriminating material for a judicial condemnation, and the writing of an unpublished manuscript was insufficient. Through his contacts at the Ministry of Health of the RSFSR, Roy was informed about the process and unsuccessfully tried to obtain changes in the commission's composition. Although the second commission did not uncover any significant psychiatric condition either, Zhores was not released and subjected to a regime of isolation. Meanwhile, the head doctor sought to convince him to renounce his "publicistic activities," which were symptoms of a "split personality." "In time, of course, the hospital will discharge you," he said, "but you must completely stop all this other activity and concentrate on experimental work. If you continue your publicistic activities, then you will inevitably end up back here with us."

However, the campaign in Zhores Medvedev's support was only beginning to gather momentum. Over the course of nineteen days, the Medvedev brothers were able to mobilize their extensive network of supporters from the scientific and literary intelligentsia, among Old Bolsheviks, within the Central Committee, and among foreign scientists. This unprecedented campaign eventually resulted in Zhores Medvedev's release. By visiting him in the psychiatric ward and openly contesting the doctors' shaky diagnosis of "split personality," and by sending dozens upon dozens of telegrams in his defense, prominent academicians and writers subjected the head doctor of the hospital and the Soviet authorities to a drumfire of protests.

Andrei Sakharov, who had become involved in human rights defense, played an important role in the campaign for Zhores's liberation. During the International Symposium on Genetics of the Academy of Sciences, he went to the black board and wrote "Academician A.D. Sakharov is in the auditorium collecting signatures for a protest against the committal of Zhores Medvedev to a mental hospital" and left his home address and phone number. As Sakharov remembered, only a few courageous people came up to him at the symposium but the next day "the whole dissident world" came by to sign his protest at Valerii Chalidze's apartment. According to Roy Medvedev, there were about twenty signatures, including those of Academicians Igor' Tamm, Mikhail Leontovich, and Semion Al'tshuler. Sakharov's intervention preoccupied the authorities, and they organized a three-hour meeting on June 12 with the USSR Minister of Health Boris Petrovskii, psychiatrists Andrei Snezhnevskii and Georgii Morozov, and Academicians Sakharov, Boris Astaurov and Piotr Kapitsa, who had protested Medvedev's committal to a psychiatric hospital. However, the scientists would not be persuaded to interrupt their campaign, and Roy believed that the meeting was a turning point leading to Zhores's liberation. When he called the head doctor in Kaluga that night, the latter promised that the biologist would be freed on June 17.

Pressure only increased when Solzhenitsyn released his own protest two days later, entitled "This is how we live."

> Because of the very *diversity* of his talents, he is charged with being abnormal, a "split personality." His very sensitivity to injustice, to stupidity, is presented as a "morbid deviation," "poor adaptation to the social environment." Apparently to harbor thoughts other than those which are *prescribed* means that you are abnormal.

In the Western media, interest in Medvedev's story was growing. On June 8, several American newspapers began to publish articles on Medvedev's manuscript on the cooperation of scientists, excerpts of which they had somehow managed to access.

But Roy was also counting on his relations within the Soviet apparatus. On May 31, he talked to his friend Iurii Krasin, who worked in the Central Committee, and who promised to take the matter into his own hands. The next day, their common acquaintance Aleksandr Bovin, a former consultant from Andropov's team and Brezhnev's speechwriter, raised the issue with the General Secretary himself. According to Bovin's own account, as he was reporting on a paper he was writing for Brezhnev, he observed that the dissident's committal to a mental hospital was a mistake: "We are making things worse for ourselves…" Usually the Soviet leader would remain composed while listening to his interlocutors, "digesting" their words without giving the slightest hint about his thoughts, but here he showed unusual vivacity and immediately rang KGB head Andropov.

> – Were you the one who gave the order for Medvedev?
>
> The answer was approximately as follows:
>
> – No, the administration overdid it. I've already received a call from the Academy of Sciences. I will sort this out.

Zhores, however, doubted that his psychiatric incarceration resulted from a lower-level initiative. This version, he believed, was launched the day after his liberation to whitewash the central Soviet leadership. While he confirmed that Roy's friends had informed Brezhnev, he doubted that the General Secretary had given the order to liberate him.

> My liberation was chiefly the result of broad and determined protests of scientists and writers, but also the growing campaign in Western media. Solzhenitsyn's intervention showed that this campaign would continue to grow, and not subside. The arbitrary was too obvious and had no medical or judicial basis. Two international biological conferences, planned for July and August in the Baltic, were under threat of boycott. The invitation of the USSR A[cademy] of M[edical] S[ciences] to the International Congress of Psychiatry in Mexico in 1971 could be cancelled as

well. Zhores Medvedev's quiet and discreet "medical isolation," intended to deprive him of access to foreign publishers and contacts with foreign scientists, failed. But no order was given to interrupt all this "psychiatric affair."

On June 17, Zhores Medvedev was finally released. Three days later, Roy was summoned for a talk at the KGB. His interlocutor, who introduced himself as "General Teplov," explained that Zhores's incarceration had resulted from a "misunderstanding" and advised him to forget about the incident. He promised that Zhores would find a new position in his field and would not suffer any consequences. Indeed, in October 1970, Zhores found a job at the Borovsk Institute of Physiology, Biochemistry and Nutrition of Agricultural Animals. But the threat had not totally subsided: even after his liberation, Medvedev remained registered as an outpatient of the Kaluga psychiatric hospital and was required to show up every month for controls. He refused to abide by these rules and felt entitled to reveal the details of his story in a book, coauthored by his brother and published in 1971 in Russian and English under the title *A Question of Madness*.

Zhores's psychiatric incarceration was a turning point in the Medvedev brothers' biography and a landmark in the history of Soviet dissent. For the first time, protests by prominent intellectuals in the USSR, buttressed by news coverage in the Western press, had led to the liberation of a dissident. Roy's and Zhores's extensive networks had played an important role in achieving this success. The campaign gave them international recognition as dissidents, a status associated with political repression. This would greatly contribute to the success of their publications in the West, even as their dissident credentials would be questioned in later years.

Works Cited

Bovin, Aleksandr. "Kurs na stabil'nost' porodil zastoi." In *L.I. Breznev. Materialy k biografii.*, edited by Iurii Aksiutin, 92–102. Moscow: Politizdat, 1991.

Zhores Medvedev, *The Medvedev Papers: Fruitful Meetings between Scientists of the World, and, Secrecy of Correspondence Is Guaranteed by Law*. London: Macmillan; St. Martin's Press, 1971.

Zhores Medvedev and Roy Medvedev, *A Question of Madness*. New York: Knopf, 1971.

Further Reading

Bloch, Sidney, and Peter Reddaway, eds. *Russia's Political Hospitals: The Abuse of Psychiatry in the Soviet Union*. London: V. Gollancz, 1977.

Theresa C. Smith and Thomas Oleszczuk, *No Asylum: State Psychiatric Repression in the Former USSR* Basingstoke: Macmillan, 1996.

CHAPTER 7

New Threads

To Soviet psychiatrists, Zhores Medvedev suffered from a "split personality": as the doctor who spoke with Roy in June 1970 put it, "He is a biologist, but is also involved with many other things which bear little relevance to his immediate responsibilities. Besides, he is always dissatisfied about something, always fighting against something." To which Roy retorted that Karl Marx would also have to be declared "abnormal" in this case. "Nearly all scholars have what you term a 'split personality'—as a rule a man cannot confine himself only to his own field. If you don't accept this, you will have to put a great many people into psychiatric hospitals."

Indeed, this characterization equally applied to Roy, who while working as an education scientist, researched the history of Stalinism and edited a samizdat political journal. In 1965, he had been appointed head of his department and started working on a new monograph on Soviet labor education in the postwar period, which could have constituted a doctoral dissertation (an advanced academic degree in the Soviet system). However, the Brezhnev leadership had turned away from labor education, and the book was withheld from publication by the Institute's Editorial-Publishing Council, presumably for political reasons. And although Medvedev was prodigiously productive in his official field of research, he estimated that he dedicated only about two days a week to his research in education, spending the rest working on his manuscript on Stalinism.

By 1967, what had begun as an earnest aspiration to contribute to the Party's de-Stalinization campaign was clearly beyond what the party deemed acceptable criticism of the Soviet past. In July 1967, Aleksandr Nekrich, a historian from the Institute of History of the USSR Academy of Sciences who had helped Roy, was expelled from the Party for his authorship of *1941. June 22*, a work emphasizing Stalin's responsibility for failing to prepare the Soviet Union for the impending German invasion. A month later, an old copy of Roy Medvedev's manuscript was discovered during a house search in the apartment of his friend Igor' Nikolaev in Leningrad. An assistant professor of history at a Leningrad institute, Nikolaev had been convening home seminars with students, during which he read aloud anti-Stalinist samizdat works, including Medvedev's manuscript. Nikolaev was arrested and sent to a psychiatric ward for three months. A friend of Medvedev's in the party apparatus informed him of the situation. Roy believed that this friendly warning came from Iurii Andropov, by then head of the KGB.

Although word of Roy's research had long reached the Central Committee of the CPSU, the confiscation of his manuscript officially involved the KGB. As a member of the CPSU, however, his case was to be examined by party instances in the first place. A report produced a year later, in August 1968, showed that Andropov was unwilling to recommend harsh action and advocated another approach in relation to Roy Medvedev. Commenting on his manuscript, the latest version of which had now fallen into the KGB's hands, he noted: "Medvedev's book, after it is finished, will undoubtedly circulate, will raise many undesired interpretations, since it is based on tendentiously selected, but authentic data, accompanied by skillful commentaries and catchy demagogical conclusions." Andropov suggested conducting a prophylactic chat with Medvedev at the Central Committee Department of Propaganda—a tactic the KGB widely used to convince dissidents to cease their "anti-Soviet" activities. But Andropov's approach was original in that he suggested co-opting Medvedev rather than repressing him: "Thus doing we should not exclude the possibility of inviting Medvedev to write a work on the period of our state's history of interest to him under appropriate party control."

By then, however, Roy Medvedev's case was being examined by the Party Control Commission (PCC), the organ in charge of investigating infringements to the party's rules. On September 21, 1967, Roy was summoned to the PCC and ordered to submit his work. "We have information about your authorship of a manuscript entitled 'In Front of the Tribunal of History,' which is written from extremely tendentious positions, and which circulates in Moscow and Leningrad," party investigator I.F. Gladnev informed him. Medvedev confirmed his authorship but denied that his work had escaped his control. He also refused to submit his manuscript to the PCC, judging that Gladnev was "not competent in theoretical problems of the history and theory of Marxism." He would only discuss his work with comrades from the Central Committee's Ideological Department or from the Institute of Marxism-Leninism.

The same day, Medvedev wrote to Mikhail Suslov, Politburo member and Soviet chief of ideology, sending the table of contents of his manuscript and asking for a meeting. He promptly received a response from F.F. Makarov, assistant of the Central Committee secretary in charge of agitation and propaganda

Vladimir Stepakov. Medvedev gave Makarov the first half of his manuscript but explained that he would submit his work to the Party's oversight only if the Central Committee granted him active support, since his research was, he believed, "very important and necessary for our Party." The report Stepakov sent to Suslov on November 14 characterized Medvedev's manuscript as a "politically harmful work," written in a wholly negative light, concentrating on "tragic events" and "monstrous crimes," and pointing not only at Stalin's responsibility, but at that of the Communist Party's as well. In his depiction of the struggle against inner-party oppositions, Medvedev took the oppositionists' side; his conclusions had a "tendentious, subjectivist character" and were "at odds with historical truth." Medvedev was prepared to work on the subject for another four years, but chapters of his manuscript had already begun to circulate in Leningrad, a circumstance which deeply concerned Stepakov. He concluded that the Moscow City Committee (MCC) should prevent the circulation of Medvedev's "mistaken and harmful research" and examine the question of his party membership.

Over the following months, Medvedev was repeatedly summoned to the PCC and to the MCC. Initially, the historian refused to submit his manuscript to these organs, arguing that they were not competent to judge his work. In return, they observed that a researcher in education sciences had no expertise to write about Soviet history. But Medvedev objected to such reasoning: of course, institutions like the Institute of Marxism-Leninism should be the ones engaging in such research, but their latest publications showed that they continued to falsify history. "If state organs stop baking bread tomorrow, private individuals will take up this work. People need truth no less than bread. And if those whose function it is to bring historical truth to light don't take care of it, private investigations such as mine will inevitably see the light of day."

On December 12, 1967, Medvedev wrote a letter to PCC chairman Arvid Pel'she, in which he pleaded for an examination of his manuscript in the framework of the Ideological Commission of the Central Committee, to which he had first written. He explained that his work was based on numerous Soviet publications that had appeared after the 20th and 22nd Party Congresses, but no secret documents or "bourgeois literature." He added that his research would only be completed in a few years. Meanwhile he had shown it to a range of witnesses, among them historians and Old Bolsheviks, some of whose names he disclosed, as well as Central Committee secretary Il'ichev, and only the Institute of Marxism-Leninism had declined to assist him.

The short review of his work that Medvedev was read out at the PCC in December 1967 only discouraged him further: he found it "tendentious" and "distorting the essence of [his] views and research." After interrupting his research for a year, he submitted the second part of his work in December 1968. By then, the invasion of Czechoslovakia had led to a crackdown on dissent. Roy certainly discussed the situation with Zhores, and in September 1968 he decided to microfilm his manuscript. After Sakharov had revealed the existence of Roy Medvedev's work in his *Reflections*, the manuscript could escape Roy's control and fall into the hands of unscrupulous editors beyond the Iron Curtain. Since the USSR had not signed the World Copyright Convention, Western editors could prey on the works of Soviet authors, giving them no control over publication and no royalties. Moreover, unauthorized tamizdat publications by anti-Soviet publishers could endanger Soviet authors. In December 1968, Zhores wrote to his Western colleague Michael Lerner, who had helped him publish his book on Lysenko, that he was worried by the possible circulation of samizdat copies of *Let History Judge* and asked him to inquire whether anyone had heard of a forthcoming publication of the book. This concern certainly accelerated Roy's decision to send his manuscript to the West for publication. In Zhores's words, the book was too important to be "released into samizdat or published by random publishers in Italy or Austria, it was necessary to conclude a contract observing all formalities with a respectable American publisher of political or historical literature."

In late 1969, Elisabeth Markstein, daughter of longtime General Secretary of the Austrian Communist Party Johann Koplenig and later translator of *The Gulag Archipelago* into German, took the microfilm to Vienna. She transmitted it to Georges Haupt, a socialist historian based in France who edited the French version of the book, published by Editions du Seuil. But since the Medvedev brothers insisted on a first edition in English, Haupt sent the microfilm on to David Zhoravsky. The American historian, who was a friend of Zhores's, edited the English version and negotiated a contract with the publisher Alfred A. Knopf. The Medvedev brothers' decision to seek out a formal contract was unusual, and the attention they paid to the choice of their publishers certainly contributed to the success of their publications. The choice of an authoritative Western historian, fluent in Russian, as Zhoravsky was, to serve as editor and representative was also crucial. To ensure that there would be no pirate editions of the work and to settle all legal questions, the Medvedevs also hired a lawyer.

Unfortunately, their correspondence was no secret to the KGB. In February 1969, the day Zhores Medvedev was called for interrogation at his workplace, Central Committee departments heads for propaganda, science and culture Stepakov, Trapeznikov and Shauro sent a new report on Roy Medvedev's manuscript to the Central Committee in response to Andropov's August 1968 report.

The authors unequivocally condemned in the harshest terms this "slanderous" manuscript, which bore a "clearly expressed anti-Soviet character." They concluded that all measures should be taken to prevent its publication abroad. There was no point in meeting the author for a talk, since this was "no isolated incident" in his party biography, and the question of his party membership should be examined.

The year 1969 marked the ninetieth anniversary of Stalin's birth and constituted the high tide of a campaign of positive mentions of the Generalissimo in Soviet media. Despite renewed rumors of an impending official rehabilitation, the Brezhnev leadership eventually settled once more for a compromise position in its December 1969 commemorative article in *Pravda*. Nevertheless, several memoirs and articles published in early 1969 raised widespread concern within the intelligentsia.

In late April 1969, Roy Medvedev sent an open letter of protest to the journal *Kommunist*, which had recently published two articles, signed by influential historians and officials, rehabilitating Stalin's wartime record and attacking historians who "blackened" Soviet history. In addition to the editor-in-chief of *Kommunist*, Medvedev addressed his nineteen-page letter to Brezhnev, Suslov, and other Party leaders. He denounced "two publications absolutely unacceptable for a party journal, unambiguously directed against the decisions of the 20th and 22nd Party Congresses." These "fractious" articles could "only complicate the situation within the world communist movement, already difficult." They would hurt the Party's prestige and complicate its relationship with the Soviet intelligentsia. The Central Committee, Medvedev concluded, should "not only disavow these irresponsible publications but also punish the guilty." In his open letter, Medvedev debunked a number of myths about Stalin and denounced attempts to discipline historians researching the dark pages of the Soviet past.

Roy Medvedev's letter immediately began to circulate in samizdat. Soviet dissident Piotr Iakir transmitted it to the West, where it was published first in the Russian-language émigré journal *Posev*, and later as a separate brochure in France under the title *Faut-il réhabiliter Staline?* This constituted Roy Medvedev's first publication in the West, and although it was not his own initiative, it certainly did not help his case, which was being discussed by the Party Control Committee. He did not make any secret of it and on May 27, he transmitted a copy of the open letter to his interlocutor in the Moscow Party Committee, Galina Perova, explaining that this text reflected his position on the Stalin question.

By then, the discussion concerning his party membership had already taken a turn for the worse. In May 1969, during a meeting with Perova, Medvedev was presented with two reviews of his work by historians from the Institute of

Marxism-Leninism, which, as he complained in a letter, were "extremely tendentious." One of these reviews called Medvedev's book "a vicious pamphlet, the goal of which is, under the pretense of criticizing Stalin's personality cult, to heap a maximum of slander on the Communist Party and Soviet society, to vilify and belittle socialism." During the meeting, Perova threatened Medvedev with expulsion from the party and told him that through his work he had already "placed [him]self outside the party's ranks." In a protest letter to Perova, Medvedev complained about these threats and reminded her that he had joined the party in 1956, after Khrushchev's Secret Speech and his father's rehabilitation. "As a party member and a historian, I invariably followed in my work the line of the 20th and 22nd Party Congresses. My work 'In front of the Tribunal of History' is written from these party, Communist positions." He also appealed to the Politburo.

These protests, however, failed to yield the expected results. When he returned from his summer vacation, Medvedev was summoned by his local District Committee on August 4. He was read, but not shown, an official report on his work. In a letter, he addressed different points raised in the document: he rejected the accusation of slander of the Soviet system and the charges that he was opposed to a one-party system, criticized Lenin or the party's struggle against oppositionists in the 1920s–1930s, or based his work mostly on foreign sources. Moreover, he expressed the regret that, despite his repeated requests and the promises he received in 1967–1968, no discussion of his work by professional historians had been organized, and a repressive course had been followed instead.

On August 7, 1969, the "Medvedev case" was heard in twenty minutes. The report accused him of writing a "vicious lampoon." Medvedev's critique of the personality cult was a mere pretext to "heap calumny on the Communist Party and the Soviet social regime" and he implied that Stalinism remained a potential threat in the USSR. He not only questioned the party's politics in relation to the opposition of the 1920s and 1930s, but also regarding the Second World War, which he described "as a series of stupidities and mistakes committed by the Supreme Commander-in-Chief." Moreover, Medvedev's research was based on "rumors" and "one-sided" quotes from Soviet authors. In a paradoxical statement reflecting the authorities' fears but also helplessness, the document concluded: "Comrade Medvedev has also declared that in case of his expulsion from the party, he would escape the control of party organs and would be free to circulate his manuscript on a larger scale and that he would not be capable of controlling the location of all copies of his manuscript." Without having so much as leafed through Medvedev's work, the committee thus excluded him from the

CPSU for "convictions incompatible with the title of communist, slander of the Soviet social and state system, unworthy methods of collection and dissemination of information."

The accusation of "slander" had a shaky base, insofar as the work was unpublished, but it could potentially lead to a conviction, and Roy Medvedev sought to avert such an outcome at any cost. In violation of party rules, his case had not been examined by his workplace's party cell, but directly dealt with at the upper echelon—probably, as Medvedev believed, to keep his colleagues from defending him. On September 22, Medvedev appealed the sentence. Despite the support of a group of Old Bolsheviks who wrote a collective letter in his support, the MCC confirmed his expulsion, but did remove the accusation of "slander." During a final appeal in front of the Central Committee's Control Commission, the two party investigators proceeded to a more serious examination of Medvedev's case, and he was able to defend himself thoroughly. The verdict, however, remained unchanged.

Surprisingly, Medvedev was not dismissed from his job at the Academy of Pedagogical Sciences after his expulsion. Such a move would have required a vote of his Institute's academic council, which Medvedev believed would have been difficult to obtain. Instead, he was given more work, so that he would have less free time to dedicate to research. Still, he would not interrupt his research. Nor did he heed the friendly advice of an acquaintance with obvious links to the KGB, who suggested around that time that he would only encounter serious trouble if his research appeared in the West. Roy concluded that, on the contrary, celebrity would best protect him from arrest.

While *Let History Judge* was being prepared for publication in the West, some concerning signals showed that the authorities were looking for an opportunity to strike. In January 1970, the Russian émigré journal *Posev* released an article entitled "The Truth about the Present Day," signed "R. Medvedev." *Posev* was a journal published by the Russian émigré anti-Soviet organization NTS in West Germany and was known for publishing samizdat works without their author's authorization, but there were also rumors about its links with the KGB. *Posev*'s publication of Medvedev's letter to the journal *Kommunist* had been an additional incriminating element justifying his exclusion from the party. Medvedev understood that this new article had been written on order to discredit him. It contained, in his view, "some reasonable economic considerations, but they were mixed with absurd affirmations, with declarations which could be judged 'criminal' according to Soviet law and even with calls to overthrow Soviet power." In its samizdat collection, Radio Liberty attributed the text to Roy Medvedev, whose name was known in dissident circles. On March 25, 1970, however, the historian disowned the article in a message to the Soviet news agency Novosti, reproduced in the *New York Times*, explaining that the text was not, as *Posev* affirmed, a samizdat document, but a "dirty forgery" and that the journal could be sued for defamation. *Posev* only belatedly published Medvedev's message with a disingenuous note affirming that the journal had never claimed that the author was Roy Medvedev: "In the Moscow phone directory there are more than eighty Medvedevs… and among them there are undoubtedly Rodions, Rostislavs, Riuriks and Romans to be found…"

Pressure did not abate in 1970. Roy not only played a key role in his brother's liberation campaign, but his own connections with Sakharov and other human rights activists made him suspicious to the authorities. In winter 1969–1970, Sakharov asked him to sign a letter to the Soviet leadership he had written with Valentin Turchin, a common friend. The signatories pleaded for a democratization of the regime and for greater intellectual freedom, which they argued were necessary for technical and economic progress in an age of technological revolution. Attempts to garner the support of prominent signatories had failed, and Sakharov had turned to Medvedev to sign the document, judging that "the conception of his book on democratization (which he was then finishing) was close to ours." But Medvedev's input was minimal, and the conception of "bridge-building" which dominated was Turchin's. This strategy, however, proved disappointing: although all Politburo members read the letter, the Soviet leadership largely ignored the call.

In February 1971, Roy also participated in two sessions of Sakharov and Chalidze's Human Rights Committee, and presented a report entitled "On compulsory psychiatric hospitalization for political reasons." In May 1972, he signed two petitions at Sakharov's request: against the death penalty and for an amnesty of political prisoners. Yet, human rights activism was not the Medvedevs' field of action: they preferred to express their views through their research.

In the spring and summer of 1971, with the tamizdat publication of *The Medvedev Papers, A Question of Madness*, and excerpts from *Political Diary*, the danger was at its greatest for the Medvedev brothers. After Roy interrupted the publication of his samizdat journal sometime in December 1970, Zhores advised him to publish it in the West, and they selected eleven of the most interesting issues. Bernard Gwertzman, correspondent for *The New York Times*, recalled in his memoirs his encounter with Zhores Medvedev at the apartment of Anthony Astrachan, from *The Washington Post*. "This time he surprised us all by emptying his pockets of dozens of 35 mm developed film cartridges. He explained that on these films are the typed publications called 'Political Diaries' that he and his brother Roy had written in recent years.

They wanted us to smuggle them out of the Soviet Union and publish them in the West."

Gwertzman and Astrachan published excerpts in *The New York Times* and *The Washington Post* on August 22, 1971. They concurred that *Political Diary*'s line was one of loyalty "to the basics of the Soviet system" and not of opposition but noted that "its editors have appeared to be at cross-purpose with the official line" on every question discussed. Western and émigré observers agreed that the journal's editors, who remained anonymous, were well-informed and probably occupied high positions, implying that their revisionist views found "echoes in the highest spheres." In an article in *The Times* entitled "Sprouting seeds of a new Revolution," Bernard Levin expressed his excitement in the face of the growth of "resistance" to the Soviet regime and his conviction that revolution in Russia would take forms similar to the Prague Spring. "And the revelations from the new Russian journal, *Political Diary*, show that the seeds of that revolution are sprouting far faster than could have been hoped even a few years ago." A Soviet report from February 1972 noted that the bourgeois press had made "a lot of noise" around this journal, said to "reflect the views of 'liberal socialists' in the USSR" and "the huge scale of resistance to the authorities in Russia."

In 1972, the "Alexander Herzen Foundation," a publishing house of dissident literature founded by Karel van het Reve in Amsterdam, published the eleven issues of *Political Diary* in Russian. In a letter to Georges Haupt, who acted again as an intermediary for the publication, Zhores initially expressed wariness of collaborating with a publisher who had been denounced in the Soviet press as "anti-Soviet." "Contact with such a group according to Soviet laws can lead to highly undesirable consequences." Nevertheless, Haupt seems to have convinced him that this was a good choice, or perhaps was there scarcely any alternative outlet for an eight-hundred-page volume in Russian.

Zhores's fears were understandable, six years after the Daniel' and Siniavskii trial. Although *Political Diary* was published anonymously, Roy Medvedev believed that the Soviet authorities suspected his authorship. Some articles from the journal had been circulating in samizdat under his name and had caught the KGB's attention. In a report on samizdat from December 21, 1970, Andropov mentioned the circulation of texts which "propagandize ideas and views borrowed from the political platforms" of Yugoslav leaders, the Prague Spring, and Western communist parties. He cited in example an article by Roy Medvedev entitled "On some sociopolitical currents in our country"—a text originally published in *Political Diary*. In March 1971, another document sent to the Central Committee mentioned a "pamphlet" by Roy Medvedev against antisemitism in the USSR circulating in samizdat and cited in the *Daily Telegraph*. Soviet reports on anti-Soviet literature mentioned the Medvedev brothers alongside Sakharov, Solzhenitsyn, and other famous dissidents whose names regularly came up in Western media reports about Soviet dissent.

The Medvedev brothers may not have been the largest fishes in the pond, but they had been systematically engaging in dissident activities. Roy's expulsion from the Party was a serious warning, but the scholar had not heeded the Party's "friendly" advice. Instead, he had sent *Let History Judge* for publication abroad, where it would undoubtedly be instrumentalized for "anti-Soviet propaganda." To arrest the author, however, the authorities needed incriminating material, which could only be obtained through a house search. To speed things up, the search was connected with an ongoing criminal affair involving Sh., one of Roy's colleagues from the Academy of Pedagogical Sciences. In late January 1971, Sh. had told him that she could help him acquire books discarded by the Lenin State Library for free. She explained that the books from the "exchange fond" could be obtained both by individuals and organizations, but the majority would just be recycled. She claimed to have obtained the necessary authorizations and offered to help Medvedev benefit from this opportunity. In a society where having the right connections was the best way to get access to scarce consumer goods, Medvedev had no reason to be suspicious. Sh. introduced him to a library employee, who showed him the catalogues and helped him select titles of interest to him. Although he found few relevant titles for himself, Medvedev invited his friends Viktor Danilov, a historian, and Vladimir Lakshin, a literary critic, to select literature for the Institute of History's library and the Union of Soviet Writers. In late April, however, he found out that Sh. had forged documents from the Academy of Pedagogical Sciences to gain access to these books. Although Medvedev tried to convince the director of his Institute to let Sh. return the books to the library and answer for her actions in front of a "comrade court," the director decided to hand the affair over to justice.

When the KGB turned up on Roy Medvedev's doorstep at eleven o'clock in the morning on October 12, 1971, they showed him a search warrant ordering the confiscation of "books stolen by A. Sh[.] from various Moscow libraries and offered to R.A. Medvedev." However, after five hours, the seven officials from the police and the KGB left with six large bags of books and documents which bore no relationship to the case. They found only one library book with a cancelled stamp among the forty items on the search inventory. The rest included the Medvedev brothers' own books and manuscripts, samizdat texts, memoirs, unpublished manuscripts, and whole folders of newspapers cuttings and other material that Roy used for his work, carefully ordered and labelled. This was a devastating blow for Roy, who had been actively collecting sources on a range of subjects for ten years. To the KGB's disappointment, though, the historian did not keep the bulk of his archive at home: he had copies hidden at trusted friends' places. The old Bolshevik Dora Zorina, for instance, kept his archive of *Political Diary*, so that no connection between Medvedev and the journal could be established. But he interpreted the search as a clear signal of an impending arrest. By the time Roy's son returned from school, the search had already ended, and he did not tell his wife anything. As a rule, he kept all his dissident affairs from her, so that in case of arrest she would not have any secrets to reveal.

A week later Medvedev received a summons to the USSR Public Prosecutor's Office. Initially, he planned to abide by it, but as he exited the house, his intuition told him that he was in danger. They may not have found any incriminating material, but they had certainly found out about his book's forthcoming publication. He remembered the warning he had received—certainly from Andropov—not to publish his book abroad. He ran upstairs, collected all the money he had and disappeared.

Roy knew how to escape surveillance and planned to hide at the apartment of his friend Suren Gazarian, but when Zhores tried to look for him, he unwillingly betrayed Roy's hiding place. The next day the Old Bolshevik told Medvedev that cars with searchlights were stationed in front of their building block, monitoring day and night exits and entrances. Roy asked Gazarian's daughter-in-law to visit Zinovii Gerdt, a famous theater artist of his acquaintance, who procured him a wig and fake beard. Roy then left the building dressed up as an old man with a walking stick. Although he soon noticed that he was being tailed, he managed to escape surveillance by getting on a crowded bus. He remained in Moscow for a few more days before travelling south to stay with friends in Odessa. He spent three months in hiding by the Black Sea, before moving on to Leningrad and Estonia, where other friends hosted him. He regularly sent his family postcards to show he was alive, but they had no way of communicating with him.

Before leaving, Roy had left a note to his wife, asking her to send on his behalf a letter of resignation to the Academy of Sciences and a letter protesting the illegality of the house search. The same day, Zhores also protested in writing the confiscation of his books and manuscripts. On October 27, the district Prosecutor rejected his complaint, arguing that no violation of legality had taken place. In a letter to the Moscow City Prosecutor, Zhores Medvedev called this response "absolutely unsatisfactory" and demanded once more a reexamination of the "lawlessness and abuse of power" that had taken place. When his complaint was rejected again, he protested the Moscow City Prosecutor's "representations of socialist legality," which were at odds with the relevant articles of the criminal code. He accused the KGB of stealing his books and threatened to engage a lawsuit. This, he warned, would give a political coloration to what was initially a criminal case, and threatened the authorities with negative international press coverage. His books dealt precisely with such violations of legality, and although he had listened to the authorities' advice and concentrated on scientific work for the past year, he warned he could reconsider this decision. "Your strange position... draws me again into legal problems and I dare assure you that should this legal discussion receive larger publicity, public opinion will hardly stand by the side of your understanding of the principles of *socialist* legality."

In January 1972, Roy Medvedev was summoned as a witness to the trial against Sh., along with Danilov and Lakshin. Through his wife, he sent a note of excuse and his written testimony, which corroborated Danilov's and Lakshin's statements to the court. They explained that they were ignorant of Sh.'s forgery and intended on legally formalizing the acquisition of literature through their organizations. As for Medvedev, he planned to return the books after reading them. All three of them were vindicated, while Sh., mother of a young sickly child, was condemned to six years of camp. Roy believed that this positive outcome was due to the personal courage of the judge, who took the risk of disregarding orders she had been given to sentence him. Yet most of all, what protected him from arrest was the publication of his book, which brought him worldwide fame. Zhores believed that at this point, the KGB decided to drop the case. He recalled being summoned to the Obninsk KGB office, where he spoke with the same General "Teplov" Roy had met in 1970. The official told him to inform his brother that he could safely return to Moscow. Roy reappeared after the trial, in late January.

The news coverage received by the affair seemed to confirm that the initial intention was to draw three independent intellectuals into a murky criminal affair. A slanderous article entitled "The criminal and the witnesses," published after the trial in *Vecherniaia Moskva* (*Moscow Evening*), threw doubts upon Medvedev, Danilov and Lakshin's innocence. Roy Medvedev had allegedly "tried to blackmail" the director of his institute to shield Sh. from punishment. And how could he have failed to notice his colleague's forgery? The author concluded that the witnesses had "if not contributed to, then facilitated the criminal actions" of Sh. In reaction to this article, Raisa Lert, a friend of the Medvedev brothers who had attended the trial, protested this "deliberate calumny" against the witnesses, which was meant to sow confusion in the public's mind. "Let the broad mass of readers, uninformed about the essence of the case, vaguely associate these names in their memory with some crime: either something was stolen from them, or they stole something…"

Once more, the Medvedev brothers played their game astutely, using their fame and the threat of publicity to evade repression. Roy's expulsion from the Party may have been an inevitable outcome, but his arrest was not, and he showed that he was prepared to play all the cards at his disposal to avoid it. Disappearing from the radar for a while was not standard behavior among dissidents, who generally privileged transparency over conspiracy. But Roy was no ordinary dissident: his friendship with Old Bolsheviks, former members of the Komintern, and even Donald Maclean, a former British spy who defected to the USSR, taught him a number of conspiracy techniques he would use in later years to conceal his activities and remain free to work in the Soviet Union.

Works Cited

Andropov, Iurii. "'Samizdat' preterpel kachestvennye izmeneniia." *Istochnik. Dokumenty russkoi istorii.* 2, no. 9 (1994): 77–78.

Astrachan, Anthony. "'Loyal' Secret Journal Chides the Kremlin." *The Washington Post*, August 22, 1971.

Golikov, V., S. Murashov, I. Chkhikvishvili, M. Shatagin, and S. Shaumian. "Za leninskuiu partiinost' v osveshchenii istorii KPSS." *Kommunist*, no. 3 (1969): 67–82.

Gwertzman, Bernard. *My Memoirs: Fifty Years of Journalism, from Print to the Internet.* Atlanta: Westwood Books Publishing LLC, 2018.

Gwertzman, Bernard. "Notes from the Russian Underground." *The New York Times*, August 22, 1971.

Levin, Bernard. "Sprouting Seeds of a New Russian Revolution." *The Times*, August 24, 1971.

Medvedev, Roy. *Faut-il réhabiliter Staline?* Paris: Ed. du Seuil, 1969.

Medvedev, Roy [Roi]. *Neizvestnyi Andropov. Politicheskaia biografiia Iuriia Andropova.* Moscow: "Prava cheloveka," 1999.

Medvedev, Roy, and Zhores Medvedev. *Nobelevskie laureaty Rossii.* Moscow: Vremia, 2015.

Priimak, P. "Prestupnik i svideteli." *Vecherniaia Moskva*, February 11, 1972.

Zelenov, Mikhail. "Otzyv G.A. Deborina na tret'iu chast' rukopisi R.A. Medvedeva 'Edinolichnoe pravlenie Stalina'. 1969 g." *Acta Samizdatica / Zapiski o samizdate* 3 (2016): 127–32.

Further Reading

Martin, Barbara. "Roy Medvedev's Political Diary: An Experiment in Free Socialist Press." *Jahrbücher für Geschichte Osteuropas* 67, no. 4 (April 2020): 601–26.

———. *Dissident Histories in the Soviet Union. From De-Stalinization to Perestroika.* London: Bloomsbury Academic, 2019.

CHAPTER 8

Into Exile

On November 7, 1971, *The New York Times* published excerpts of Roy and Zhores Medvedevs' memoir *A Question of Madness*, and on November 28, a review by Alan M. Dershowitz entitled "The Mental Hospital as the new Siberia" boasted the "brilliantly conceived" dual-autobiographical format of the book, which the Medvedev twins had written in duet, each from his own vantage point. As the author observed, Zhores Medvedev had only recovered his freedom thanks to the broad publicity of his case, as Soviet "bureaucrats apparently feared massive condemnation by the international community" at forthcoming large scientific conferences. His committal was certainly not unique—over the years, the much more serious cases of Soviet dissidents Natal'ia Gorbanevskaia, Vladimir Bukovskii, General Piotr Grigorenko, or Leonid Pliushch would come to light—but it was the first one to be broadly advertised in the West. Zhores's story had ended well, he was released and granted a new job, but his account revealed a practice that would be widely used to stifle dissent in the Soviet Union in the 1970s. Dershowitz concluded: "…both Zhores and Roy risked their freedom by writing and circulating this document, which is likely to embarrass the Soviet Government but is certain to benefit the people."

Although Zhores had resumed his scientific work at his new laboratory in Borovsk, and the authorities expected him to cease his publicistic activities, the tamizdat publication of *The Medvedev Papers* and *A Question of Madness* demonstrated his determination to pursue his denunciation of the failings of the Soviet system. To prevent him from smuggling new manuscripts to the West, the decision seems to have been taken to isolate him from his international colleagues, and this implied preventing him from attending international conferences, even in the USSR.

The fifth Congress of the International Association of Gerontology (IAG), of which Zhores Medvedev was a member, was taking place in Kyiv in July 1972, and the biologist had been invited to give an introductory lecture to the session on nucleic acids. After sending the text of his lecture in June 1971, however, he tried in vain to contact the organizers in Kyiv. On March 28, 1972, they informed him that, given the large number of applications to the Congress, his talk had been cancelled. The President of the IAG, Nathan Shock, was embarrassed: the IAG Executive Committee had indeed pre-selected Medvedev, but the Soviet organizing committee was free to introduce quotas of speakers for its own nationals. Nevertheless, Zhores was eager to meet his Western colleagues to discuss his new theory of cell aging processes, a summary of which had just appeared in the journal *Nature*. He decided to travel to Kyiv as planned, not on an official mandate from his Institute, but on a private trip during his vacation. The Congress's sessions were public and there was no reason to expect that he would be prevented from attending. He informed his friends among Western gerontologists about his intention of disregarding the cancellation of his talk. Leonard Hayflick expressed concern and warned him that he might be detained if he tried to attend.

Zhores arrived in Kyiv on June 29, 1972, two days before the conference opening. When he registered as a Congress participant, he was told that his name was not on the list of official guests. Nor was his lecture in the conference program. The conference organizers seemed embarrassed by his unexpected presence in Kyiv. After taking a walk in the city, he unexpectedly met David Gershon, a colleague from Israel, and informed him about the situation. Gershon gave him his invitation card to the conference opening, which was not specific to an individual. The next day, Medvedev visited Nathan Shock and explained the situation. Shock promised to talk to the Congress president.

On July 2, when Medvedev showed up at the Ukraina Hotel on Kyiv's main square for the Congress opening, he was immediately surrounded by a policeman and a group of plain-clothed men, who ordered him to follow them. When he protested, the policeman intervened and warned him against "disturbing public order." Medvedev was dragged into a car and carted off to a local police station. The police officer explained that they had received instructions to "protect the Congress from outsiders and undesirable elements." Two "bystanders" could testify that the biologist had been causing public disturbance and resisted arrest, and these circumstances could easily warrant a sentence of ten to fifteen days in prison. Yet the officer was embarrassed to hear that Medvedev was in Kyiv on vacation, had every right to attend the Congress and even had a letter of invitation. After a phone call to his superiors, he changed strategies and tried to convince Medvedev to return home the same day. Medvedev unsuccessfully tried to use the threat of undesirable publicity, which his arrest would certainly produce once it became known at the Congress, but eventually gave in and was escorted to the train station.

Meanwhile, David Gershon, who had noticed Zhores's absence, alerted his colleagues. Some delegates had witnessed his arrest and wanted to present the organizers with an ultimatum: either Medvedev was allowed to attend, or they would boycott the Congress. After getting home, Medvedev sent a telegram to his colleagues Shock, Gershon and Hayflick in English, expressing the regret not to be able to attend the Congress after his meeting with "Profess. Kidnapper"—a code name he made up to designate the KGB. Bernhard Strehler called Medvedev on July 5 and informed him that about five hundred delegates were prepared to boycott the Congress, but the dissident preferred to avoid any scandal. Nevertheless, Medvedev's Western colleagues called a press conference and informed the media about the events. The same day, Medvedev sent a letter with an account of his mishaps to his Western colleagues. Alex Comfort, one of the recipients, told him he had just passed on the information to the editor of *Nature* "for immediate action" and assured him: "In view of the injustice to yourself and the gross affront to the International Committee, we are moving to ensure that no further international conference should be attended until this kind of things stops." The op-ed in *Nature* commented:

> Plainly, the Russian authorities are bent on harassing Medvedev. A decade ago, this awkward customer would no doubt have been dealt with much more harshly, but it remains intolerable that a scientist should have been prevented by the intervention of the police from participating at an international gathering of scientists. The Russian authorities must recognize that their treatment of Medvedev will put in hazard the willingness of scientific societies everywhere to collaborate in the holding of international conferences in the Soviet Union.

Medvedev's arrest, however, could have caused yet a greater scandal if the Congress had been boycotted by one fifth of its participants. In his memoirs, Zhores hypothesized that the operation had been planned by the same organs as his psychiatric hospitalization, perhaps the Ideological Department of the Central Committee. "The failure of this operation and the unjustified risk of disruption of the Congress's work and the outbreak of an international scandal could only arouse anger and some new actions. I understood that they would not leave me in peace even in Borovsk."

For the Soviet authorities, it became clear that Zhores Medvedev would not remain quiet. Détente had led to an increase in cultural and scientific contacts with the West, which were necessary for scientific progress, but the adverse effect from the point of view of the regime was the increase in informal contacts between Western scientists and Soviet dissidents. In the early 1970s, the Soviet human rights movement was regularly making headlines in the West, and Western publishers were keen to publish works by Soviet dissidents. The prosecution of famous figures, such as Piotr Iakir and Viktor Krasin, who were arrested in 1972 and publicly recanted at their trial a year later, could have a demoralizing effect on the movement. But it could also have adverse consequences when Western public opinion pressured decision makers into protesting political repression in the Soviet Union. The KGB had to try to find alternative ways to repress dissent without endangering détente with the West, and they started using a method that appeared both humane and efficient: exile.

For the past years, Zhores Medvedev had been getting invitations from Western colleagues to visit their laboratories. Particularly enticing was an invitation from the National Institute of Medical Research in London, received in 1972, but his Institute's hierarchy informed him that the Soviet "instances" judged this trip "inexpedient." In September, however, the director announced that the "instances" had now authorized his departure on a one-year academic leave. Medvedev had no intention of defecting to the West: his wife and younger son Dima, aged sixteen, were allowed to accompany him abroad, but they had to leave behind Sasha, nineteen, who was in prison.

Zhores understood that his request had been approved in the hope that he would choose to remain in the West and apply for political asylum. For the past two years, the Soviet Union had been allowing an increasing number of Soviet citizens with Jewish roots to emigrate to Israel. Many dissidents were tempted to leave, even though this meant renouncing their Soviet citizenship. Forced emigration, however, had yet to become a staple of the Soviet repressive arsenal. As Zhores was leaving, news came out that Valerii Chalidze had just been stripped of his Soviet citizenship while on a conference tour in the United States. But Chalidze was a human rights activist who had been criticizing the Soviet Union in the West, and Medvedev believed that if he refrained from any political activity during his stay, he would not be prevented from returning to the Soviet Union.

Initially his main fear was to fail to get an exit visa. Had he not repeatedly tried to travel abroad in the 1960s, only to see his requests turned down one after another? However, on December 4, 1972, he suddenly heard on the BBC that Zhores Medvedev had been authorized to travel abroad for a year. There was little ground to question the veracity of the information: no doubt Soviet officials had sold the information to Western news agencies. Three days later the official confirmation came in. But there were disturbing signals: although Medvedev had paid the rent for his apartment for a whole year in advance, on December 15, strangers showed on his doorstep, asking to visit the apartment. They claimed to have received an offer to occupy the flat after the Medvedevs' departure. The biologist sent a vehement protest to the local authorities, insisting that he was leaving his furniture, library and archives on site and planning to return.

In expectation of his departure, Zhores visited his friends, who entrusted him with various tasks, mostly related with their publishing affairs in the West. Sakharov asked him to find out if he could recover part of the royalties for the publication of his *Reflections* to fund the studies of his stepchildren at Harvard University. Solzhenitsyn also counted on Medvedev to contact his Swiss lawyer and help him oppose the publications of his ex-wife's memoirs, used by the Soviet authorities as a weapon against him. The Nobel laureate also asked him to publish in the Western media an article in his defense concerning his divorce, and a review of a recently published unauthorized biography of him. As they kissed goodbye, Solzhenitsyn said: "Don't fool yourself, Zhores, they won't let you back…"

On January 8, 1973, however, three days before departure, Medvedev was still waiting for his British visa. He asked to meet the British consul and warned that if he did not receive a reply the same day, he would give a press conference and announce that his trip was cancelled. The diplomat took the threat seriously and called the British Minister of Foreign Affairs the same day. By five o'clock in the evening, the issue was settled, and the consul handed Medvedev his visas. On January 11, Rita, Dima and Zhores boarded a train to the West, leaving behind their family, friends, and a lifetime of memories.

Upon his arrival by boat in Liverpool, Zhores was welcomed by Robin Holliday, Head of the Genetics Division at the National Institute for Medical Research, and by James Right, editor at Macmillan, his publisher. They helped him settle into his new life and took care of his financial and work issues. Medvedev met his new colleagues at the Institute located in Mill Hill, north of London. At first, however, he only had the status of guest researcher and no budget to conduct experimental research. It took him several months to secure the authorization to conduct experiments with mice.

Zhores Medvedev. London, 1973. OKhDLSM, F. 333, op. 14, d. 39, l. 1.

The biologist also had the pleasure of reconnecting with Western colleagues working at British universities, and he hoped to be able to attend the 13th Congress of Genetics in San Francisco, planned for August 1973. But this required an authorization from the Soviet embassy, which he was refused. Medvedev refrained from issuing a public protest, which could have been interpreted as "anti-Soviet" action. With this concern in mind, he turned down countless invitations from the media or universities to give lectures on Soviet dissent. His position was uncomfortable: his dissident friends in the Soviet Union could not understand his cautiousness, nor even his desire to return to the USSR.

Regular provocations, such as suspicious "advice" from a Radio Liberty employee encouraging him to apply for asylum, showed that both the KGB and the CIA had an interest in keeping him in the West. A new warning came in May, when Medvedev received a visit from a Soviet colleague he had not seen in years. During an evening walk, G. asked him what his plans were. When Medvedev explained that he planned on returning home at the end of the year, G. unexpectedly suggested that he move to the United States. "Why return to Borovsk? Conditions are much better here. You can also ask your son to join you… I expect they would let him go…" These words, coming from someone who had always been cautious and loyal to the regime, sounded odd to Medvedev.

Half a year after his departure, the Soviet authorities were losing patience. His defection to the West would have been advantageous, whereas stripping him of his citizenship without any pretext would undoubtedly throw discredit onto the Soviet regime. Yet one thing was clear: they would not let him return to the Soviet Union.

Zhores realized that one way to avert this outcome would be to receive diplomatic immunity. In 1964, he had received a proposal to apply to become a member of one of UNESCO's scientific expert councils, but his application had not passed the barriers of postal censorship. Acquiring a status of expert for UNESCO or the WHO would now protect him from repression. With the recommendation of prominent scientists, including a Nobel prize laureate, Medvedev applied to UNESCO again. This time, however, his application was turned down on the request of Soviet members of the directors' board. He tried to apply for similar positions at the WHO and other UN agencies.

The Soviet authorities, however, decided to call the game off. On August 6, the biologist was summoned to the Soviet Embassy. Under the pretext of settling the issue of his travel to the Genetics Congress in San Francisco, the secretary asked him to bring his passport. As soon as he was in possession of the document, however, the official read him out a decree adopted by Presidium of the Supreme Soviet of the USSR on July 16, 1973, stripping Medvedev of his Soviet citizenship "for actions defaming the title of citizen." He was accused of having been involved for years "in the fabrication, the expedition to the West and circulation of slanderous materials, defaming the Soviet state, its social system, and the Soviet people."

Zhores was shocked both by the decision and the secretary's petty deception. He wrote a protest to the authorities: "I consider it unworthy of a great country to take away its citizen's passport through such humiliating fraud. These are swindlers' practices, not state officials'. Soviet or Russian citizenship belongs to me by birthright, and no one can deprive me of the right to a homeland." On August 8, Roy Medvedev wrote a protest against this "absurd procedure, devoid of any decency." While "any country would be proud of such a citizen" as Zhores Medvedev, the Soviet authorities had preferred to inflict harm on the USSR's prestige. Zhores himself gave interviews but refrained from any harsh condemnation of the Soviet regime, perhaps in the hope of a reversal of the decree, or because his son was still imprisoned. On August 9, the Soviet News Agency TASS publicized the news, and the report was reproduced in major Soviet newspapers.

The dissident had to organize his new life in the West on a more permanent basis. The director of his institute Arnold Burgen proved sensitive to his plight:

he found him a grant and promised to do whatever he could to help him after the end of his stay as an invited scholar. In his correspondence with his brother back in Moscow, filled with requests for books, articles and arrangements concerning his Obninsk apartment, Zhores expressed the hope that "after a given delay it will be possible to restore my Soviet citizenship. Meanwhile I will have to settle here on a more stable basis in expectation of the next two to three years at least." He assured his Soviet friends: "I will definitely return. Of course, not with such honors and possibilities as [Juan] Peron in Argentina, but still in better times."

In the fall of 1973, Zhores received from the British authorities an identification document for temporary residents, which allowed him to travel abroad. He also benefitted from a grant to pursue his research. In July 1974, he was offered a position of senior researcher at the National Institute of Medical Research. After a one-year trial period, his contract could be renewed for five years and eventually made permanent. His grant included funds to hire a lab assistant, and he also invited his wife to work on his team on a voluntary basis.

After his situation stabilized, Zhores began to travel abroad for conferences, combining the pleasures of discovering new destinations with that of giving lectures on a range of subjects: gerontology and aging processes, but also Soviet science and Soviet dissent. During a trip to Paris in December 1973, Medvedev gave his first lecture on a subject which would raise considerable interest on his conference tours: longevity and the phenomenon of "super centenarians." A recent publication by Alexander Leaf in *National Geographic* about exceptional longevity in the Vilcabamba valley in Ecuador had popularized the theory that life in mountain valleys could foster exceptional longevity, up to one hundred forty years. However, as Medvedev showed in his lectures, the phenomenon of super-centenarians was due to faulty birth registrations and a cultural tendency to inflate one's age.

In her letters to Roy's wife Galina, Rita described their new life. At first, everything seemed new and strange, from the intense car traffic to the variety of clothes worn by Londoners, but soon she adapted to this new reality. Zhores had started working with his new team almost immediately: "[He spends] the whole day at the Institute, and in the evenings, as usual, he works until late at night at home ... Dima and I have a hard time dragging him out for a walk. He is always busy." She had been taking English classes but had little time for lessons between her job at the Institute and the household chores. She still found it hard to speak the language, although she recognized that life in London was possible even without good English skills: "Nearly all shops function in self-service, everything is packed and labelled, with indications of ingredients, calories and how to cook." There were signs and maps in public transport, so that

Zhores Medvedev and Margarita Medvedeva, outside their first London home, early 1970s.
Courtesy of Dmitry Medvedev.

Zhores Medvedev and Margarita Medvedeva on vacation in Southern France, 1970s.
Courtesy of Dmitry Medvedev.

there was no need to speak with anyone. Dima had also adapted to his new school and mastered the language faster than her. She could not forget, however, that she had left a son behind, and she longed to visit the USSR. After a year, once the feeling of novelty passed, she missed her loved ones who remained behind the Iron Curtain. In 1975, following a steep increase of their rent, Zhores and Rita decided to buy a semi-detached cottage on a quiet lane on Mill Hill, on the northwestern outskirts of London, within walking distance of the Institute. The Medvedevs would remain in this modest house with a pleasant backside garden until the end of their lives, growing vegetables in their garden plot.

Zhores Medvedev had never intended to emigrate, but he had taken the risk of leaving, knowing he might not be able to return. For a scientist who already had a solid reputation, living in the West was easier than for writers or even scholars in the humanities, who found it harder to adapt, especially without language skills. The Soviet authorities may have hoped to neutralize Zhores Medvedev by sending him into exile, but he had no intention of scaling down his political activism. Most of all, his presence in London allowed his brother Roy to pursue the career of an "independent scholar."

Works Cited

Dershowitz, Alan M. "The mental hospital as the new Siberia," *The New York Times*, November 28, 1971.
Medvedev, Zhores. *Opasnaia Professiia*. Moscow: Vremia, 2019.
Medvedev, Zhores, and Roy Medvedev. "A Question of Madness," *The New York Times*, November 7, 1971.
"Zhores Medvedev and the Reputation of Russian Science." *Nature* 238, no. 5359 (July 1972): 61–62.

Further Reading

Martin, Barbara. "A Struggle across the Iron Curtain: Soviet Dissidents in Exile in the 1970s." In *Mobility in the Russian, Central and East European Past*, edited by Roisin Healy, 95–107. London: Routledge, 2019.

CHAPTER 9

Carving a "Third Way" in the Cold War

A new kind of civil celebration appeared in dissident circles in the 1970s, halfway between a baptism and a funeral: the so-called *provody*, or "seeing-off." Those who applied for an exit visa through Israel made the difficult choice of leaving their loved ones and friends behind without any prospect of seeing them again. At the same time, they were reborn to a new life in the West, which, however, often proved more challenging than expected. Emigration was a hotly debated issue in the Soviet dissident movement. Except for those, like Zhores Medvedev, who had incurred the regime's wrath and were forced to leave the country, emigration was open only to Soviet citizens of Jewish or German descent, and with a large number of restrictions. For Russian patriots like Solzhenitsyn, emigration was not an option. Nor did it make sense for Roy and Zhores Medvedev, who believed in achieving a democratization of the Soviet system, rather than just personal freedom.

For those dissidents who remained in the Soviet Union, 1973 was a year of renewed repression, which dealt a heavy blow to the movement. This was also a time of affirmation of various political platforms among dissidents, ranging from liberal democratic to Christian Russophile or socialist reformist views. While in the 1960s dissidents stood united behind by the rallying call to fight against Stalin's rehabilitation and defend human rights, in 1973 Solzhenitsyn, Sakharov and the Medvedev brothers parted ways ideologically. As they began to take stances on domestic and foreign policy issues and to publish programmatic essays, they were bound to step into opposition to each other.

Roy Medvedev was the first to draw the lines of his program for the democratization of the regime in an essay entitled *On Socialist Democracy*. Written in the wake of the Prague Spring, it was published in Russian, French, German, and English between 1973 and 1975. After analyzing the various opposition currents both within and outside the party, Medvedev gave a detailed overview of the reforms he called for: greater inner-party democracy, an increased role of elected executive and legislative bodies, a democratic and independent judiciary power, less bureaucracy, greater freedom of the press, and freedom of movement and decentralization of decision-making in the economy.

Roy Medvedev's limited course of reforms did not threaten the Party's monopoly on power, but it was bold enough for the early 1970s. Medvedev insisted that his program was more realistic than the radical course of action advocated by other Soviet dissidents. Reforming did not mean starting from a *tabula rasa* but gradually purging the existing system of its flaws.

> Something new can only be fashioned out of what has come before in previous stages of social development... It is in no way a question of destroying the values of the Revolution. Rather we must restore and purify them; they must be reinforced and built upon. Only if there is a systematic and consistent democratization of the whole of our political and social life on a socialist basis will our country be able to regain its role and influence among the progressive forces of the world.

With the publication of this essay, Medvedev affirmed himself as a political analyst. American Sovietologist Frederick Barghoorn considered Medvedev's study "one of the most important *samizdat* works to come out of the USSR ... an extraordinarily rich source of information on emerging trends in Soviet public life and public opinion." British scholar and socialist peace activist Ken Coates also hailed the book, calling Medvedev a "modern, rational, and passionately democratic thinker."

Although his critique of the regime was moderate, Roy Medvedev had grounds to be concerned in the summer of 1973. He had been officially unemployed since October 1971 and could easily be arrested on charges of "parasitism" or "anti-Soviet propaganda." With Piotr Iakir and Viktor Krasin's trial, which began in Moscow on August 27, 1973, pressure was mounting against dissidents of all stripes. The son of a repressed Red Army commander, Iakir had himself spent five years in a youth penal colony under Stalin. In the 1960s, he became an outspoken dissident and human rights activist. However, after their arrest in June 1972, he and Krasin yielded to pressure and agreed to cooperate with the investigators: they testified against hundreds of dissidents and pleaded guilty of anti-Soviet agitation, for which they received a "light" sentence of three years of imprisonment. On September 5, they repeated their confessions of guilt during a televised press conference. This trial was a huge demoralizing blow to Soviet dissident circles and heralded new repression.

On August 31, 1973, Roy Medvedev wrote to his brother:

> My name and yours are not cited anywhere anymore in print, but in August, during an instruction meeting of newspapers and journals editors, the speaker, as I was told, explaining the reasons for depriving you of your citizenship (according to [Soviet News Agency] TASS's press release), said that Zhores Medvedev's brother Roy also writes books defaming [the Soviet regime] and that he will also be expelled from the USSR.

The historian added that one of his acquaintances had been arrested and that many house searches had taken place in relation to the Iakir-Krasin trial. Fortunately, none of his manuscripts had fallen into the KGB's hands. But during interrogation, one of his acquaintances had been told: "Roy M. has gone over to the other side of the barricade, he doesn't work and doesn't want to work, but lives off royalties sent to him from abroad." Therefore, to avoid any accusation of "parasitism," Roy had decided to send a job application to the Academy of Pedagogical Sciences.

While Roy preferred to lie low, Solzhenitsyn and Sakharov were taking the fight to the barricades. Sakharov had followed an evolution common to many Soviet dissidents, from calls for democratization to human rights rhetoric. The change was less one of goals than one of methods of action: when his appeals to the Soviet leadership proved inefficient, he decided to put the authorities under pressure by publicizing his grievances in the West and using the combined pressure of Western public opinion and politicians to obtain change in the USSR. Indeed, the new policy of détente with the West made the Soviet leadership more sensitive to criticism of its human rights record.

In the early 1970s, Brezhnev had initiated a rapprochement with West Germany and the United States. During US President Richard Nixon's visit to Moscow in May–June 1972, the two leaders had signed a package of disarmament treaties, along with a Soviet-American Trade Agreement. The ratification of the latter, however, ran into unexpected difficulties. Détente faced the opposition of a broad range of political forces on both sides of the Iron Curtain, from human rights activists to Cold Warriors. In a context of increased political repression, the Soviet-American rapprochement appeared to many premature, if not downright cynical. In the United States, Senator Henry Jackson, who opposed Nixon's "quiet diplomacy" with the USSR, championed the right of

Soviet Jews to emigration through a linkage between human rights and trade. The Soviet authorities, who had granted over thirty thousand exit visas in 1972, had imposed in August 1972 a "diploma tax." The law, which required financial compensation from prospective emigrants for the cost of their higher education, raised an uproar in the United States and gave fuel to Senator Jackson's rhetoric. With the support of Charles Vanik in the House of Representatives, he introduced an amendment to the Trade Act making the granting of Most Favored Nation Status to non-market economies conditional on a liberalization of emigration. Despite intense negotiations between Moscow and Washington over this question and the tacit suspension of the "diploma tax," no accommodation could be found. The Soviet leadership would not accept any quotas and Senator Jackson would not be soothed by vague promises.

In the summer of 1973, Sakharov stepped up his rhetoric, openly criticizing the Soviet regime in interviews with Western journalists and calling for a liberalization of emigration, an issue he had been advocating since 1971. He warned the West against granting economic concessions to Moscow without strings attached. The reaction to Sakharov's interviews was a ferocious smear campaign unleashed against him in Soviet media, accusing him of "*de facto* siding with the most reactionary imperialist circles." Despite the violence of the blow, Sakharov was undeterred, and launched on September 14, 1973 an appeal to the US Congress to adopt the Jackson-Vanik Amendment. He did not believe that the amendment would imperil détente or be interpreted as interference in Soviet internal affairs. On the contrary, renouncing international law would represent "total capitulation of democratic principles in the face of blackmail, deceit and violence" and would have dire consequences for "international confidence, détente, and the entire future of mankind." Senator Jackson hailed Sakharov's appeal, which, he declared in front of US Congress, "has challenged each of us to higher levels of conscience and responsibility."

Sakharov was not alone to be targeted in Soviet media. Solzhenitsyn had become "dissident number 1" since the publication of several of his works in the West and after receiving the Nobel Prize for Literature in 1970. In 1968, he had sent a microfilm of *The Gulag Archipelago* to Paris but preferred to delay its publication. In late August 1973, however, the KGB arrested his typist, who revealed under duress where she had hidden a copy of the manuscript. Driven to despair by her forced confession, she committed suicide. As a result of this tragedy, the writer sent word to the West to release the book, which came out on December 28, 1973. In his memoirs, Solzhenitsyn conveyed the violence of the struggle he and Sakharov led against the Soviet authorities in September 1973: "There was an uproar in the press. Blows fell thicker on Sakharov, but I got my share. East and West, our names were coupled, and everything that he said was attributed to me too." Such violence was not unusual in the Soviet press, of course, but times had changed: "This was the first time in fifty-five years, I think, that people hounded by the Soviet press had dared to bark back."

In these circumstances, Soviet dissidents all gathered around the figureheads of the movement. On September 5, Solzhenitsyn nominated Sakharov for the Nobel Peace Prize, and several dissidents openly supported this nomination, describing him as "an outstanding fighter for real democracy, for the rights and dignity of man, and for a genuine, not an illusory peace." The Medvedev brothers, however, remained awkwardly silent. Roy judged that Sakharov was mistaken, both in his views and in his interlocutors, and he felt the need, for his own safety, to publicly dissociate himself from Sakharov's views. On September 30, 1973, he wrote to Zhores: "I want to expose my opinion on many questions, on which Sakharov and Solzhenitsyn have so often spoken up, and express, in a loyal way of course, my disagreement with their conception." During a propaganda lecture condemning Sakharov's declarations "one of the district committee secretaries, explaining Sakharov's political activism, said that it can be explained by the great influence on him of Medvedev 'who was recently deprived of Soviet citizenship.'" Clearly, the propagandist had mixed up the two brothers, but for Roy, "this showed once more that I have to formulate and publish my point of view, which I will do soon." Despite Zhores's advice not to take a position against Sakharov and Solzhenitsyn, the historian made his views public in the Western press.

In an article entitled "Problems of Democratization and Détente," first published in October 1973 in the West German newspaper *Die Zeit*, Roy Medvedev criticized Solzhenitsyn's and Sakharov's recent statements. He regretted that the threat of arrest had led some dissidents to "express more and more extremist viewpoints, to put forward less and less constructive proposals, being moved more by emotions than by considerations of political efficacy." Particularly counter-productive, in his view, was Sakharov's appeal concerning the Jackson-Vanik Amendment. The US Congress had no interest in the development of an economically strong and democratic USSR, in Medvedev's view. He predicted that the amendment would lead to a deterioration of US-Soviet relations, with adverse effects on emigration policy. Détente, on the other hand, was a process to be encouraged for its own sake, which would in the long run lead to a democratization of the USSR. By increasing the role of public opinion in "shaping the internal affairs of each power," détente gave added weight to protests. Medvedev considered that "the relaxation of international tensions is in itself a very important pre-condition, though not the only one, for the development of democracy in Soviet society." He was skeptical about the prospects for democratization as a result of pressure from below: Soviet dissidents were too isolated from the masses, and in this context, outside pressure could be counterproductive. Change was more likely to result from the action of progressive forces within the leadership, and Medvedev hoped that the new Soviet Constitution would contain additional provisions for human rights. Although the Soviet authorities constantly violated their own legislation, human rights activists could use these laws as levers of pressure on the regime.

Roy Medvedev deemed his criticism of Sakharov and Solzhenitsyn "careful and tactful." He had shown Sakharov the text, and the dissident had not objected to it. Nevertheless, the publication unleashed in the émigré press a storm of "open letters to the Medvedev brothers" from fellow dissidents. The first to strike was Vladimir Maksimov, a dissident writer whom Medvedev had criticized in his article. He was indignant at Medvedev's attack against Sakharov and Solzhenitsyn, "Russia's moral pride," launched precisely when their lives were at risk. "Who are you working for?" Maksimov asked rhetorically, thus inaugurating a long list of accusations of collaboration with the Soviet regime formulated against the Medvedev brothers. Sakharov issued a statement in support of Maksimov's position: "By their pragmatism, the Medvedevs have placed themselves in opposition to those who lead today a struggle for the right of a person to live and think freely." In an interview with *Time*, Solzhenitsyn joined the chorus, judging Medvedev's expectations that a new generation of leaders would bring change "pure nonsense." In an interview to the émigré weekly *Russkaia mysl'*, Zhores Medvedev took up his brother's defense, expressing regret that the discussion had turned into violent personal attacks reminiscent of Stalin era antisemitic campaigns.

This episode put an end to the relationship between Sakharov and Roy Medvedev, who had been growing apart since the early 1970s. In his memoirs, Sakharov commented: "By saving Zhores [from psychiatric incarceration], I showed my loyalty to dissident solidarity. However, later, both personal and ideological relations with the Medvedev brothers became hostile. They definitely lost my sympathy." In April 1974, Roy Medvedev clarified the nature of his differences with Sakharov, which were less ideological than tactical, and he agreed that his own approach was "pragmatic."

> Academician A.D. Sakharov considers his positions and demands as "purely moral." It is of considerable importance to declare moral demands, and this is natural for a learned physicist.

But for people devoting themselves professionally to the political and social sciences moral indignation alone is not enough. While studying Soviet society, they must seek realistic possibilities and realistic routes for its democratic development.

A realist approach meant going beyond the mere expression of "feelings" and to "proceed from the real state of things." Change had to be achieved, bearing in mind "*this* people, *this* youth, *this* intelligentsia, *this* ruling elite, and *this* regime, which will not be routed by statements and books, but which can (although this task is extremely difficult) be gradually transformed to secure the establishment of socialism 'with a human face.'" Medvedev did not consider economic pressure an effective lever: economic progress would only be slowed down by the absence of Western credits, not halted. Conversely, he reasoned, "the expansion of international trade and international division of labor based on mutual concessions can hasten this process [of democratization] somewhat," provided it does not come in the form of ultimatums.

Roy Medvedev's affirmation of his difference of views with Sakharov, and later with Solzhenitsyn, was both necessary and inevitable, once the united front of opposition to Stalin's rehabilitation had given way to a variety of political currents. Beyond the affirmation of a concrete political program, what he emphasized was his method of action, which was gradual and relied on the combined effect of détente and reform from above to lead to a progressive democratization of the regime. Although Zhores was less outspoken about his political views, the twin brothers generally saw eye to eye in matters of political strategy. While discussions over the Jackson-Vanik amendment were still raging, Zhores received an opportunity to defend his and Roy's conception in the US Congress.

Zhores had been planning a trip to the United States since late 1973, after receiving several invitations from colleagues in the United States: Nathan Shock, Bernard Strehler, Michael Lerner, and Leonard Hayflick. He also hoped to meet his friends David Joravsky, Max Delbrück, Alex Comfort, Valerii Chalidze, and Theodosius Dobzhansky. When Medvedev ran into difficulties in getting a visa, his friend Jeremy Stone, a professional lobbyist from the Federation of American Scientists, solved the issue by calling Henry Kissinger. During this first American tour, in April–May 1974, the dissident visited New York City, Albion (MI), Chicago and the Argonne National Laboratory, Evanston (IL), Harvard and Boston Universities, Baltimore, Bethesda (MD), Washington D.C., Kansas City, Los Angeles, Santa Barbara, Stanford University, UC Berkeley, Toronto, Minneapolis and Yale University. Everywhere he stayed for a day or two to give one or two talks, combining lab visits and lectures on scientific, historical, and political themes. For reasons of cost and to better enjoy the journey, Medvedev opted during this and his following trip to the United States for transatlantic boat travel and interstate train journeys.

Zhores Medvedev with American colleagues, 1974. Courtesy of Zhores Medvedev.

More than his expertise on gerontology and aging, Medvedev's experience as a dissident scientist was in high demand. He was cautious, however, to avoid topics which could possibly harm his reputation in the West, provoke unnecessary debates, or endanger his family in the USSR. He refused to speak about specific dissidents or various currents of Soviet opposition, a question he felt he could not yet handle with the necessary distance and objectivity. He also turned down lectures on Soviet politics or religion. But he did touch upon the question of political repression in his lectures on Soviet science, the topic on which he was most often invited to talk.

During Zhores's stay in Washington D.C. in May 1974, Jeremy Stone took the opportunity to organize an encounter with Senator Jackson. The meeting lasted for three hours. Zhores Medvedev explained his and his brother's position: the concessions that Jackson was demanding from the USSR were not realistic, they would require substantial legislative changes, which the Soviet authorities would never agree to. Moreover, any outside pressure would be interpreted as interference in Soviet domestic affairs. "The loss of prestige is more dangerous for party leaders than the loss of possible credits," argued Medvedev. But Jackson objected that it was too late to make any substantial changes to his project. The House of Representatives had already adopted the amendment on December 11, 1973, by a four fifths majority, and the vote in Senate was expected to take place in the fall.

In late June, Zhores Medvedev gave an interview to *The Christian Science Monitor* in which he discussed the question of détente and the Jackson-Vanik Amendment. He argued that Henry Kissinger could obtain greater concessions from Soviet leaders than Jackson, because his demands did the not have the character of an ultimatum. Following the publication on July 9, he received a phone call from the assistant of Senator J. William Fulbright, Chairman of the US Senate Committee on Foreign affairs. He was invited to take part in public hearings on détente organized by this committee from August to October 1974, and to give a thirty-minute talk on the Jackson-Vanik Amendment. Other speakers included Henry Kissinger, George Kennan, Averell Harriman, and George Meany. Medvedev replied that he would be honored to take part in the hearings, the timing of which allowed him to combine his participation with attendance of the World Gerontology Congress in Portland, Oregon. Soon, his program filled up with new invitations to speak about aging, genetics in the USSR, détente and the Jackson amendment, and intellectual life in the USSR, at Duke and Harvard Universities, Buffalo, Cleveland, and Cornell University.

Zhores Medvedev spoke in front of the Senate Commission on October 8, 1974, the day before the closing of the Hearings. He repeated in his presentation his previous arguments: the right to emigration, as advocated by the Jackson-Vanik Amendment, amounted to no more than a deprivation of Soviet citizenship, without any right of return to one's homeland. Moreover, Jackson's demands required reforms of Soviet legislation pertaining to access to state secrets or military service and constituted an obvious interference into Soviet domestic affairs. Since US-Soviet trade volumes were insignificant, adoption of the amendment would certainly result in a cancellation of the Trade Act by the Soviet Union, along with the disarmament agreements. Emigration would be cut down to a minimum and the Cold War would resume.

The Medvedev brothers' position on détente coincided by and large with that of Henry Kissinger and President Gerald Ford, who had just replaced Nixon in the wake of the Watergate scandal. Public opinion, however, was on Jackson's side and he won the vote. The Senate adopted the amendment on December 20, 1974, and President Ford signed the Trade Act into law on January 3, 1975. Shortly thereafter, however, the Soviet Union repealed the treaty, as the Medvedevs had predicted. The same year, only thirteen thousand exit visas were granted to Soviet emigrants, a clear decrease from the preceding year. In his state of the Union address, President Ford regretted: "Legislative restrictions, intended for the best motives and purposes, can have the opposite result, as we have seen most recently in our trade relations with the Soviet Union."

Yet, with every public intervention, the Medvedev brothers became more isolated. Zhores's speech in front of the Fulbright Commission unleashed a new storm of protests in the émigré press. The object of the most heated comments was his declaration that repression against dissidents "is not growing but diminishing and changing its character (terroristic and judicial methods are giving way to administrative methods)." Under Brezhnev, he reasoned, information exchanges over the Iron Curtain had increased thanks to the development of broadcasting technologies, and samizdat and tamizdat had weakened the effectiveness of censorship. Sending dissidents into exile, a practice which had come to replace incarceration in many cases, was "a more humane method than confinement in prison or a mental hospital." Medvedev conceded that "to this day dozens of people in the USSR are imprisoned on political charges," but in his view what had changed was less the level of repression than Western awareness and sensitivity to it, thus "creating the illusion that the general level of repression is rising."

After hearing his brother's speech broadcast on radio, Roy expressed his general agreement with the text, which, he believed, could annoy only a few "extremists" such as Vladimir Maksimov and the likes. Still, he admitted that Zhores could have strengthened in a couple of places his criticism of censorship and political repression. He feared that the cuts altered his brother's ideas, and he asked him to send the full translation of the text to circulate it among his friends. However, the text dissatisfied more than a few "extremists." Upon returning to London, Zhores Medvedev received a long letter from Lev Kopelev and Lidiia Chukovskaia, two Soviet writers who had chosen him as their literary representative in the West and whom he considered friends. They accused him of helping the "executioners, instead of their victims" and of being on the side of "Sakharov's persecutors." Although they wrote that their letter was private, in circumstances which remain unclear, a distorted account of the letter was leaked to Western radio stations and published in *The Guardian*.

Zhores felt deeply hurt by the breach of confidence and addressed what he deemed unfair accusations in a reply to Kopelev and Chukovskaia's letter sent privately, through diplomatic channels.

> Some "dissidents" have started too easily taking upon themselves the responsibility of accusing others of the most revolting sins and doing this in the rudest and most unworthy expressions. In their view, there is no need for proofs in "Samizdat," and information agencies will spread unproven accusations through the whole world, [Radio] Liberty will broadcast them in Russian. But this is called "slander," these are the methods of those we dislike so much, methods of snitches who wrote to the newspapers in the 1930s. Only you are not threatening my life now, with this vile word "accomplice of perpetrators," but my reputation.

Roy suspected that Sakharov's wife Elena Bonner, who was well-connected with newspaper correspondents, had leaked the letter to the news agency France Presse in the form of a one-page summary written by memory. Chukovskaia also claimed to have kept the letter with her at all times and had only shown it to four people, including Sakharov and his wife. "What happened? A misfortune. You and I were betrayed, sold, cheated and dumped into the mud... Surveillance devices? They can overhear but cannot add what wasn't said. Therefore—people... nearby." Kopelev believed it was a ploy of the KGB, which overheard their conversations during the preparation of the letter and transmitted it to Western media through a staffer of France Presse of Russian origin. "We also read the forged text and noticed that it contains only a few excerpts of sentences from the original letter: the rest is only a deliberately rude and distorting 'retelling'..." Zhores, however, was unconvinced by these explanations. He had found out that *The Guardian* had received the text through United Press International, which had received the Russian original through a "reliable source" in Moscow, which Zhores believed to be Chukovskaia herself, and had published it with cuts, which distorted its meaning. He replied through a letter to *the Guardian*, published under the title "Nobel or ignoble?"

Around this time, Zhores told his brother about difficulties his son Sasha was experiencing in prison. He only received his father's letters irregularly, worried about his fate and experienced breakdowns. Zhores feared that local authorities might be using the situation against him. He warned that this would only give opposite results and advised Roy, if he felt the hand of the KGB, to call officials, such as General "Teplov," the high-ranking KGB official with whom Roy had had a conversation in 1970. He did not want the Soviet authorities to believe the rumors which explained his political position by the fact that his son was held "hostage."

The Medvedevs' vision on détente and socialist democracy was widely shared by European left-wing intellectuals, although some of them disagreed with his top-down approach to change in the USSR, at odds with the Marxist canon. In 1975, Ken Coates, chairman of the Bertrand Russell Peace Foundation, edited a volume of essays by prominent socialist intellectuals and political actors in response to Roy Medvedev's article "Problems of Democratization and Détente." All of them stood for socialist democracy and opposed Soviet authoritarian rule, yet they differed with him on the question of the methods of action.

Both Roy and Zhores privileged collaborations with left-wing publishers and intellectuals, who shared their values. Their position, however, became unpalatable to the majority of Soviet dissidents and recent émigrés, who considered the Medvedev brothers objective allies of the Soviet regime. While Sakharov's human rights advocacy fell on sympathetic ears in the West, the socialist democracy advocated by Roy Medvedev elicited little enthusiasm among late Soviet intellectuals. In the wake of the Soviet invasion of Czechoslovakia, the socialist idea had lost much of its power of attraction. Finally, there was certainly a personal component to these polemics: the Medvedevs' personality, their measured discourse and cautiousness, but also their critical attitude towards fellow dissidents aroused irritation and often hatred among their opponents. Their ostracization only increased when Solzhenitsyn turned from a friend into one of the Medvedevs' fiercest critics.

Works Cited

Barghoorn, Frederick C. "Medvedev's Democratic Leninism." *Slavic Review* 32, no. 3 (September 1973): 590–94.
Coates, Ken. "The Moscow Democrat." *The Guardian*, August 7, 1975.
Medvedev, Roy. "Democracy and Détente." In *Political Essays*, 13–29. Nottingham: Spokesman Books, 1976.
———. "Dissent and Free Discussion." In *Political Essays*, 30–42. Nottingham: Spokesman Books, 1976.
Medvedev, Roy, and Zhores Medvedev. *Nobelevskie Laureaty Rossii*. Moscow: Vremia, 2015.
Medvedev, Zhores. *Opasnaia professiia*. Moscow: Vremia, 2019.
Sakharov, Andrei. *Sakharov Speaks*. Edited by Harrison E. Salisbury. London: Collins & Harvill Press, 1974.
———. *Vospominaniia*. Vol. 1. Moskva: Prava cheloveka, 1996.
Solzhenitsyn, Aleksandr. *The Oak and the Calf*. Collins/Fontana, 1980.
———. "Ugodilo zernyshko promezh dvukh zhernovov. Ocherki izgnaniia. Chast' 1 (1974–1978)." *Novyi Mir*, no. 9 (1998): 47–125.

Further Reading

Bergman, Jay. *Meeting the Demands of Reason: The Life and Thought of Andrei Sakharov*. Ithaca: Cornell University Press, 2009.

Kelley, Donald R. *The Solzhenitsyn-Sakharov Dialogue: Politics, Society and the Future*. New York; Westport Conn: Greenwood Press, 1982.

Levin, Geoffrey P. "Before Soviet Jewry's Happy Ending: The Cold War and America's Long Debate Over Jackson-Vanik, 1976–1989." *Shofar* 33, no. 3 (2015): 63–85.

Martin, Barbara. "The Sakharov-Medvedev Debate on Détente and Human Rights: From the Jackson-Vanik Amendment to the Helsinki Accords," *Journal of Cold War Studies* 23, no. 3 (August 9, 2021): 138–74.

CHAPTER 10

Solzhenitsyn: The End of a Friendship

After the confiscation of his Soviet passport in August 1973, Zhores Medvedev expected a gesture of support from Solzhenitsyn. After all, just a few months earlier, they had parted as friends, and Zhores had fulfilled several of the writer's requests once in the West. In February 1973, he had published in *The New York Times* an article entitled "In Defense of Solzhenitsyn," defending his "good friend" against unfair attacks orchestrated by Soviet propaganda in the Western press. At the writer's request, he had also published a review of David Burg and George Feifer's unauthorized biography of Solzhenitsyn, underlining the distortions it contained. Finally, together with Solzhenitsyn's lawyer Fritz Heeb, he had tried, unsuccessfully, to prevent the publication of Solzhenitsyn's ex-wife's memoirs in the West, which had been instrumentalized by the KGB.

However, when Zhores received a letter from Solzhenitsyn through confidential channels, it contained words of outrage, not at the Soviet authorities' decision, but at Medvedev's recent declaration to a Canadian journalist, a translation of which he had heard on the radio: "What we have in the USSR is not a regime, but the same government as in other countries, and it rules based on the constitution." Medvedev claims this was a distortion of his declaration, which may have been mistranslated into Russian, but his original words were not devoid of ambiguity either. This was but the first in a long series of controversies between the Medvedev brothers and Solzhenitsyn.

When Solzhenitsyn's literary research *The Gulag Archipelago* was published in Paris in December 1973, Roy Medvedev was the first Soviet author to review it. He received the book from Hedrick Smith and Robert Kaiser, correspondents for *The Washington Post* and *The New York Times*, with whom he had good relations, and who gave him the book days after its publication in Paris. In a week, Roy had written a seven-thousand-word review, excerpts of which appeared in the Western press, and which circulated in samizdat. As Solzhenitsyn was being subjected to another smear campaign in the Soviet press, Roy Medvedev emphasized the truthfulness of his work. "I cannot agree with some of Solzhenitsyn's judgements or conclusions. But it must be firmly stated that all the main facts in his book, and especially all the details of the life and torment of those who were imprisoned, from the time of their arrest to that of their death (or in rarer cases, their release) are perfectly correct." In private, however, the Medvedev brothers were more critical: in January, Zhores wrote to Roy: "The book disappointed me. The form is great, the material is rich, but there are many mistakes and incorrect interpretations." Roy agreed: "From what I know, I can conclude that in the book you write about there is much that is subjective and inaccurate. And the conception itself will hardly satisfy anyone here, it's unrealistic, utopian and not very original." Still, he wrote a review which he considered balanced enough: "I essentially dispute the author's main theses, but I think that I managed to adopt the right tone in this polemic and support everything that constitutes a criticism of Stalinism."

Following Solzhenitsyn's arrest, on February 13, 1974, Roy Medvedev issued a short statement of protest. Praising Solzhenitsyn's "courage and tenacity," he called for his liberation, warning that a trial against "the great writer and great citizen" would be a "disgrace" for the USSR. The Soviet authorities were aware of the adverse publicity that the political trial of a Nobel laureate would have, and they chose instead a "milder" option. On February 14, Solzhenitsyn was forcefully deported to West Germany. This was the first time a dissident had been exiled from the country since Lev Trotskii in 1929. Soon, the writer settled in Zurich, under the relentless gaze of the Western press.

Zhores Medvedev planned to travel to Italy in March 1974, and he intended to stop in Switzerland to meet his friend. However, Solzhenitsyn refused, on the pretext that he needed isolation and tranquility to concentrate on his work. In his letter to Roy, Zhores expressed his disappointment: "This is another one of his fits of megalomania in light form, it will pass in a few weeks…" In his memoirs, Solzhenitsyn was blunter: he had refused to meet Zhores because he did not wish to "sustain the outside illusion" of a friendship, which unduly "confused Europeans, blurred all boundaries." For Solzhenitsyn, the Medvedev brothers' stance on détente had definitely placed them in the adverse camp, and in his memoirs, he called Roy Medvedev's 1973 article a "stab in [Sakharov's] back." Yet he also understood that the division of Soviet dissent into three main currents, socialist, liberal and Russophile, represented by Medvedev, Sakharov and himself, was inevitable.

In March 1974, Solzhenitsyn published a "Letter to the Soviet leaders," which had a programmatic character. Initially addressed to the Soviet leadership in

September 1973, it had been modified for publication in the West. The text caused widespread incredulity and some degree of derision. While his call to abandon Marxist ideology and forgo imperialist rule over non-Russian lands could find echo in the West, the letter's anti-Western spirit and critique of democracy were unpalatable to a Western audience. Moreover, Solzhenitsyn's concern over war with China and proposal to abandon industrial and urban civilization and resettle Russia's population in the Northeast of the country failed to convince, even among his friends, according to Zhores Medvedev. The writer had greatly harmed his image in the West through this text. Both Sakharov and Medvedev published critical responses, which laid out the differences in their approach to political change in the USSR. Zhores had tried to dissuade Roy from writing a critique of Solzhenitsyn's letter. "No one is taking it seriously here, it is food for jokes and satires." One of them was a satirical article entitled "Aleks, Baby!" published in *The New York Times*, which began with the following satirical address to Solzhenitsyn: "As the press agent and promotion man for your American publishers, it behooves me to tell you that your latest fifteen thousand-word open letter to the Kremlin has been a public relations disaster here in the U.S.A."

Despite his brother's advice, Roy did write a critique of Solzhenitsyn's letter in May 1974, at the request of the West German journal *Der Spiegel*. Medvedev agreed that the alarming situation of agriculture in central Russian villages had to be remedied. However, he found Solzhenitsyn's proposal of directing part of the Soviet military budget towards thawing out the lands of North-East Siberia utterly absurd. Neither did he agree with Solzhenitsyn that Orthodox religion would constitute the moral basis for the spiritual rebirth of the Russian nation. Although he regarded freedom of conscience as a fundamental right, Medvedev considered religion a relic of the past, which had "no future in our country," but should be left to die a natural death rather than repressed. Neither the restoration of capitalism nor the return to national and religious values of seventeenth century Russia were a realistic program for Russia. "Solzhenitsyn rejects for the USSR not only the prospect of socialism but even that of democracy. Yet this is the only rational alternative and the only possible road for real progress by all the nations of our country." After half a century of Soviet rule, the majority of the people favored a "socialist path of development." The only option was therefore "the transition from primitive bureaucratized variants of socialism and pseudo-socialism to socialism with a human face." Marxism-Leninism could not be blamed for all the shortcomings in the Soviet system; it was not a dogma, but a science, which had to evolve with its time, but also had a "right to err." Medvedev continued to hope that the Soviet leadership would implement the necessary reforms to solve the existing contradiction between scientific-technical progress and excessive centralism and bureaucratization. He also hoped that in time, a new socialist party would appear, which would differ both from social-democratic and from Communist parties and would constitute "a loyal and legal opposition to the existing leadership and help to renovate the Communist Party of the Soviet Union and restore it to health."

What Roy Medvedev believed to be an intellectual debate on the ways of reforming the Soviet Union was for Solzhenitsyn a personal attack. And from then on, he would ensure that any blow the Medvedev brothers inflicted on other dissidents would be met accordingly. In September 1974, as Zhores Medvedev was giving a lecture at the Nobel Institute in Oslo, he was asked whether he supported Sakharov's candidacy to the Nobel Prize for Peace. Since the Nobel Institute had specifically asked him not to comment on the subject, Medvedev gave a non-committal response, to the effect that he could not make comparisons, since he did not know the candidates from other countries. In his memoirs, Zhores wrote that the question was a provocation staged by a member of the anti-Soviet émigré organization NTS, who circulated to Russian émigré media and Radio Liberty a transcript in which Medvedev's words were distorted beyond recognition. It read: "You must analyze and weigh up how great a contribution Academician Sakharov made to the cause of peace and how great—to kindling the flames of war."

Vladimir Maksimov, who received a copy of the report, hurriedly called Solzhenitsyn to ask him to react immediately to this new attack against Sakharov. Solzhenitsyn did not take the trouble to verify Maksimov's account: "As always in such hastily transmissions and nervous requests there was no accuracy, no text, no written record—and where and when could I find it?" Despite having "neither heard nor read" the original speech, he wrote a letter of protest, attacking Medvedev and highlighting Sakharov's role in defense of human rights in the USSR. "In an astounding way, Zh. Medvedev always knows what the Soviet government likes to hear and says precisely that, in a more appropriate and cleverer way than the entire paid Agitprop apparatus of the C[entral] C[ommittee] could do . . . And if what is needed is to denigrate our national hero, then the most convenient place is chosen, the Nobel Institute." Solzhenitsyn sent his letter to the London *Times*, but the newspaper refused to publish a text containing unbuttressed accusations which could qualify as slander. It only appeared in the Norwegian newspaper *Aftenposten* and the Russian émigré press, with a short account in *The Daily Telegraph*. Zhores Medvedev sent letters of protest to these newspapers, defending his reputation.

There was always a rivalry between Roy Medvedev and Aleksandr Solzhenitsyn as authors of the two main dissident histories of Stalin-era repression. As their relationship soured, the Medvedev brothers became less cautious in their criticism of *The Gulag Archipelago*, the main conception of which greatly differed from the central motive of *Let History Judge*. Roy Medvedev studied the genesis and consequences of Stalinism as a phenomenon restricted in time, which he believed to be akin to a disease or deformation of Socialism. He believed it could be cured, provided the reasons for its appearance were given due attention. For Solzhenitsyn, however, the fateful turn had taken place with the February 1917 Revolution, and Stalin only walked in the footsteps of his predecessor.

In his review of the second volume of *Gulag*, published in September 1974, Roy Medvedev strengthened his criticism. As he wrote to his brother: "in the second volume there is too much obvious tendentiousness, bias, which imperceptibly drifts here and there into untruth. It is the same 'party spirit' the other way round. An objective demonstration of all crimes would have had a stronger effect." Roy disagreed with Solzhenitsyn's condemnation of party members who had died in the repressions and believed that among them "were also not a few who were misguided" by "the cult of party discipline." He concluded: "One should clearly state that no man deserved the terrible fate that befell the leaders arrested in 1937–1938. And it is impossible to relish the thought of their humiliation and sufferings, even if one does know that many of them deserved the penalty of death."

In December 1974, Solzhenitsyn travelled to Stockholm to receive the Nobel Prize for Literature he had been awarded in 1970. During his press conference, the writer expressed at length his disagreement with Roy Medvedev and those Old Bolsheviks whom the historian represented.

> Roy Medvedev has written a huge, voluminous book, *Let History Judge*, researching the Stalin era—well, mostly what happened in the party and to the Bolsheviks... Out of sympathy the Western media speaks about it as a scientific work. I don't see any signs of scientificity in it. It is a publicistic, political book following narrowly the party line... Now, trying to save the Soviet Marxists, he has come up with such a solution: "We need a new socialist party, free of responsibility for the crimes of the past." That is, one party has already killed sixty million people, it's already impossible to wash its hands, therefore let's form another [party] and start all over again. Roy Medvedev's "renaissance of Marxism"

> is approximately as if in Germany now a publicist tried to demonstrate that Hitler's theory was correct, only the execution was unsuccessful ... Roy Medvedev spoke up essentially against *The [Gulag] Archipelago* ... because he has to save Lenin, the idea of communism and defend those very same Old Bolsheviks who until the last day before their arrest helped the grinding machine destroy others; then suddenly they were seized and imprisoned as well. He now calls them victims. But one may ask: if the victim helped the executioner until the last moment and sent others to be slaughtered and held the ax—to what extent are they victims or also perpetrators?

Using the label of "dissident" in relation to Roy Medvedev, as the Western media did, was unjustified, in Solzhenitsyn's view. "Nothing threatens him personally because he, in general, defends the regime in the best way—in a more clever and flexible way than the official press can." And "no Soviet propagandist and agitator could have justified repressions in the USSR as boldly" as Zhores Medvedev had done in front of the Fulbright commission.

The Medvedev brothers were dumbfounded when they read the text of the interview. Solzhenitsyn gave quotes from *Let History Judge* in which the author allegedly justified the use of violence—but these quotes were pure inventions and distorted its content. The page numbers he provided corresponded neither to the manuscript, nor to the published book. It was unclear who had compiled these quotes for Solzhenitsyn, who had obviously never read the book. Zhores remembered showing him the manuscript in 1968, but after looking at the table of contents, the writer had declared: "I have another conception on the subject, and I don't want to change it." Solzhenitsyn himself writes disdainfully in his memoirs: "I have not read Roy's party book."

The opposition between the two men crystallized around the figure of Mikhail Iakubovich, a former Menshevik, whose testimony about the show trial of the so-called "All-Union Bureau of the Mensheviks" figured prominently in both Roy Medvedev's and Solzhenitsyn's works. From the use of torture to extract confessions about imaginary crimes to the staging of a public trial, all the ingredients of the show trials of the late 1930s against prominent party figures were already present in this 1931 political prosecution. In his petition for rehabilitation, written in 1967, Iakubovich told his tragic story: after enduring inhuman torture and attempting suicide, he had agreed to "play his role" dutifully in the forthcoming trial. In Solzhenitsyn's rendition of Iakubovich's story in *The Gulag Archipelago*, however, the accused was depicted as a convinced Communist who had agreed to collaborate with the prosecution out of ideological considerations, before even being tortured.

Roy Medvedev, who had known Iakubovich since 1965 and published his petition in full in *Let History Judge*, was shocked to see that Solzhenitsyn had distorted the old Menshevik's account. It was not simply illogical, it was clear slander against Iakubovich, with whom Medvedev was still in contact, and whose interest he took upon himself to defend. Their correspondence testifies to Iakubovich's resentment towards Solzhenitsyn, which was easily exploited by Soviet propaganda. The Soviet news agency APN first shot an interview with him, in December 1974, then encouraged him to write a text against Solzhenitsyn and in defense of Roy Medvedev. This could have been a first instance of direct exploitation of the conflicts among dissidents to discredit one of them, but the authorities apparently deemed this strategy too risky, or perhaps the fact that Iakubovich remained unrehabilitated hindered his instrumentalization by Soviet propaganda.

Roy, however, remained bent on whitewashing the old man's reputation. When he started editing a new samizdat journal entitled *Dvadtsatyi vek* ("Twentieth century"), in 1975, he opened his pages to Iakubovich, publishing in English the first part of a forty-page essay entitled "From the history of Ideas." Zhores could thus claim to represent Iakubovich's interests in the West. In 1978, as he was preparing a second volume in English, published by Merlin Press, Zhores noted that the editor was intent on including other essays by Iakubovich. However, to defend Iakubovich's honor, the Medvedev brothers wished to add an introduction pointing out the distortion of his affair in *Gulag*. Since this could possibly lead to a legal confrontation, Zhores asked his brother to send him a letter from Iakubovich confirming his version of the events. Eventually, the biologist realized that the only way to obtain justice for Iakubovich was to exercise pressure on Solzhenitsyn through his publisher, to induce him to change the text of *Gulag* in future editions. Solzhenitsyn accused Iakubovich of having changed the sequence of events in his petition from his earlier account and claimed not to have read Iakubovich's text but, eventually, he agreed to add a footnote. This was not enough for Zhores.

For several years, however, the Medvedevs were left without news from Iakubovich. As they found out through a friend, the old man had suffered a heart attack. The lack of explicit declaration from Iakubovich kept Zhores from acting decisively on his behalf, but when a new letter from him came in, Zhores sent a copy to Solzhenitsyn's English publisher to prove that he was still alive. In it, Iakubovich bitterly complained: "My case is presented in the rendition of an enemy, who crept to me under the guise of a friend." Zhores warned that

Iakubovich could hire a lawyer and sue the publisher. "This was bluff, of course. Iakubovich lived in Karaganda [Kazakhstan] and was almost ninety years old. But I had a few of his letters. Neither I, nor he, could afford to hire a lawyer, it is terribly expensive. But it would have been worth it." Eventually, Solzhenitsyn gave in, and all the following editions of *Gulag* featured Iakubovich's story with the correct sequence of events. In his memoirs, however, Solzhenitsyn presented the Medvedevs as being solely interested in financial compensation, and he concluded. "And Zhores fell silent for now. There was no trial against the *Archipelago*."

The confrontation between Solzhenitsyn and the Medvedev brothers was as much a battle of egos as an ideological struggle. Given their fame, their skirmishes played out on the pages of the émigré newspapers and sometimes the Western press. By 1975, the Medvedevs had lost much of their credit in the Russian diaspora, although they were still considered authorities on Soviet politics and dissent in the West. Thanks to his works *Let History Judge* and *On Socialist Democracy*, Roy Medvedev had acquired the label of figurehead of the "socialist" branch of Soviet dissent. But as some dissidents acerbically pointed out, he was a general without any troops. When the need for political allies was felt, he decided to found a new samizdat/tamizdat journal.

Works Cited

Medvedev, Roy. "Solzhenitsyn's 'Open Letter.'" In *Political Essays*, 93–109. Nottingham: Spokesman Books, 1976.

Medvedev, Zhores. *Opasnaia Professiia*. Moscow: Vremia, 2019.

Safire, William. "Aleks, Baby." *The New York Times*, March 11, 1974.

Solzhenitsyn, Aleksandr Isaevich. *The Gulag Archipelago: 1918–1956*. Vol. 1. Glasgow: Harpers and Row Publishers, 1974.

———. "Ugodilo zernyshko promezh dvukh zhernovov. Ocherki izgnaniia. Chast' pervaia (1974–1978). Glavy 4–5." *Novyi Mir*, no. 2 (1999).

———. *Publitsistika v trekh tomakh*. Vol. 2. Iaroslavl': Verkhne-Volzhskoe knizhnoe izdatel'stvo, 1996.

Further Reading

Fireside, Harvey. "Dissident Visions of the USSR." *Polity* 22, no. 2 (Winter 1989): 213–29.

Martin, Barbara. *Dissident histories in the Soviet Union: from de-Stalinization to Perestroika*. London: Bloomsbury Academic, 2019.

CHAPTER 11

Finding and Losing Political Allies

In November 1974, Roy Medvedev told his brother that a group of "Marxist theoreticians, some of them quite well-known," had decided to create a Marxist quarterly journal. The emigration of a growing number of dissidents had led to the displacement of the democratic movement's center of gravity to the West and to a gradual replacement of samizdat by tamizdat. New publications of various orientations had seen the light of day, adding to an existing Russian émigré press. In 1974, Vladimir Maksimov had launched in Paris *Kontinent*, a Christian liberal-democratic, anti-Communist quarterly journal with an initial print run of seven thousand copies. At the end of 1974, Aleksandr Solzhenitsyn and Igor' Shafarevich also released the collection *From under the Rubble*, containing a range of essays by Russophile and Orthodox authors. It drew inspiration from the early twentieth-century collection *Vekhi* ("Landmarks"), published in Moscow in 1909 by Russian religious philosophers who questioned the Russian intelligentsia's role in history. To offer a left-wing counterpart to these publications, and particularly to Solzhenitsyn's volume, Roy Medvedev had agreed to take part in the creation of a socialist journal. As he wrote to Zhores, he had neither the time nor the energy to lead the project, but he was ready to write articles and collect materials. He also enquired whether a socialist publisher in the West would be ready to publish this quarterly in Russian in a small print run. Zhores, however, warned him that "it won't be easy to seriously help from here, under the influence of its own economic and political problems the West has lost its burning interest towards what is happening in the USSR, if it concerns little-known figures and minor events, which abound here as well."

A month later, after reading *From Under the Rubble*, Roy decided to take the project's lead. He added that "a few very good theoreticians have agreed to take part as well, but under pseudonyms." Frequent statements from Soviet dissidents to the effect that Roy Medvedev was a "one-man opposition," the last socialist dissident, convinced him of the need to gather some of his supporters around a common liberal Marxist publication. By January 1975, he had an approximate table of contents for the first samizdat issue and a title, *Dvadtsatyi Vek* ("Twentieth Century"). The publication would discuss "contemporary Soviet history, events of the recent past and possible perspectives" and include political, historical and economic articles, along with excerpts from literary works, mostly memoirs. He hoped "to give an outlet to accumulated intellectual energy, conserve some of the good literature and lead to an exchange of thoughts." Roy also planned on publishing the journal in tamizdat, which would allow him to pay small royalties to the journal's authors, who were mostly living on modest pensions or unemployed, waiting for an emigration visa. To give Zhores more freedom for the publication of selected articles abroad, he decided on a non-periodical format. The introduction to the first tamizdat issue stated: "Guided by the concern for the development of a just society and socialist thinking in the USSR, setting as their main goal the combination of socialism and democracy, a group of like-minded people" begins the publication of a "sociopolitical and literary almanac."

By March 1975, Roy had put together two samizdat issues and decided to inform foreign correspondents. From the outset, Medvedev had wanted to give an "anti-Solzhenitsyn" orientation to the publication: it featured several articles critically reviewing *From under the Rubble* and Solzhenitsyn's novel *August 1914*, in addition to an essay by Lev Kopelev, Solzhenitsyn's former friend and campmate, entitled "A lie can only be conquered by truth." In this critical analysis of the "Letter to the Soviet Leaders," Kopelev expressed his disagreement with the writer's approach to Communist ideology. "To accuse Marx, Engels, or even Lenin of responsibility for 'ideological agriculture' that is, for destructive collectivization, for the miscalculations and the incoherence of industrial development" was as illogical as blaming Darwin for Hitler's crimes for the sole reason that the dictator had appealed to the scientist's doctrine of "natural selection." Several publications came from Roy's portfolio: Mikhail Iakubovich's memoirs on the preparation of the October Revolution; Dmitrii Vitkovskii's Gulag memoirs *Half a lifetime*, which Tvardovskii had entrusted to him after the author's death, and two portraits of Russian writers with tragic fates by Boris Iampol'skii. Medvedev himself had contributed a review of Vladimir Maksimov's novel *Quarantine* and chapters from his recently completed manuscript questioning Mikhail Sholokhov's authorship of *Quiet flows the Don*, which had earned him the Nobel Prize in 1965. The writer was known for his political loyalty and public attacks against dissidents. More unexpected was "Commodity number 1," a sociological study of the consumption of alcohol in Soviet society pointing to the state's interest in perpetuating high levels of vodka consumption, published under the pseudonym of A. Krasikov by M.D. Baital'skii. Several pieces were also signed by Raisa Lert, a socialist dissident. Although Roy did not mention her in his letters to Zhores, presumably as a conspiracy measure, Lert seems to have been the initiator and at first the co-editor of the journal.

For a few years, the KGB had left Roy Medvedev in peace. However, the preparation of a new samizdat journal, coupled with the circulation of his book on Sholokhov among Moscow writers, were bound to irritate the authorities. Once he made the existence of *Dvadtsatyi vek* public, the reaction was swift. On March 14, 1975, Roy was summoned for a five-hour interrogation. In the account he made of his talk in a confidential letter to his brother, he called the conversation "quite peaceful, without threat or warnings." "I had the impression that they are still probing and that other steps may follow next. Therefore, I want to act quickly and have three [journal] issues ready by April 10–15 and then go on vacation in May." On March 21, he was summoned to the Moscow Prosecutor's Office for another five-hour interrogation. Afterwards, he was asked to sign a written injunction, in which he was described as a "citizen without specific occupation" and was enjoined to "stop his slanderous activity directed against state interests and take up work useful to society." Medvedev refused to sign and protested that he neither considered himself "without specific occupation," nor found his activities "slanderous." He informed his friends but asked them to keep it secret. However, the next day, foreign radio broadcasts mentioned the incident.

On April 7, the historian expressed further concern in a letter to his brother. He had heard that the authorities were discussing repressive measures against him but did not seem to have come to an agreement yet. A lady of his acquaintance who worked at the Ministry of Health had warned him that the question of his psychiatric hospitalization was under discussion.

> All these are just conversations, but it is important to take them into account. I have of course consciously begun editing the journal precisely now (after the book on Sholokhov) and have assumed authorship of *Political Diary*. In for a penny, in for a pound. All of this immediately raises the stakes in this political game that I have to play, and if I win, then it will be very important for everyone. But I might also lose, and I am also prepared for this.

This time, Roy did not intend on going into hiding, as he had done in 1971. On the contrary, he felt that staying in the limelight was crucial for his safety and his journal's survival. He warned his brother that an interruption in their correspondence could mean that something had happened to him. Ten days later, Roy wrote more cold-bloodedly that, although the authorities were annoyed by the journal and the success of his book in samizdat, he was under "no real threat." He would go on holiday as planned. "It will be better to demonstrate full tranquility and assurance than alarm. And it would make a negative impression on potential authors... I have the impression that the authorities are precisely expecting me to be alarmed, try to 'hide,' etc. But following my old rule, I always have to act the opposite way than expected."

Some time later, early in the morning, KGB officials rang his doorbell for a house search. However, this time, Medvedev refused to let the officials leave with whole bags of files as they had done in 1971. He insisted on them observing legal regulations, which foresaw that documents seized should all be itemized separately; and after locking away his papers in his desk and cupboard, he threatened to offer physical resistance if rules were broken. But the officials had obviously no warrant for arrest, and after a phone call to their superiors, they left with only a few tamizdat books. Although Medvedev kept copies of his most important documents at trusted friends' places, he kept current work material and books at home, some of which could be considered anti-Soviet. Still, the losses were insignificant compared to 1971. Medvedev felt that the authorities expected him to protest the search. He decided to keep silent, however, for his journal's sake, and the pressure ceased. The materials seized apparently did not warrant a new summons to the Prosecutor's Office.

Despite the threats, Roy microfilmed the first three journal issues and sent them to London in April 1975. Zhores had created a small publishing house under the name "T.C.D. Publications" for the purpose of publishing the journal in Russian. Two volumes appeared under this label: the first one, published in 1976, was released in one thousand copies. It bore both the names of Roy Medvedev and Raisa Lert as editors and included two essays on the themes of the current divisions of the dissidence, formulated in echo to each other: "Questions that are of concern to all" by Roy Medvedev, followed by "… And to which there are no simple answers" by Raisa Lert. Both authors noted that the unity that had characterized the dissident movement in the 1960s, based on a common critique of the regime, had in the 1970s given way to a diversity of positive programs for reform and, as a result, polemics between representatives of various political currents had arisen. But while Medvedev's contribution only added fuel to the fire, Lert sought on the contrary to refocus the democratic camp on its struggle against a common adversary.

In his article, Roy Medvedev reiterated his position concerning détente, emigration, and the perspective of "changes from above," emphasizing his differences with other dissidents. He regretted that the dialogue with the authorities had taken only one form, that of KGB interrogations but noted that the Soviet government, which had never been monolithic, now included a group of "technocrats," who, provided they allied with the "moderate" group of Brezhnevites, could possibly bring about democratization. Noting that the new, "third wave" of Russian emigration, unlike the first two, was in a position to exercise some influence on both sides of the Iron Curtain, Medvedev examined its main currents. While praising Solzhenitsyn's literary talent, he mocked him for posing as a "prophet," warning that he would "have even fewer followers than L.N. Tolstoi." He criticized *Under the Rubble* for its "intolerance towards dissent, narrow-mindedness and dogmatism, that is in the end the same party spirit of the worst kind, only with a different content," but also Solzhenitsyn and Shafarevich's "hatred towards socialism, which allows any means in the struggle with its opponents." He was no kinder towards *Kontinent*, which, he felt, was addressed mostly "to the West, and its main task is the denunciation of Marxism in the eyes of Western intelligentsia and youth." Overall, he found both publications' Russian messianic line inadequate: just as Russia's salvation could not come from outside, Shafarevich, Maksimov and Solzhenitsyn could not claim to teach mankind.

Raisa Lert considered such criticism unproductive and called for a shift from "the criticism of platforms conceived for the future," and therefore utopian to a large degree, to "a criticism of today's 'unsatisfactory situation in the country,'" and more specifically the "denunciation of forces and tendencies that oppose democratization." While she essentially agreed with Medvedev's views, she chastised him for exposing them in such a way that his main adversaries appeared to be not Soviet bureaucrats, the KGB and anti-Semites, but Senator Jackson, Maksimov and Solzhenitsyn.

This first tamizdat issue was thus less the affirmation of a positive political platform than a critique of other dissident projects. Clearly, two years of battle between the Medvedev brothers and Solzhenitsyn had taken their toll, and Roy Medvedev seemed bitter, to the point that he sometimes lost sight of his real adversaries. Another confrontation with Solzhenitsyn occurred with the publication of Solzhenitsyn's memoirs *The Oak and the Calf* in 1975. This chronicle of his long-standing opposition to the Soviet regime painted a negative picture of those "half-dissidents" who had compromised with the system for the sake of advancing their pawns, in particular Aleksandr Tvardovskii and *Novyi Mir*. Vladimir Lakshin, a literary critic who had belonged to Tvardovskii's editorial team, was particularly shocked by Solzhenitsyn's depiction of his former benefactor, whose support had been crucial for the publication of *Ivan Denisovich*. Roy was friends with the literary critic and shared his indignation but left it to Lakshin to criticize Solzhenitsyn's memoirs. Although Lakshin hesitated for a long time to release his text in samizdat, fearing the consequences, he found the alternative, an instrumentalization of his protest by the Soviet Press Agency APN, to be ethically unacceptable. Medvedev also suspected that Lakshin was afraid of alienating that part of the intelligentsia "for whom Solzhenitsyn is still an idol." But Lakshin's essay finally appeared in the tenth samizdat issue of *Dvadtsatyi vek* and Zhores arranged for its publication as a separate brochure in France, later translated into English.

Roy Medvedev released a total of eleven issues of *Dvadtsatyi Vek* into samizdat in 1975–1976, and the first tamizdat issue came out in London in 1976. Meanwhile, the historian was subjected to new direct threats. In late 1976, in preparation for the forthcoming sixtieth anniversary of the October Revolution, repression against dissent increased. Two authors of *Dvadtsatyi Vek* publishing under pseudonyms were subjected to house searches and their personal papers were seized. One of them was Mikhail Baital'skii, the author of a two-part essay on alcohol sales in the Soviet Union. Shortly thereafter, in November, Medvedev was summoned again to the Moscow Prosecutor's Office. He was shown a tamizdat copy of his journal and ordered once more to stop the publication. This time, Medvedev decided to take the warning seriously: it seemed clear that instructions had been sent from "above" to deal a decisive blow to samizdat periodicals. In December 1976, he told his brother he wanted to end the samizdat publication. It had been almost two years since he had launched the periodical, ten issues had come out, and he felt like he had fulfilled his plan. He had never intended on devoting more than one or two years to this time-consuming project.

This, however, did not mean the end of tamizdat publication: they now had sufficient material to publish a few anthologies in the West, which would reach a wider readership. In England, "Merlin Press" which published *The Socialist Register*, an authoritative theoretical journal, released two volumes under the title *The Samizdat Register*. The French socialist publisher "François Maspero" and the Italian left-wing "Giulio Einaudi Editore" released collections of articles, and further volumes in German and Japanese also appeared. By 1977, Zhores was sending small sums of royalties to be dispatched to *Dvadtsatyi Vek*'s authors. In February 1977, Roy was still giving instructions to Zhores to prepare a third tamizdat issue in Russian, with a note explaining that the samizdat publication had ceased. "You may indicate various reasons, the weakening of samizdat, financial difficulties for publication and the difficulty of sending materials from both sides."

Overall, the publication was not a lucrative endeavor. Although the second volume in Russian was, of Zhores's admission, more interesting than the first, it was, as Zhores stated in June 1977, "selling slowly, as the price is high and the main Russian émigré libraries are not ordering, visibly scared because of the critique of their idol [Solzhenitsyn]." The Medvedevs had become odious figures to many Russian émigrés, and the journal's audience was mostly constituted by Sovietologists, for whom the material published presented only marginal interest. Roy also explained the end of the tamizdat publication by another bout of pressure on him: the Soviet Immigration Department (OVIR) through which Zhores's wife had applied for a visa to visit their elder son in the USSR, had made the visa conditional on the complete liquidation of the publication. Roy did not feel it legitimate to deny a son the right to see his mother and yielded to blackmail.

Another reason for the journal's disappearance may have been dissensions within the editorial collective, which already transpired in the first issue. By 1977, when the second volume in Russian appeared, Raisa Lert's name had vanished from the cover, on her request: according to Roy, she argued that "she could not determine [the journal]'s line and [Medvedev] decided on everything mostly by himself." The historian explained that attributing her the title of "editor" in the first volume had been a typo; they had actually agreed she would fulfill the function of a secretary, but she could not accept such a subordinate function. Medvedev concluded: "It is much easier to lead this affair alone, and what if there were an editorial team?"

Lert's version of this conflict appeared in an open letter by Petr Abovin-Egides, a close friend of hers. Abovin-Egides identified himself as an author of *Dvadtsatyi vek*, who shared Medvedev's striving for democratic socialism and had long looked up with hope towards the dissident. But he deplored the dissident's drifting to the right over the past years and regretted the Western media's representation of Roy Medvedev as the figurehead of socialist democratic dissent in the USSR. Medvedev may have claimed to have remained loyal to the same ideas since the 1950s, but the failure to react to Soviet society's evolution and adapt his stance was in itself "backwards evolution."

Abovin-Egides found fault with Roy Medvedev's tactical moderation, which he deemed immoral. Why always bury his boldest ideas under a thick layer of "old dogmatic rubbish," to the point that they become almost invisible to his readers? "Of course, you may make a merit out of your ability to safely pronounce some not quite harmless words. But if one considers not one's safety, but the interests of the struggle for the democratization of our country, this tactic is harmful." And if the tactic was morally unsound, no higher moral goals could justify it. From a tactical consideration to avoid provoking the authorities' anger, Medvedev went one step further, "turning against dissidents the blade of his criticism, once directed against those who stifle freedom." All too often, his discourse, whether regarding dissidents, Soviet foreign policy, or the absence of economic rights in the West, coincided with the official Soviet position.

The same problems arose with *Dvadtsatyi vek*. According to Abovin-Egides, the idea of a samizdat journal of socialist orientation "had been in the air" and he and Lert had discussed it with Roy Medvedev several times. Although the historian initially judged the project "utopian," he suddenly announced, "that the journal will be, and that it will be called 'Twentieth century' and that [he] is its sole editor and publisher," refusing the creation of an editorial committee and taking everything into his own hands. First, Abovin-Egides thought he could accept such a format, but soon he was disappointed by the journal's orientation, and by Medvedev's refusal to discuss it. "The journal's line became yours: avoid complicated domestic questions, step up the polemics not against official policy, but against dissidents of other currents than yours." Lert's and Abovin-Egides's attempts to contest this line were in vain and Lert's decision to resign from her position of editorial secretary had no impact on Medvedev. The journal had eventually died "a natural death: as you declared yourself, by lack of content. Indeed, who would want to publish in a *samizdat* journal, which denounces predominantly... Carter, Jackson and Solzhenitsyn? For this there is the official press."

Abovin-Egides concluded that Medvedev's line, wrongly interpreted as representative of the socialist democratic opposition, could drive young people away from democratic socialism. By adopting an ambiguous position in relation to the authorities, Medvedev gave ammunition to those who considered him and his brother KGB agents. While Abovin-Egides rejected these "dirty inventions," he still felt entitled to ask what could explain Medvedev's strange "extraterritoriality." His popularity in the West could not be the decisive factor. "I think that, more importantly, in recent years your position, your 'tactic' not only does not preoccupy our authorities but is even extremely *convenient* to them. It is almost *advantageous* to have such a dissident." Medvedev's criticism of other dissidents looked "more convincing" than if it had been printed in the official press.

> Of course, the silent union between the dissident Roy Medvedev and our authorities arose incidentally, spontaneously. I am certain that you did not conclude any agreement, either open, or

secret, with them, you did not take on any obligations. It just worked out this way: you softened your criticism of the regime and directed it against dissidents—they left you alone and gave you the possibility of "devoting all your time to historical works." They like the taste of the *pâté* that your articles and interviews constitute (20 percent of criticism of the regime and 80 percent of criticism of dissidents and foreign state actors).

This was neither the first, nor the last time that such accusations were formulated against the Medvedev brothers, but this time, it came from his own camp, not from Solzhenitsyn or Maksimov, but from those he had once considered his allies. Abovin-Egides's letter appeared in *Poiski* ("Searches"), a samizdat journal of democratic orientation, which he and Lert co-edited. Founded in 1978, *Poiski* appeared in response to the conflicts that had divided the dissident movement, a symptom of which had been the failure of Abovin-Egides and Lert's collaboration with *Dvadtsatyi vek*. The full title of the journal was "In Search of Mutual Understanding" and its line was one of convergence of various viewpoints, perspectives.

Roy Medvedev, however, had little understanding for Lert and Abovin-Egides's frustration. The latter had shown him this letter before publication in Spring 1978 without giving him a copy. As he complained to Zhores: "I told him that there are factual errors, even calumnious sentences, but that he can write whatever he wants, it became a fashion to write you and me all kinds of letters. Their main complaint is that I consider that there is socialism in the USSR, albeit with a mix of bureaucracy and false socialism. He wants me to write not what I consider necessary, but what he considers necessary."

By September 1978, when the letter came out in *Poiski*, Roy was furious, especially as it came amid a KGB-orchestrated campaign of anonymous letters, which had not only played on his own nerves, but also impacted his wife's health. In a letter to his brother, he called Abovin-Egides "a cowardly and unfertile philosopher" who had waited until retirement to publish under his real name. He was convinced that Lert had strongly edited Abovin-Egides's letter and resented the fact that she had published the letter in *Poiski* without giving him a right of response. On September 23, after a four-hour conversation with Lert, Roy wrote her an open letter, which he circulated among his friends and explicitly made public. He conceded that the letter was "rather harsh, albeit still polite."

Medvedev addressed his letter to Lert, because the letter contained much information that only she could have communicated to Abovin-Egides, whom Roy had met but three or four times in his life. The historian argued in his defense that the views that he expressed were indeed his, and not a measure of protection from repression.

> But, unfortunately the thing is, I have always written and will write only what I thought and think myself. There is no diplomacy or disguise here. The views that Egides wants me to profess at the moment are absolutely not my views. These are Egides's own views and conceptions. It is quite possible that precisely my theoretical views have always been, and continue to be wrong, especially concerning the nature and elements of socialism in the USSR. It is quite possible that in this case Egides is right. But then let him sit at his desk and try to expound his own conceptions coherently and convincingly.

Medvedev could not take seriously the theoretical pretenses of an author whose first work published under his own name was his "open letter to Roy Medvedev." And Lert's arguments that Egides could not publish his earlier works openly because he was only one year away from retirement sounded funny. Had Medvedev not started writing his own books over twenty years before retirement? "And what would our 'democratic' movement be if only pensioners participated in it?"

Secondly, he rejected the idea that his career as a dissident historian was a "phenomenon." It felt like Egides "is trying at least in his own eyes to justify his own creative inferiority" by arguing that "for some reason they <u>let</u> Medvedev write his books and articles, whereas <u>they don't let</u> me!" Even if the authorities did let the Medvedev brothers publish their books, twenty of which had come out in the past ten years, this still demanded considerable work. Moreover, Lert knew very well the measures of pressure to which the Medvedevs had been exposed, from house searches to anonymous letters. "I just don't consider it necessary to tell foreign correspondents or the majority of my friends about these actions." It was particularly painful to see these accusations in print "now, when I, my friends and my close ones became victims of particularly sophisticated harassment, when the question of how to silence Roy Medvedev is being discussed at the highest level."

Finally, Medvedev considered it unfair to accuse him of not having expressed his opposition to the Brezhnev regime. Admittedly, he had not been on Red Square to protest the Soviet invasion of Czechoslovakia in August 1968, but then neither Sakharov, nor Solzhenitsyn had protested. Medvedev had expressed his views on the question on the pages of *Political Diary*, which Lert read at the time.

He concluded that writing open letters to the Medvedev brothers appeared to have become a new literary genre, but this was the first time that people who called themselves his friends had written him such an epistle. He therefore encouraged Lert to show his letter to others and even to publish it on the pages of her journal if she wished.

Lert's reaction, according to Roy, was to call him and express relief that he had written the letter. She promised to make sure that his reply be included in the issue of *Poiski* that had just been sent abroad for publication. Whether her contrition was heartfelt or contrived is unclear, but soon the polemics surrounding the letter grew considerably, for another reason.

In his open letter to Lert, Medvedev not only settled his scores with her and Abovin-Egides, but also expressed his frustration with the Soviet human rights movement at large by sharing his critical comments on the recent trial of Aleksandr Ginzburg. The dissident was condemned in July 1978 to eight years of imprisonment for managing the Fund of Assistance to Political Prisoners, created by Aleksandr Solzhenitsyn and funded through the royalties he received for *The Gulag Archipelago*. Medvedev was on vacation when the trial happened, and he had only just read an account of it. He took the opportunity of his open letter to Lert to express his views, which pertained not just to the Ginzburg case, but to such questions as conspiracy and transparency in the dissident movement.

Medvedev questioned the attitudes of dissidents who willingly exposed themselves to the risk of imprisonment. Ginzburg's "sacrificial nature" may have been praised when he compiled a "white book" on the trial of Iulii Daniel' and Andrei Siniavskii, for which he received his second camp sentence in 1967. But the qualities required to managed Solzhenitsyn's Fund were different: someone distributing financial assistance to thousands of relatives of political prisoners throughout the country should have, most of all, been concerned with observing utmost secrecy. Ginzburg, instead, had compiled an extensive card index containing the personal data of recipients, their addresses and the sums received, and, what is more, he had kept this index at home, making it an easy catch for the KGB. Medvedev was horrified to see that the transparency characteristic of the Soviet human rights movement led some dissidents to show "carelessness" in their handling of personal information about donors, thereby imperiling "many honest people, especially in the provinces, who could be of use to the human rights movement." In Medvedev's view, after taking responsibility for the Solzhenitsyn Fund, Ginzburg should have remained as discreet as possible. Given his situation, he should have striven not to draw the authorities' attention in any way. Instead, as the trial had shown, he had used part of the funds allocated to organize "lavish banquets" for his own birthday. Medvedev concluded:

> I am of course indignant about the extremely harsh sentence that A. Ginzburg received in Kaluga. But I am no less pained to think of how many people throughout our country could suffer because of Ginzburg's carelessness, negligence, and, let's speak frankly, vainglory. A. Ginzburg had to avoid at any cost what is called in revolutionary circles a "failure." Instead, he often almost consciously drew upon himself repression in relation to himself and his close ones.

This kind of behavior was not unique to Ginzburg, it was also characteristic of other dissidents who formed organizations and groups without "taking into account all the complexity of such an affair in our country." What was needed was a deep knowledge of the "rules of the game."

> Unfortunately, among our dissidents a wholly false value system is progressively becoming commonplace. One begins to judge a person not based on what he did for the movement but based on how many times he was subjected to interrogations, house searches, how many years he spent in a camp, in exile, in prison or in a psychiatric clinic.

Roy Medvedev transmitted his open letter to the dissident writer Georgii Vladimov, whom he had recently met, and who headed the Moscow section of "Amnesty International." Although he certainly hoped for support on his part, the writer answered through an "open letter to Roy Medvedev" of his own, in which he denounced the historian's accusations against Ginzburg. Vladimov defended the human rights movement's strategy of transparency, which from the beginning departed from the conspiracy practices of revolutionary movements, such as the Bolsheviks' in Tsarist Russia. By refusing to retreat into the underground, human rights activists had already triumphed morally over a "terrorist underground organization," which was not "persecuted by the government but stands in power," intimidating dissenters through blackmail, forgeries, perlustration of correspondence, anonymous letters, and other immoral methods. Medvedev's insinuations that Ginzburg had used the Fund's finances in his own interests, a calumny based on the accusations formulated at the trial, showed that Ginzburg's careful accountancy was indeed necessary.

On October 27, Roy Medvedev answered through an "open letter to G. Vladimov," not, as he emphasized, because he was offended, but because the writer raised in his letter a series of important points concerning the orientation and methods of action of the dissident movement, and he wished to clarify his views on this topic. He began by denying that it was immoral to discuss the conduct of someone who was under arrest or imprisoned. Had dissidents not discussed—and condemned—the behavior of Iakir and Krasin, who had denounced hundreds of their peers? Secondly, Medvedev explained his reservations against the creation of dissident organizations. Not only did these contradict "one of the most anti-democratic articles of the Constitution," which demanded that all social organizations be placed under the CPSU's supervision, but the risk with such organizations was also the growth of all kinds of "unnecessary documentation," as well as infiltration by KGB informers. The dissidents' most important weapon was, in Medvedev opinion, "the truthful word," and to spread this word, no organization was needed: it was sufficient to compile the same documents without announcing the creation of an organization. Medvedev acerbically noted: "It is a bit strange to observe the behavior of people who declare to all who care to hear that they live in a totalitarian and police state, but who continue to behave as if they lived in France or England."

Concerning the question of conspiracy, Medvedev explained that he did not call for the use of illegal methods of action but for reasonable self-protection from the state's interference. Dissidents could not obey all laws, and the regime itself did not respect its own legislation. But why take the risk of discussing sensitive questions on one's private phone when it was well-known that the authorities monitored telephone conversations? "We cannot lead human rights defense activities in such a way as to increase at the same time the number of political prisoners, of people dismissed from their jobs or even just deprived of phone access (and this is now a common form of repression)." Nor was it necessary to expose, by neglecting elementary rules of precautions, foreign correspondents or other intermediaries who transmitted letters through non-official channels. "The indirect result of all this 'imprudence' is the fact that today almost none of the foreign correspondents will endeavor to help us in our correspondence with our friends abroad," lamented the historian.

Creating card indexes with thousands of names and addresses was no less imprudent. It was wrong to pretend, as Vladimov did, that those who stepped into contact with Ginzburg knew what they were risking and were already under KGB surveillance anyway. Medvedev received a lot of visitors from the provinces, and some of them used assumed names, and whispered or wrote their messages on pieces of paper to avoid being identified. He personally knew of several people who had been interrogated after their names had been found in Ginzburg's card index; some of them had never even been in contact with him, and two of them had been arrested as a result. For state security, such card indexes were a real find, which helped the KGB cast its nest ever further into the provinces. In fact, Medvedev argued, the only reason why the Solzhenitsyn Fund was allowed to exist for so long was not that the state had an interest in an inflow of foreign currency, but rather that it allowed the KGB to place under surveillance a very broad network of dissidents throughout the country.

These exchanges of letters did not remain unnoticed, and Medvedev received new open and private letters of protest from several former friends, including Lev Kopelev. On October 26, during a press conference with foreign correspondents, Elena Bonner and representatives of the Moscow Helsinki Group issued a declaration denouncing Roy Medvedev's position, pointing out that his accusations against Ginzburg coincided with the KGB's charges. This statement appeared in *Kontinent*, along with Vladimov's letter and a letter by Lert. She accused Medvedev of "using [her] name to participate in the currently growing official campaign of discreditation of the human rights movement" and publicly broke off her relations with him. In his letters to Zhores, Roy vented his frustration with the whole dissident movement: "People who are not occupied with real activities and cannot fulfill their potential on a professional level simply degrade... Hence, as a compensation, attempts to create all kinds of toy organizations." In retrospect, Roy expressed regret at having yielded to the temptation to answer Lert's open letter: as a result, "a whole stream of 'open letters' and 'declarations' flowed in my address," each more hurtful than the other.

This was not the last attack launched against the Medvedev brothers. With the publication of the first volume of *The Political Diary* in Russian, in 1972, they had gained a new enemy: Abdurrakhman Avtorkhanov, the author of a samizdat "bestseller," *The Technology of Power*. Avtorkhanov was a Chechen historian who had emigrated to West Germany in unclear circumstances during the war after his release from Soviet jail. His book, mixing memoirs about Soviet political life in the late 1920s and political analysis, had produced a very strong impression on General Piotr Grigorenko, a socialist dissident, who, of his own admission, had launched it into samizdat. In *Political Diary*, however, Roy Medvedev called the book "anti-Soviet" and pointed out contradictions between Avtorkhanov's account and testimonies of Old Bolsheviks. Medvedev brought up the rumor according to which the KGB willfully circulated radioactive copies of the book to trace its presence with Geiger counters. He also mentioned that Avtorkhanov had defected to the Nazis' camp during the war—an episode Avtorkhanov later mentioned in his own memoirs. When *Political Diary* appeared in the West,

Avtorkhanov came across the review and violently denounced the Medvedev brothers as "false dissidents" in the preface to the second edition of his book.

But the affair received a new development in 1978 when Grigorenko, recently exiled to the West, denied in an interview given to *Kontinent* that he and Roy Medvedev shared the same ideas and declared that he would not even sit next to someone who did not observe "a minimum of decency" in his relations with other dissidents. When he was incarcerated in a psychiatric hospital, Grigorenko remembered being shown a copy of Medvedev's *On Socialist Democracy*, in which the historian described Grigorenko's views as "semi-anarchist" and identified him as the person circulating's Avtorkhanov's anti-Soviet book. This was, in his view, a direct "denunciation" in print.

Following the publication of Grigorenko's interview, Avtorkhanov renewed his attack with greater violence, through an article entitled "R. Medvedev: Slanderer or provocateur?" published in the Paris-based weekly *Russkaia Mysl'* in December 1978. Avtorkhanov wished to destroy the "myth" that Medvedev was a Marxist dissident and show that he was "Brezhnev's mask," the KGB and Central Committee's mouthpiece, able to relay "disinformation" in much more efficient ways than the regime could. Medvedev's occasional critiques of the regime were meaningless, what was significant was the fact that he was not interrogated and left free to publish his books in anti-communist publishing outlets. For Avtorkhanov, the Kremlin had "deployed intensive propaganda in the West to turn Medvedev into 'one of the great dissidents' of the USSR," and Medvedev had copied his "philosophy" from Brezhnev's six-volume collected works. Whether Medvedev used calumny, as he did against Ginzburg, or told the truth, as in Grigorenko's case, in both cases he was an informer.

Avtorkhanov's accusations, on the pages of one of the most read newspapers of the Russian émigré press, were a mighty blow. Zhores defended his brother on the pages of *Kontinent* and *Russkaia Mysl'*. He pointed out that Roy had only cited from Grigorenko's "Declaration to the Prosecutor of the USSR," a document circulating in samizdat in which Grigorenko publicly defended Avtorkhanov's work, and which Avtorkhanov himself cited at length in the preface to the second edition of his book.

The Medvedev brothers spent a lot of energy trying to counter attacks made against them in the émigré press, which they took to heart. They chronicled these conflicts in a three-hundred-page memoir which they coauthored in 1980. Entitled *In search of common sense*, it covered the 1970s with an alternation of chapters written by each of the two brothers, a format similar to *A Question of Madness*. A contract was signed with the publisher Norton Inc., yet for some reason the book was never published. There was still talk about the publication in their correspondence in 1983; the English translation was taking longer than expected, and they considered updating the content. However, Zhores Medvedev believed that the publication had been cancelled after Sakharov was exiled to Gorkii in 1980. It may have been related to the hunger strikes which the physicist undertook in 1984–1985, which seriously threatened his life and made the publication of such a memoir undesirable.

Instead of gathering allies around him, Roy Medvedev's experience with *Dvadtsatyi vek* only deepened his isolation within the dissident movement. Just as Solzhenitsyn had alienated the Western public through his statements in the West, Medvedev lost much of his credit through his denunciation of his dissident adversaries. Moreover, by remaining silent about the harassment he was enduring at the KGB's hands, he created the myth of his own "extraterritoriality," which then proved difficult to dismiss.

Works Cited

Abovin-Egides, Petr. "Molchalivaia uniia (Otkrytoe pis'mo Roiu Medvedevu)." *Poiski*, no. 4 (1982): 30–43.

Avtorkhanov, Abdurakhman. "R. Medvedev: Klevetnik ili provokator?" *Russkaia Mysl'*, December 14, 1978.

———. *Tekhnologiia Vlasti*. 2nd ed. Frankfurt/Main: Posev, 1976.

"Interv'iu s Petrom Grigor'evichem Grigorenko." *Kontinent*, no. 17 (1978): 395–417.

Lert, Raisa. ". . . I na kotorye net odnoznachnykh otvetov." In *Dvadtsatyi Vek. Obshchestvenno-politicheskii i literaturnyi al'manakh. Izbrannye materialy iz samizdatnogo zhurnala "XX Vek,"* edited by Roy Medvedev and Raisa Lert, 1:33–40. London: TCD Publications, 1976.

[Medvedev], [Roy]. "O Knige A. Avtorkhanova 'Tekhnologiia Vlasti.'" In *Politicheskii Dnevnik. 1964–1970*, 509–15. Amsterdam: Fond imeni Gertsena, 1972.

Medvedev, Roy. "Voprosy, kotorye vol'nuiut kazhdogo." In *Dvatsatyi vek: obshchestvenno-politicheskii i literaturnyi almanakh. Izbrannye materialy iz samizdatnogo zhurnala "XX vek,"* edited by Roy Medvedev, Vol. 1. London: T.C.D. Publications, 1977.

Further Reading

David-Fox, Michael. "Memory, Archives, Politics: The Rise of Stalin in Avtorkhanov's Technology of Power." *Slavic Review* 54, no. 4 (1995): 988–1003.

CHAPTER 12

Under the KGB's Watch

While Soviet human rights activists privileged transparency (*glasnost'*), Roy Medvedev followed the tradition of Bolshevik revolutionaries and was a master of conspiracy. The historian had carefully studied secret police and espionage techniques, based on his discussions with ex-Komintern members and with former spy Donald Maclean, who had defected to the Soviet Union in 1951. This knowledge gave him an advantage over KGB agents, allowing him to effectively escape surveillance.

The first time Roy noticed that he was being followed, he used a simple trick to escape the KGB agent's attention: he entered a restaurant, sat down to drink a coffee and gave a tip to the waiter, asking him to show him the backdoor exit. Over time, Medvedev became an expert at "losing" his tails. When he decided to "disappear" after his house search in 1971, the dissident tried to escape surveillance by dressing up as an old man, but when he noticed that he was being followed, he took a small footpath to the next bus stop and jumped at the last minute into a crowded bus through the back door. Medvedev was particularly careful when he visited friends who kept some of his archive for safekeeping or his typist. Evgeniia Ogorodnitskaia lived in an eleven-floor apartment block with twenty entrances, which were connected by a long corridor on the top floor, and Medvedev was always careful to enter and exit through different entrances. She was never called in for interrogation. And when Medvedev wanted to minimize the risk of being followed, for instance to visit famous writers, he solicited the help of his friend Aleksei Tsybuliatskii, who worked as head of the garage of the USSR Academy of Sciences and had a police accreditation. He greatly enjoyed speeding through the city in his Moskvich car to escape vehicles which tried to tail them. This cat-and-mouse game apparently intrigued the KGB. Roy once met at the Lakshins' a renowned medical specialist who had been called on duty to the office of Filip Bobkov, head of the KGB section in charge of dissidents. The physician told him that when he entered Bobkov's office, he noticed a large Moscow map with flags indicating locations where Roy Medvedev had been spotted.

This surveillance was justified both by the need to monitor his numerous contacts with Western correspondents and to keep him under pressure. Arresting him was not a good option for the regime, because of the adverse publicity it would create in the West, but the KGB tried to restrict his freedom of movement. Yet the historian played his game astutely and he believes that his sources of information and the channels through which he transmitted his manuscripts abroad remained secret.

In the 1970s and 1980s, Roy Medvedev published on average one book per year. After *Let History Judge* (several augmented editions of which appeared, in 1974 in Russian, and in 1989 in English) and *On Socialist Democracy*, he turned to Khrushchev's biography. Coauthored with his brother, he published in 1975 *Khrushchev: The Years in Power*, the first chapters of which had appeared in *Political Diary*, followed by a full biography of the Soviet leader in 1982. For this second book he benefitted from the active support of Khrushchev's son, although the latter judged the final product too critical of his father's action, especially in the agricultural field. After the publication of his book on Sholokhov and his samizdat journal *Dvadtsatyi Vek*, Roy turned to the history of the Russian Revolution (*The October Revolution*, 1979) and the Civil War (*Philip Mironov and the Russian Civil War*, 1978, coauthored with Sergei Starikov). He also wrote portraits of Stalin's contemporaries: his opponents (*Nikolai Bukharin: The Last Years*, 1980) and his colleagues and henchmen (*All Stalin's Men*, 1983), along with an additional volume *On Stalin and Stalinism* (1979). In the 1980s, he returned to political philosophy with *Leninism and Western Socialism* (1982). His close contacts with Italian journalists Piero Ostellino and Giulietto Chiesa also resulted into the publication of books of interviews (*On Dissent*, 1980; *Time of Change: an insider's view of Russia's transformation*, 1989). Finally, he returned to his youth interest in China and published *China and the Superpowers* in 1986.

The publications of these books, translated into several languages, in addition to articles commissioned by Western newspapers, provided Roy Medvedev with a comfortable income. Roy remembered that he received his first advance on royalties of one-thousand dollars from the German writer Heinrich Böll in 1970. The logistics of such operations was complex, as Soviet citizens were not authorized to own foreign currency. Böll bought Medvedev consumer goods in a Soviet "Beriozka" special retail store, which he transmitted through friends. Over time, these contacts were facilitated: after settling in London, Zhores closely supervised his brother's publishing affairs, serving as his representative with publishers, signing contracts and managing his finances. In exchange, he received 30 percent of his brother's earnings. Until 1976, it was relatively easy to wire money to the Soviet Union from the West through the USSR Foreign Trade Bank. This system was mostly intended for Soviet citizens employed abroad: they could transfer their wages, and then withdraw them in the form of certificates, which could be used to buy consumer goods at "Beriozka" special shops. Ironically, a number of dissidents began to use this system to receive foreign royalties and thus had access to restricted stores selling scarce goods. The situation ended in 1976 when a 30 percent tax was imposed on such transfers. Soviet authors' royalties' payments were exempted of this tax only for works published through legal (censored) channels. The Medvedevs, however, found ways to circumvent these restrictions: in addition to books, in the 1980s, Zhores started sending his brother electronics, which Roy could sell on the black market. Foreign correspondents also bought him goods in "Beriozka" shops as a payment for articles the historian had written for their newspapers.

Since international phone calls were expensive and dissidents' phone lines were bugged, the twin brothers exchanged almost daily letters. As correspondence sent through the Soviet post was subjected to censorship and could be intercepted, the Medvedev sent registered letters, which they numbered (to check whether they arrived), containing only information of minor sensitivity. Confidential information was usually sent through foreign correspondents, who had access to diplomatic pouches. Through them, Roy received foreign journals to which he subscribed, and parcels with books or stationery. Occasionally, Western scholars travelling to and from the Soviet Union could also transmit packages or microfilmed manuscripts. To ensure that manuscripts sent through regular mail arrived, they were often duplicated and divided into several parts sent separately.

How could the Soviet authorities allow Roy Medvedev to pursue such a successful career as an independent historian unimpeded? How come he remained the last prominent dissident at large, after Solzhenitsyn's expulsion from the USSR in 1974 and after Sakharov was sent to Gor'kii in internal exile in 1980? There are various explanations to this paradox, and this chapter and the next will provide some clues, but the short answer was that Roy Medvedev's brand of dissent was much less threatening to the Soviet regime than Solzhenitsyn's or Sakharov's. Moreover, unlike them, Roy Medvedev deliberately restrained his criticism. He may have denied that his caution was calculated, but there was certainly some truth to Abovin-Egides's allegations that it was by avoiding "dangerous" themes that Medvedev had escaped arrest. Indeed, throughout his career, the historian always kept sight of the red lines that he knew he should not cross if he wanted to remain free to write and do research. Hedrick Smith, correspondent for *The New York Times,* accurately pinpointed Roy Medvedev's specificity. The journalist was impressed by "the careful calibration of his protest, his calculated tactic of refraining from extremes that would make the authorities feel compelled to garrot him." He called Medvedev "a pragmatist, a gradualist who envisions reform evolving slowly in the Soviet system"; in short, he constituted "the loyal opposition" to the Brezhnev regime.

Although Roy Medvedev remained free to write while many others were imprisoned or forced to emigrate, there was nothing predetermined in this outcome. His freedom was always relative and came at the price of caution and self-restraint. In retrospect, he admitted that he exercised self-censorship: he never wrote Lenin's biography, because he knew he could not afford to criticize the Soviet leader, and he only wrote critical biographies of leaders who were no longer in power. His second rule was to always act on his own and never form any organization, which he knew would be most severely punished. After the signature of the Helsinki Accords, in 1975, Soviet human rights activists had formed Helsinki groups to monitor their implementation; other activists had created a Soviet branch of Amnesty International, but all these initiatives were mercilessly repressed. Third, he and Zhores agreed not to deal with press and media organs that the Soviet regime identified as "anti-Soviet," such as Radio Liberty or the publishing house "Posev," owned by the anti-Soviet émigré organization NTS. They preferred to publish in left-wing media and with publishers of socialist orientation, academic and commercial publishers and the Western "bourgeois" press. Finally, Roy never criticized foreign newspaper correspondents, who were among his most faithful allies. Although they betrayed his trust more than once for the sake of sensation, Medvedev knew that without them, he would have lost the publicity necessary to protect him from arrest. Yet this was a fine line to walk, and he knew that even his moderate criticism of the regime could get him into serious trouble.

Indeed, pressure on Roy Medvedev and his family remained a reality throughout the Soviet years, increasing at times and diminishing at others, in unpredictable ways. For tactical reasons, Roy rarely made these instances of pressure public, thus sustaining the myth that he enjoyed special treatment. In some situations, publicity was the best defense, but in others, he used alternative tactics in his arsenal to outmaneuver the KGB, displaying great shrewdness.

His correspondence with Zhores, however, shows that he was regularly harassed and threatened. The two house searches of 1971 and 1975 were followed by new attempts to convince him to stop his publications. In Spring 1976, the dissident heard from his friend Lakshin that several measures were planned against him and his family: his son would be barred from entering university, his family's plan to move into a new cooperative apartment would fail, and his wife would face obstacles in defending her doctoral dissertation. "And this is only being considered as a first warning," added Lakshin, the final goal being to force him into exile abroad.

Roy's son Aleksandr planned to study at the Petrochemical Institute. He had successfully passed the chemistry and mathematics exams and only had a literature exam left. After hearing the warning concerning his son, Medvedev called the KGB and asked to talk with an agent. He had a trump card and was ready to use it in a show of strength with the KGB. He had heard through his friend Norair Ter-Akopian, head of department at the Institute of Marxism-Leninism, that during recent disarmament talks between the United States and the USSR in Washington, the Soviet negotiators had lost face and been forced to give in when the US delegation proved to be acquainted with secret information that they themselves ignored, as a result of the lack of transparency within the Soviet apparatus. When an agent took up the call, he started shouting at him:

> How dare you meddle into some petty intrigue—not to admit my son into his institute, when you should be dealing with the protection of state interests! What kind of work are you doing, when the Americans, as it turned out, know our secrets better than we do! You send people to work on some petty questions regarding Roy Medvedev and let important secrets escape.

An hour later, Medvedev received a call back from a high-ranking officer, who asked very politely:

> – Roy Aleksandrovich, did you find out about this from American or from Soviet sources?
> – I found out about it from Soviet sources, but of course I will never tell you who told me this.
> – Thank you, we congratulate your son on being accepted into his institute.

This episode shows that Medvedev's access to information through his broad network of contacts could also allow him to blackmail the Soviet authorities. However, he had less success with his move into a new cooperative apartment. As he explained in a letter from October 1976, his wife Galina had come up with a scheme: in exchange for their apartment in the northern Khovrino district, she had bought shares in a cooperative which was building new apartments in the

Novye Cheremushki neighborhood, south of Moscow. But after they had been assigned an apartment, the District Executive Committee had refused to grant the Medvedevs authorization to move in. This was a complex real-estate transaction, as was often the case in the Soviet Union, where having the right network of contacts was crucial to obtain scarce goods, and not fully legal. While, according to Medvedev's information, the authorities had closed their eyes on several cases of corruption involving a party official in the same cooperative, they would show no such leniency in relation to him. In his letters, which he knew were being read by the KGB, he warned he would make sure that the authorities were informed of these wrongdoings. Roy hoped to put the authorities under pressure again: in November 1976, he was warned not to give an interview to foreign media on the occasion of Brezhnev's seventieth birthday. In a letter he sent to Zhores through regular mail, he warned that he would take measures in his own defense: "But I hope that this will help avoid intrusions into my affairs, such as the cooperative, etc. If I have to face obstacles with such trifles... then I will give a TV interview in such a way that it will strongly spoil [Brezhnev's] birthday." But by late November, the District Executive Committee had approved all new cooperative members, except for Galina, arguing that the Medvedevs already had an apartment. Roy did not intend on fighting but considered that this was "important as a symptom of relations" with the authorities. Despite the *modus vivendi* that had seemed to arise, the tendency was still to put pressure on him in all possible ways, including through his family. He feared that this might also impact Rita's chances of being allowed to travel to the Soviet Union in the future. In December, Galina decided to appeal the District Committee's decision in court, but her attempts remained unsuccessful, and she gave up on the cooperative apartment.

Galina was a Communist party member and secretary of her party organization. At work, few of her colleagues knew that she was the wife of a famous dissident, because she had kept her maiden surname. The Party tried to exercise pressure on Medvedev through her. But these efforts backfired: Roy warned his wife that if she tried to meddle into his work, he would have to leave her. Attempts to influence Roy through his childhood friends Ter-Akopian and Simongulian yielded even fewer results: Caucasian friendships proved stronger than the KGB's threats.

In the anniversary year of 1977, marked by numerous arrests and searches, Roy Medvedev kept a low profile. Soon, however, serious attempts were made to cut the precious lifeline between the Medvedev brothers. In February 1978, Roy noticed that Zhores's letters and parcels had stopped reaching him. In a letter sent to Zhores through regular mail on February 12, he sent a warning to the KGB: "This week I will send a written complaint to the International Post Office and the Min[istry] of communications. After receiving copies of receipts and registration numbers I will sue the post office and will make this whole affair public." He added that he had sent a complaint to the Prosecutor's Office to request that work material seized during the 1975 house search be returned to him and intended on sending the same complaint concerning the house search of 1971.

> I didn't say anything when all these years I didn't receive foreign correspondence—not from you, but from other people. I didn't protest [the fact] that letters from Soviet citizens, except for my relatives, didn't reach me, although I received phone calls from many cities and some of the letters were registered... But now if I stop receiving your letters and parcels sent through regular mail and without any violation of postal regulations, I will be forced to react to such nonsense.

He continued to discuss various options to break the mail blockade, but his letters did not reach Zhores. By late March, however, Roy noted that almost all delayed parcels and letters had reached him. "In the end, I can always find a way to send you letters and manuscripts besides the post, but I don't want my basic right to correspondence to be violated." To ensure that all letters safely reached his brother, he sent three separate copies of each through several channels.

By August 1978, however, the KGB's harassment had taken new, creative forms. Roy's wife and son, but also his friends and his friends' families had begun to receive obscene verses featuring him and women of his acquaintance. Although Roy could hardly be described as a womanizer, the anonymous correspondent pictured him as a Don Juan. The dissident warned his friends about the letters, which were particularly upsetting for his wife and the women who received them. Some were sent by registered mail, including to work addresses. Strangely enough, one letter involved a certain Natasha, who turned out to be the wife of Georgii Vladimov, a dissident writer with whom Medvedev was not even acquainted and who was also subjected to such harassment at the time. The unexpected outcome was a friendship with the writer, who was forced to emigrate in 1983. But the "moral terror," as he called it, which seemed calculated to isolate him, also resulted in former friends and colleagues turning away from him as a result of these letters.

The KGB was clearly at work: the verses reached even the writer Lev Kopelev, who was subjected to a mail blockade at the time. Most troubling was the fact that these letters were based on authentic personal information, obtained through "operative" means, whether through informers or surveillance of his phone calls and visitors. Medvedev had noticed that for the past ten years whenever a foreign correspondent visited him, the janitor was either chatting with a neighbor in the corridor or had her door left ajar. Clearly, the KGB had information about private visits he had received. Medvedev thought he had identified some of these informers. Through them, Medvedev gained a better sense of the kind of information that the KGB was looking for. In his youth, some of his former schoolmates had joined the NKVD and he had learned through them some of the state security's techniques. To gain Medvedev's trust, informers had to pass off as fellow dissidents and give him some useful information. After getting them to drink enough alcohol, he was able to get them to talk more than they should have, and some even unwittingly provided him with information for his research.

In summer 1978, another unpleasant incident indicated that the authorities wanted to interrupt Roy Medvedev's unofficial connections with the West. The KGB intercepted a package addressed to *New York Times* correspondent David Shipler containing letters from American historian Stephen Cohen to Medvedev and several books intended for him. The detailed protocol of the content seized was transmitted to the US Embassy in Moscow. Medvedev concluded that the goal of this maneuver was to intimidate Western newspaper correspondents and discourage them from transmitting materials to and from dissidents. But there may have been a political dimension as well. The letters by Stephen Cohen, the author of an acclaimed biography of Nikolai Bukharin, were addressed to Bukharin's son Iurii Larin. Since 1978 marked the fiftieth anniversary of Bukharin's execution, the package's interception could be connected with an attempt to denounce the campaign for his rehabilitation. Cohen and Medvedev both subscribed to the view that the Bolshevik leader could have constituted a more humane, democratic alternative to Stalin. The two historians had first met in 1975; Cohen described their relationship as a friendship of two colleagues: "He had knowledge I needed about historical events, people and materials; I knew the Western literature that he did not. It was, we agreed, an excellent collaboration." In 1978, as Medvedev was writing a book on Bukharin, he read the Russian translation of Cohen's biography. In 1982, Cohen published a selection of articles from *Political Diary* in English under the title *An End to Silence*.

Apart from Cohen, Medvedev was acquainted with Robert Tucker and other Western historians. These connections gave him added protection. The authorities knew that in case of arrest, Medvedev would benefit from the active support of these colleagues, who would ensure that Western public opinion was informed about the situation, in the same way that Western scientists had defended Zhores Medvedev in 1970 or signed petitions in defense of Andrei Sakharov throughout the 1970s and 1980s.

This tacit support was Medvedev's trump card, which he played whenever necessary. In October 1978, he adopted a more vindictive tone in his letters to Zhores:

> If I see that my letters stop reaching you, I will begin to send 4–5 registered letters with return receipt with copies and separate pages of my articles, and then I will file claims or a lawsuit. In the end, the secrecy of correspondence is guaranteed by law, and every citizen has the right to use postal services if he has rightfully paid these services. In this regard, mail does not differ in any way from public transportation and its use may be limited only for individuals under arrest.

Although the Medvedev brothers were generally careful in their correspondence sent through official channels, in October 1979, Roy revealed to his brother that excerpts of Zhores's private letters in which the latter criticized other dissidents were cited in a work of propaganda with a print run of one hundred thousand copies entitled *Straight talk* (*Razgovor nachistotu*). Although his name was not mentioned, he was described as "one of those deprived of his Soviet citizenship in recent years." Roy noted that these letters had not been seized and he kept his correspondence safely stored at a friend's place. This was the "first instance of such unceremonious acknowledgment of constant perlustration." With the growth of repression against dissidents, Roy wrote that in case of renewed house search, he would not let the KGB seize his archive a third time. "Only in case there is, in addition to a search warrant, a warrant for arrest."

Roy Medvedev was dependent on foreign journalists and diplomats for his correspondence with the West, and he knew that the media were his best ally, for the publicity given to his statements and publications in the West afforded him the best protection from arrest. He developed a number of long-lasting collaborations with Western newspapers, from the *Los Angeles Times* to *L'Unita*, and when he remained the last free prominent dissident in the USSR, his comments on Soviet politics were particularly appreciated. In the 1970s–1980s, he published two books of dialogues with the Italian communist and correspondent of *L'Unita* and *Stampa* Giulietto Chiesa and one with Piero Ostellino, from the conservative Italian daily *Corriere della Sera*. While Ostellino was interested in what Medvedev had to say about the Soviet dissident movement, for Chiesa and many others, Medvedev was first of all a very attentive observer of Soviet political life, who sometimes possessed insider information. As Chiesa recalled later on: "When I went to Moscow in October 1980 I was not yet personally acquainted with Roy Aleksandrovich. But I had already read many of his books and articles, therefore even before meeting him his opinion was authoritative for me . . . Later as well, under Andropov and Chernenko, he gave an astonishingly exact forecast of events, which was always confirmed! Then I asked him to start working on our first common book. It's amazing, but everything that he said then was fully confirmed later on, after 1985."

Roy Medvedev in his office, 1981. Courtesy of Roy Medvedev.

Other foreign correspondents helped him publish various texts about current Soviet politics and paid him honoraria. They brought him mail and parcels, bought items on his behalf in the "Beriozka" shops. Given this relationship of interdependence, Medvedev maintained his loyalty towards them, although some of them occasionally misused his trust. He recalled a few such episodes, which were a source of embarrassment to him and could have had serious consequences.

In 1975, an English journalist from the newspaper *The Observer* asked to meet Roy Medvedev and his friend the dissident physicist Valentin Turchin. According to Medvedev, the correspondent explained that he was new in the USSR and wanted some off-the-record information about the Soviet system. He and Turchin spoke very openly, without any of the self-censorship Roy usually exercised in his comments to the Western press. Three weeks later, however, Zhores called his brother to inform him that *The Observer* had published an article entitled "How I would run the Soviet Union" by Roy Medvedev. In it, he made disparaging comments on Sakharov's lack of a political program and expounded the measures he would take if he came to power. Needless to say, such an interview not only further antagonized other dissidents, but could have had serious consequences for Medvedev. Zhores wrote that the tape of the conversation had also been transmitted to Radio Liberty, but he had demanded its destruction. "It speaks of the dishonesty of correspondents, and you can protest to [the journalist]—he is permanently in Moscow."

Another embarrassing incident was connected with the visit of a correspondent of the newspaper *The Washington Post* in 1978, who asked to see an article Roy was preparing for an Italian newspaper. Some time later, however, *The Washington Post* published an article entitled "Nikita Khrushchev: 'Dictator on a Pension.'" It summarized Medvedev's essay, which, according to the journalist, was "now circulating privately in Moscow."

Medvedev believed that he was not arrested because he possessed information, which he could occasionally use to put pressure on the Soviet leadership. Although the authorities accused him of revealing state secrets to foreign journalists, Medvedev explained he did not have access to any: most of the time, he only gave his analysis on events, based on information which was not readily accessible from the Soviet press. This insider knowledge came from his friends among writers, who had connections in the military and in the Central Committee and attended various ideological conferences. Medvedev had an excellent memory and could use relevant information years after hearing it when put under pressure. It occasionally served him in his dealings with the KGB.

Foreign diplomats and journalists valued Medvedev's insider knowledge, but the historian insisted that he was careful not to depend on them. He believed he had identified secret agents among them and was wary of the use made of the information which he provided. He recalled meeting the vice-director of the CIA at the apartment of a journalist following Brezhnev's public disappearance, in the 1970s. He answered several invitations from American ambassadors, who asked him to comment on Soviet political figures, for example after Andropov's designation as General Secretary of the CPSU. However, soon after this encounter, Medvedev's comments appeared in the American press: it turned out that another guest, whom the ambassador had introduced as his personal friend, was a journalist.

Roy Medvedev's position was unique within Soviet dissent: indeed, he managed to be at once an insider and an outsider, receiving information from high-placed confidential sources while at the same time remaining an independent scholar publishing in the West. The handling of his case therefore required more nuances than for Solzhenitsyn and Sakharov. There was one man in the Soviet apparatus who knew that Roy Medvedev was more useful free than in prison: Iurii Andropov. His tacit protection seems to have saved Roy from arrest more than once, even as the KGB intensified its crackdown on dissent in the early 1980s.

Works Cited

Cohen, Stephen F. *The Victims Return: Survivors of the Gulag After Stalin*. Exeter, New Hampshire: Publishing Works, 2010.

Medvedev, Roy. "Nikita Khrushchev, 'Dictator on a Pension.'" *Washington Post*, December 18, 1978.

Medvedev, Roy. "How I Would Run the Soviet Union." *The Observer*, June 15, 1975.

Smith, Hedrick R. *The Russians*. New York: Ballantine Books, 1977.

Further Reading

Sharlet, Robert. "Dissent and Repression in the Soviet Union and Eastern Europe: Changing Patterns since Khrushchev." *International Journal* 33, no. 4 (1978): 763–95.

CHAPTER 13

Andropov's Protection

In his essay *On Socialist Democracy*, Roy Medvedev formulated a program for reform of the Soviet system. Unlike Sakharov's, his position was not one of purely moral opposition: his vision of political change was reformist, grounded in the reality of Soviet political life. Yet a yawning gap remained between his moderate criticism and the position of reformists within the Soviet apparatus, and the system did not foresee any possibility of political action for oppositionists. Even though, formally, alternative candidacies were allowed, without the party's endorsement running for a seat in the Soviet Supreme Soviet, the puppet parliament in charge of rubberstamping decisions from the Central Committee, seemed like science fiction.

It therefore came as a surprise when, in late January 1979, a delegation from the independent trade union SMOT (an acronym standing for "Free Interprofessional Union of Workers"), which had formed a group called "Elections-79," visited Medvedev to ask him to run in the name of their organization in the upcoming election on March 4. Their second candidate was Liudmila Agapova, an engineer. This initiative, launched by the photographer Vladimir Sychev and the driver Vadim Baranov, followed the logic of "civil obedience" put forward by such human rights activists as Aleksandr Esenin-Vol'pin in the late 1960s: they called on the Soviet authorities to abide by their own laws. Since there were elections, candidates and voters, why should reformist candidates not seize the opportunity to run and act as though the regime really allowed for an alternative? With Medvedev's approval, the group "Elections-79" prepared the necessary documents and asked the Sverdlovsk District in Moscow to register "their" candidate. Medvedev remembered that the head of the Electoral Commission laughed at the proposal; he asked them "whether they knew in which country they were living" and advised them to "descend from the heavens onto this sinful earth." But since the group insisted and had submitted the required documents, their application was accepted.

Group "Elections-1979" in front of a polling station. Photograph by Vladimir Sychev. OKhDLSM, F. 333, op. 3, d. 23, l. 2.

A week later, however, Sychev and Baranov were summoned to the Electoral Commission and told that for their application to be accepted, it had to be presented by an organization registered by the City Executive Committee. The group therefore studied the legislation to become registered as an organization and adopted a charter acknowledging the CPSU's leading role and stating that their goal was "to increase voters' activeness and their political conscientiousness." While the group was in the process of trying to register its organization, however, the deadline for the registration of candidates passed. The last option that remained was for members of the group to show up at the Sverdlovsk polling station, to cross out the name of the official candidate on their voting bulletin and to write in Medvedev's name instead. In addition to the twenty-eight members of the group, a number of dissidents and sympathizers voted for Medvedev and Agapova in the two districts where they were running for seats. Those one or two hundred votes were much too few to get Medvedev elected, but the symbolic impact of the action, which was reported by Western radio stations and newspapers, was not negligible. The publicity contributed to a process of emulation. After the election, Medvedev found out that a group of two hundred war veterans from Sochi had sought to register him as candidate as well, but their letter asking for his written consent was only delivered after the election. He believed that similar groups had appeared in the Vladimir region and in Lithuania as well. Although the group "Elections-79" had planned to repeat the operation in 1980 for the elections to the Supreme Soviet of the Russian Federal Republic, Baranov and Sychev emigrated to the West in October 1979.

Roy Medvedev, 1979. Courtesy of Roy Medvedev.

On June 11, 1981, Anatolii Churganov, one of the Sochi World War II veterans who had supported Medvedev in the 1979 election, was arrested. This Soviet "whistleblower" had been collecting compromising information and writing denunciations to the Central Committee of the CPSU against several local political figures, including the Krasnodar Regional Committee First Secretary Sergei Medunov, whom he accused of corruption. During the search conducted at Churganov's apartment, the KGB seized several tamizdat books, including *Let History Judge, On Socialist Democracy* and *The Secrecy of Correspondence is Guaranteed by Law*, which Medvedev had given him. During the interrogation, Mikhail Gaevets, a KGB colonel, demanded that he write a denunciation of Medvedev, whom Gaevets called a "dissident-*antisovietchik*" who disseminated his anti-Soviet works. Although the interrogation lasted for an hour, Churganov refused to write the denunciation, arguing that it was his right to befriend whomever he wanted. Churganov was eventually condemned to six years of camp and three years of exile. Although Medunov was excluded from the Central Committee two years later for covering up a whole system of corruption organized by the "Sochi mafia," which Churganov had been denouncing, the political prisoner was not released from the camps.

The early 1980s were a time of renewed onslaught on Soviet dissent. On December 25, 1979, the USSR invaded Afghanistan, putting an end to détente with the West. Andrei Sakharov, who had protested the invasion, was arrested on January 22, 1980 and sent to Gor'kii in internal exile. Roy Medvedev did not share his indignation.

> I felt that the military operation in Afghanistan was justified to some extent by historical circumstances, "the international duty" of a socialist state... The revolution in Afghanistan seemed to me a democratic event. I supported the revolution in Afghanistan and Babrak Karmal's politics, whose errors I only understood later on. Therefore, although I had opposed the Soviet invasion of Czechoslovakia, I did not oppose Afghanistan's.

Following Sakharov's exile, Roy Medvedev remained the last free prominent dissident. Western journalists and diplomats regularly visited him, often without forewarning, using public transportation to evade surveillance. On November 10, 1982, Medvedev received the visit of CBS News correspondent Walter Cronkite, a highly influential newsman. These visits were not to the taste of the authorities. The next day, news of Brezhnev's death and Iurii Andropov's designation as new General Secretary came out, and on November 13, following the publication of an article in which Medvedev denounced the crackdown on Soviet dissent, the dissident received a visit from KGB officers, who warned him to "sit tight" and not "give out any more slanderous statements."

Roy Medvedev with Walter Cronkite, 1982. OKhDLSM, F. 333, op 14, d. 39. L. 4.

When Brezhnev died in 1982, two literary agents turned to Zhores to ask Roy to write an "express biography" the new Soviet leader. The historian declined this offer, which could have exposed him to repression. However, Zhores decided to write such a biography himself, which he offered directly to trusted publishers, under conditions of absolute confidentiality. He understood the necessity of writing the text directly in English, to ensure that the Russian text did not end up in samizdat. Nevertheless, Roy's participation was essential: he knew several consultants in the Central Committee who had closely collaborated with Andropov: Fedor Burlatskii, Aleksandr Bovin, Georgii Arbatov, Iurii Krasin, Georgii Shakhnazarov and Iurii Kariakin. Zhores began work on the biography in mid-December 1982, and Roy communicated the necessary information to him.

However, the KGB was probably aware of the project, and on January 18, 1983, Roy Medvedev was summoned to the office of the Prosecutor General of the USSR for a "prophylactic" chat. Twice before he had received warnings from this office, but this time, he was advised that this was a direct message of the Soviet leadership. Their patience was coming to an end and the ultimatum was clear: "Either you stop writing such articles and books or we put you in jail." He was asked to sign a statement ordering him to cease his "anti-Soviet activities which are harmful to the interest of the Soviet state." These accusations clearly hinted at a possible prosecution under Article 70 of the penal code, which punished "anti-Soviet agitation and propaganda."

But Medvedev knew that he could use his fame in the West to protect himself. He refused to sign the text and handed a protest letter to the authorities. The same evening, he convened a small press conference with foreign journalists and gave them a copy of his protest. The text addressed the accusations formulated against him: he argued that his research had been only conducted for "the common good," yet being a historian was no easy task in a country plagued by endemic corruption, violations of legality, and abuse of power both in its judicial system, the security services, and the higher echelons of power. He concluded:

> In a country like the Soviet Union, an honest historian must not only be a researcher but an investigator and a judge as well, making political and moral judgments regardless of whether those in power like them or not. I am little troubled by the evaluation of my work by the prosecutor and by the KGB. Any honorable and independent historian should care only about one thing—the search for truth. The prospect of punishment does not frighten me, so it is pointless to issue me warnings or make threats.

For an hour, he answered the journalists' questions. When asked if he considered emigration an option, he answered negatively. "I have not received any invitation from abroad, and if I were to receive such an invitation, I would not accept it at present. Moreover, I have never applied to emigrate. I don't think the Soviet authorities would forcibly expel me, and I will never voluntarily leave for abroad." Nor did he find expulsion a likely outcome in his case. There were only two such precedents in Soviet history: Trotskii and Solzhenitsyn. The regime was cautious about its image and sought to avoid the bad press associated with the arrest of a famous dissident. Medvedev's strategy proved effective. As he wrote to his brother on January 22: "There is no sign of liberalism. But personally, if I manage to withstand the current pressure, I will be able to gain more leeway. For the new leadership I am a prominent figure, whereas Brezhnev possibly didn't know who the Medvedev brothers were."

Indeed, Medvedev was then left in peace until Andropov's death. During the Second Congress of People's Deputies of the USSR, in 1989, Roy Medvedev met "General Teplov," the KGB official he had first met in 1970, after Zhores's psychiatric incarceration. His real name was Ivan Abramov, and he turned out to be a high-ranking figure of the Fifth Directorate of the KGB, in charge of suppressing dissent. Now Abramov made this strange confession: "We wanted to arrest you, but Andropov was opposed to it. What we wanted to find out was through which channels you sent your manuscripts to the West. For this, we had to institute criminal proceedings, with all the consequences it entailed. But Iurii Vladimirovich categorically rejected this proposal." Medvedev was not surprised by this revelation. As long as Andropov was head of the KGB, he had sent him several times "messages" of caution through intermediaries, which Medvedev chose, however, to disregard. Later, he would hear from a former Central Committee official that when they had emptied Andropov's office after his death, they had found the manuscript of *Let History Judge* among secret documents.

Andropov's protection probably resulted less from a personal favor than from a clever calculation. Why imprison a famous intellectual whose views were profoundly socialist and who knew the limits he should not cross? Moreover, it seems likely that the authorities exploited the divergences between dissidents. Medvedev's frequent polemics with Solzhenitsyn and Sakharov contributed to discrediting the movement as a whole, so the logic went. Medvedev remembered that during a KGB interrogation he was once shown a letter from a good acquaintance containing harsh words about himself. The goal was obviously to sow conflict between the two men. Medvedev replied that they lived in a country where the secrecy of correspondence was guaranteed by law, and he did not wish to be shown other people's letters.

Nevertheless, the threat of deportation from the country remained real. In March 1978, Roy Medvedev received an invitation from Bruno Kreisky, Austrian Chancellor, to give lectures in Austria. Although the invitation was not official and had been transmitted through the Austrian cultural attaché, it could be feared that the Soviet government would take the opportunity to deport Medvedev to Austria, should the invitation be made public. As Zhores Medvedev travelled to Vienna for a conference in May 1978, he met the Chancellor's assistant and asked him not to renew any invitation to his brother, for fear of involuntarily causing him harm. But in March 1983, following a request by Ken Coates, from the Bertrand Russell Foundation, Kreisky intervened with the Soviet leadership on Medvedev's behalf. His letter most certainly contained a proposal to grant Medvedev asylum in Austria, as German Chancellor Willy Brandt had done for Solzhenitsyn in 1974. At the time, in the context of détente, the writer's case had raised heated discussions in the Politburo: while the hawks wished to imprison the dissident, the doves feared for the USSR's international prestige.

By 1983, however, détente was but a distant memory, and most Soviet dissidents were either behind bars or abroad. A report by KGB chief Viktor

Chebrikov and Prosecutor General of the USSR Aleksandr Rekunkov from April 8, 1983, reflected the view that the time had come to take radical measures against Roy Medvedev. He was described as a "convinced opponent" of the regime, whose "hostile activity" consisted in "systematically preparing and publishing in the West writings, which are constantly used against the Soviet Union." Although Medvedev tried to make his "anti-social activities" more palatable to the Soviet authorities by collaborating with publishers affiliated with European Communist parties, he also maintained contact with many foreign correspondents in Moscow. Not only did he send his "slanderous writings" to the West through these "illegal channels," but he also supplied Western media with "insinuations about domestic political events in the country, spreads anti-Soviet fabrications and prejudiced evaluations on the USSR's position in relation to international issues." His latest provocation made it necessary to "stop Medvedev's criminal activity" through criminal prosecution. Should protests arise in the West and some foreign government offer to take Medvedev, he should be expelled from the country. If not, then a sentence of internal exile should be pronounced. However, it seems that Andropov refused to give his assent to this plan.

In his reply to Ken Coates, Chancellor Kreisky reported on May 17, 1983:

> I have now received an answer from the Soviet authorities concerning the situation of Mr. Roy Medvedev. The activities of Mr. Medvedev are in their view directed against the interests of the Soviet Union and he is supposed to have established contacts with foreign agencies which are considered detrimental to the interests of the Soviet state. According to this information the Soviet Attorney General already several times had the intention to open legal proceedings against Mr. Medvedev but up to now it has been possible to avoid such action.
>
> In view of this situation, I have furthermore been informed that in case Mr. Roy Medvedev should express the wish to leave the Soviet Union for another country this application would be considered favourably if it should be supported by us.

The Soviet leadership certainly would have liked Roy Medvedev to join his brother in the West, yet the dissident showed no desire to leave the USSR and Andropov was not prepared to expel him by force. According to Zhores, Andropov always discussed such repressive measures in the Politburo, and the absence of record of such a discussion suggests that he had other priorities at the time, such as the struggle against corruption.

Andropov's rule, however, was short-lived. When Konstantin Chernenko was designated General Secretary of the Party in February 1984, Roy Medvedev did not refrain from criticizing him in his comments to Western media. As Robert Cullen, a *Los Angeles Times* correspondent, remembered: "Sitting in his *kabinet*, Roy, at my request, once gave me an interview in which he correctly assessed the election of Konstantin Chernenko as a reversion to the stagnation of the late Brezhnev years. He knew that by doing so he flirted with personal disaster, but he told the truth as he saw it." A week later, on February 20, Medvedev received the visit of two KGB officers, who issued him a strict warning and accused him of being a "paid informer of Western correspondents and secret services." Medvedev rejected the accusation: he only gave his analyses on well-known facts and did not have access to any secret information; moreover, he was only paid for his books and articles, not for his conversations with journalists. Nevertheless, an hour after this visit, he found a group of policemen stationed on the staircase outside his door. For the next fifteen months, his apartment would remain under constant surveillance by two or three police officers under KGB orders, who controlled his visits and kept foreigners out. They communicated by radio with other KGB agents stationed in neighboring buildings and with two police cars stationed in front of his block and at the street entrance, following him, his wife, and his Soviet visitors. Medvedev estimated that, overall, about thirty people were involved in the surveillance of his flat, night and day.

Medvedev was not under house arrest: this would have entailed a judicial decision, which Chernenko obviously tried to avoid. He was free to leave the house, but he and his wife were shadowed wherever they went. Once, Medvedev somehow managed to escape surveillance by leaving at five o'clock in the morning to visit Giulietto Chiesa in the city center, and the KGB went looking after him as far as Kalinin, a city 180 kilometres north of Moscow where he had family. Medvedev tried to persuade the "secret curators" who read his mail that the measures did not affect him in the least. In a letter sent to this brother through open mail on February 25, he wrote that he would not issue any protest. "It would be funny to protest the fact that foreign correspondents don't visit me. And many of them were only in the way, asking for my 'opinion', taking up time but always refusing to help me in any way, even if I asked them to find me a good German textbook or some medication I need, etc."

Since the historian was prevented from meeting foreign correspondents, his correspondence with London was complicated. Zhores only received his February and March letters in June. The tone was markedly different: "My situation is not very good. I don't tell journalists everything and don't write any protests. I can't act like last year and repeat myself. I have to act in an unexpected manner." He noted that it would become more complicated to send mail through diplomatic channels and to receive books and parcels. But he had enough material for two years, should he be cut off from his sources of information. He and Zhores could write their memoirs, and then he also had plans for two philosophical works in case he was sent into internal exile. A month later, he declared in a letter sent through regular mail:

> My situation hasn't changed, and I don't think that it will (if it does, then probably for the worse). But I am taking things serenely. This is not the same situation as in 1970–71. I have written my main works, I have done the most important things I wanted to do. Therefore, any strict repression could only give the authorities more trouble than to me personally. If someone "up there" reflected more sensibly, they would offer me an official position at the Institute of History, or even better, Philosophy. I would be happy to spend 5–7 years of my life working on philosophical problems, which I have had in mind since my student years.

His call to the authorities for a compromise solution to the crisis was reminiscent of Andropov's 1967 proposal to co-opt Medvedev instead of repressing him, but it yielded no results.

According to Zhores, the authorities feared that the Medvedev brothers would publish Chernenko's biography, as they had done with Andropov, Khrushchev, and were preparing to do with Brezhnev. Yet, Roy understood that in his situation, he had to avoid any provocation. He stated in his letter that he preferred to put on hold his plans to write a biography of Brezhnev with portraits of his contemporaries. Writing about figures currently in power could be a dangerous game for a dissident who, unlike Western Sovietologists, was directly exposed to repression and under close surveillance. In confidential letters, however, he instructed Zhores to finish this book and publish it under both of their names, should something happen to him. The biography ultimately came out in 1991.

Meanwhile, despite the ban on foreign visitors, Medvedev continued to meet some foreign correspondents and diplomats outside his home. Except for his assistant, Soviet visitors were allowed. As Robert Cullen remembered, after the publication of Medvedev's interview and the repressive measures taken against him, "I was afraid I would be expelled, and I was prepared to stop visiting him.

Roy, who was so much more vulnerable, refused to be intimidated. He simply took to meeting in a nearby park, quietly speaking his mind when asked and continuing to operate as if both he and the police believed in the flowery statements of citizens' rights in the Soviet constitution."

On April 3, Roy wrote that the KGB had stopped following him when he went out. The costly operation was ineffective since he always managed to "lose" his "tail." Harassment through phone calls also ceased. By June, the police officers on his staircase were obviously bored with their mission, playing dominos and listening to music during their long shifts. For two weeks Medvedev had not had a single visitor: he told people not to visit him before the fall, and for important affairs he went to Moscow himself. However, when Zhores's wife Rita visited from London, she was let in, and she and Roy went shopping together. In October, Medvedev wrote that the police surveillance from neighboring buildings had ceased, but his phone line had been cut again.

The authorities also made attempts to draft his son into the army, although he had been exempted from military service on medical grounds, and put pressure on Medvedev's friends, his assistant, and his daughter-in-law's family. Roy was adamant: "This is a very vile and veiled campaign. The pressure is obviously also on me. Maybe they want me to emigrate, which I will not do. I am not going to celebrate my birthday and generally I ask people not to visit me. Let them sit idly." By December 1984, the agents stationed on his doorstep had been equipped with a TV set and seemed there to stay. When Rita tried to travel to the USSR as a tourist in December 1984, she was refused a Soviet return visa. Despite the pressure, Roy continued his work unimpeded. He prepared a book of interviews with Giulietto Chiesa, and reeditions of *Let History Judge* and *Khrushchev*.

On December 15, 1984, Mikhail Gorbachev visited London with a delegation of deputies of the Supreme Soviet. Ken Coates, who had consistently supported Roy Medvedev, decided to use the opportunity to appeal once more on his behalf. He organized a petition of Labor MPs, which he planned to transmit to Gorbachev after his speech in the British Parliament. Tony Benn, former Secretary of State for Industry, supported the initiative and offered to speak about Roy's situation with Gorbachev during a meeting at the Soviet Embassy and to send a letter to the Soviet Ambassador. The result of these appeals is unknown, but a few months after Gorbachev came to power the police station on Medvedev's doorstep was removed.

Roy Medvedev's position was certainly privileged when compared with Sakharov's precarious life in exile or with the fate of thousands of less famous dissidents who filled the camps. The price of his freedom was a measure of caution, self-censorship, and clever maneuvering in critical situations. This strategy, rather than collaboration with the KGB, as has often been alleged, explains Medvedev's survival in times of near-complete crackdown on Soviet dissent. While Roy was under close watch from the KGB, Zhores drew the attention of the British counter-espionage agency. The suspicion increased when the dissident raised a highly sensitive topic: the safety of nuclear plants.

Works Cited

Medvedev, Roy. *Neizvestnyi Andropov. Politicheskaia Biografiia Iuriia Andropova*. Moscow: Izd. "Prava cheloveka," 1999.

Medvedev, Zhores. *Opasnaia Professiia*. Moscow: Vremia, 2019.

Cullen, Robert, "Traveling in Style. The Insider's Moscow: The Real Russia Begins Where Intourist Stops," *Los Angeles Times*, June 2, 1991.

CHAPTER 14

The Nuclear Threat

When he returned from America in late 1974, Zhores Medvedev received a call from the British Foreign Affairs Office. He was summoned for interrogation by the MI5, the British counter-intelligence service, in January 1975. Accusations launched by other dissidents against the Medvedev brothers probably raised suspicion. Had Zhores been sent to London on a special assignment? During the seven-hour talk, the Security Services asked him about his connection with Gerald Brooke, a British teacher arrested in the USSR on espionage charges and exchanged for Soviet spies in 1969, whom Zhores had met only once at a reception. Other questions concerned Medvedev's talk in front of the Fulbright Commission and Sakharov. The biologist understood that the MI5 had received its information from US intelligence, but he was surprised to see his conflicts with other dissidents attract so much interest.

After attending the Tenth International Gerontological Congress in Jerusalem in June 1975 and the European biochemical congress in Paris in July, Zhores Medvedev began to plan a new trip to the United States. He had received an invitation to deliver a talk on Soviet science at the University of Utah in the framework of the prestigious lecture series "Frontiers of Science." Several Nobel Prize laureates had been among invited speakers since the series' creation in 1967 and the lecture was to be recorded and broadcast in several states. Medvedev combined this invitation with the Annual Conference of the Gerontological Society of America in New York, and lectures on gerontology and Soviet science at Princeton University, Connecticut State University, in Evanston (IL), at Indiana University, in Burlington (VT), and at the City University of New York. As Rudolf Tőkés, a specialist of Soviet dissent, explained to Medvedev, dissidents had ceased to interest the American public now that they had turned into immigrants in the West. In Washington, Abraham Brumberg from the US State Department invited Medvedev to speak in front of a group of state officials and scholars about his and his brother's vision for Russia's future and their differences with other dissidents. Fearing unfavorable headlines in the émigré press, Medvedev accepted on condition that the conversation would remain confidential.

The main event of Medvedev's 1976 tour, however, was his talk at the University of Utah, for reasons he had not quite anticipated. During his lecture in Salt Lake City, Medvedev first talked about the history of Russian and Soviet science before providing an overview of the development of nuclear industry in the postwar period. He mentioned the nuclear accident caused by an explosion of radioactive waste at the Maiak plutonium production site near Kyshtym, in the Urals region, in 1957. Rated 6 on the International Nuclear Events Scale (INES), this nuclear catastrophe remains to this day the third most serious of its kind after the Chernobyl and Fukushima disasters. Medvedev had first heard of this catastrophe through his supervisor Vsevolod Klechkovskii, who had been sent to the Kyshtym zone in 1958 to organize a secret experimental station and measure the territory's radioactivity, through Evgenii Fedorov, a friend and former colleague of Medvedev's, also sent there for work, and from Timofeev-Resovskii, who conducted radioecological research at the Urals branch of the Academy of Sciences in 1957. Medvedev had no idea that the catastrophe remained a secret not only in the USSR, but also in the West. Up to this point, the most serious known nuclear accident known in the West was the fire at the Windscale nuclear facility in England in 1957, ranking 5 on the INES.

Most questions Medvedev was asked after his lecture concerned the Ural nuclear catastrophe, and judging by his interlocutors' reaction, the dissident could tell that his account failed to convince. The local newspapers reporting on his lecture made no mention of it. Medvedev believed that someone had already given orders not to let the press publish information about it. As he later found out, Peter Gibbs, a theoretical atomic physicist from Utah University, had called the Hanford nuclear site in Washington state to ask their opinion on Medvedev's account. "If anything of the kind had really happened, we would know about it" was their reply. In his lecture in Bloomington, four days later, Medvedev raised the subject again, with more evidence to back up his claims. He gave more details, based on Klechkovskii's account. The next day, Medvedev discussed the question with Sovietologist Alexander Rabinowitch, and the latter promised to speak with his editor about ordering a book on Soviet science from Medvedev, based on his lecture. The book eventually came out in 1979.

By the time Medvedev reached New York, on November 4, the latest issue of the journal *New Scientist*, featuring a shorter version of Medvedev's lecture, had appeared. In his article, Medvedev provided the example of the catastrophe to explain why Soviet nuclear scientists, shocked by the human consequences of nuclear irradiation on large populations, had lobbied Khrushchev to obtain the legalization of classical genetics, at least in the fields of radiology, radiobiology, and medicine, leaving the agricultural field to Lysenko. On November 7, *The New York Times* was titling "Exiled Soviet Scientist Says That an Explosion of Buried Atomic Wastes in the Urals in 1958 Killed Hundreds." All over the media, declarations of skeptical scientists appeared, commenting on Medvedev's claim. Sir John Hill, Chairman of the UK Atomic Energy Authority, declared Medvedev's assertions to be "pure science fiction" and "rubbish." He excluded the possibility that nuclear waste could have produced such an explosion. On December 7, 1976, the eyewitness account of a recent Soviet émigré living in Israel, Lev Tumerman, was reported worldwide. The scientist, whom Medvedev knew, had driven between the cities of Sverdlovsk (nowadays Ekaterinburg) and Cheliabinsk through the irradiated territory, on his way to a summer school on genetics organized by Timofeev-Resovskii in the Ural region.

> About 100 kilometers from Sverdlovsk, a highway sign warned drivers not to stop for the next 20 or 30 kilometers and to drive through at maximum speed. On both sides of the road, as far as one could see, the land was "dead": no villages, no towns, only the chimneys of destroyed houses, no cultivated field or pastures, no herds, no people ... nothing.

Tumerman also confirmed that the scientists who had informed him about the catastrophe had affirmed that it had been caused by negligence in storing nuclear waste. Western nuclear specialists, however, continued to deny the validity of this thesis.

In April 1977, Zhores Medvedev was summoned by the MI5 once again. This time, the interrogation lasted for two days. The questions dealt with the Urals catastrophe, but also the Medvedev brothers' actions and Soviet political life. Medvedev believed that some questions were inspired by denunciations against him sent by Soviet émigrés related to the anti-communist organization NTS. One such letter, which Medvedev had received from a British journal, hinted at the fact that the Medvedevs' criticism of Sakharov and Solzhenitsyn was part of a scenario planned by the Soviet authorities. Medvedev's explanations seem to have convinced his interlocutors; at any rate, two months later he received a letter informing him that he could now reside permanently in the United Kingdom and apply for a new travel document instead of his one-year identification document.

To back up his claims and to write his book *Soviet Science*, Zhores decided to conduct a work of investigation, using the means available to him in the West.

He went through the publications of Soviet scientists who had studied the consequences of irradiation on the territory near Kyshtym. These studies had apparently started in the late 1960s, following the designation of the irradiated territory as a protected area. Soviet scientists could not indicate the location of the territory studied, but it could be inferred based on the information provided about the fauna and flora. Some of these were very large-scale studies, one focusing on twenty-two types of mammals over two years, including such rare animals as weasels and ermines, another studying fish populations from several large lakes. On this basis, Medvedev could calculate that the radiated territory was too large to have been experimentally contaminated, it could be no less than several thousand square kilometers, and based on the type of fauna and flora, encompassing two hundred species, it had to be in the south Urals or Western Siberia. All the studies pointed to the same irradiation dates, around 1957. In June 1977, based on this information, Medvedev published a new article in *New Scientist* entitled "Facts behind the nuclear Disaster." It contained a hypothetical map of the irradiated territory, spanning about ten thousand square meters eastwards of Kyshtym, through the Cheliabinsk and Kurgan regions.

As a result of this publication, Medvedev received an invitation from Stanley Auerbach from the Oak Ridge national laboratory, a major nuclear research center located in Tennessee, to give a talk on the Urals catastrophe in November 1977. Soon, similar invitations came from Brookhaven National Laboratory, Argonne National Laboratory and the Princeton Center for Environmental Studies. Medvedev combined these visits with attendance of a Gerontological Congress in San Francisco. Since the phone conversation with Auerbach had shown that American scientists continued to doubt his findings, Medvedev decided to look for new evidence. He found another study on traces of radioactivity in migratory birds of the Urals region and published an article in *New Scientist* on this basis. If these birds, which included about a million cranes and geese, migrated to southern Europe, their level of radioactivity could be measured on their overwintering sites. Meanwhile, however, in October 1977, Medvedev received a reply to several Freedom of Information Act requests he had placed for the declassification of CIA intelligence documents related to the Urals catastrophe. The documents described measures taken to protect the local population from the dangers of irradiation in Spring 1958, from food radioactivity measurements to bans on drinking water from a contaminated river.

Medvedev's first talk, at the Brookhaven National Laboratory, went smoothly, without much discussion. At Princeton University the conversation concerned the ecological consequences of the accident, rather than its causes. After several other lectures in Washington D.C. and Texas, Medvedev flew to Nashville for his lecture at the Oak Ridge National Laboratory on November 8. His host Stanley Auerbach, the founder of radioecology as a scientific discipline, had the authority to determine how the Urals catastrophe would be considered, not only in the United States, but in other countries as well. The nuclear scientists Medvedev had talked with so far were mostly concerned with disproving his claims. "The fact of such a large accident, which landed by its scale into a hitherto unknown category of catastrophes, changed the history of nuclear, military, and energetic industries," Medvedev remembered. It was at the time the largest accident of this kind and implied a revision of methods of nuclear waste storage and disposal. Medvedev's talk, which featured not only data analysis from Soviet publications but also a copy of CIA documents, was greeted by a round of applause. As Auerbach later wrote in a report on the talk, which he sent Medvedev, he and his colleagues were impressed by the courage of a man who, without being himself a specialist in the field, took the risk to alert the world scientific community concerning this important event. The Oak Ridge Laboratory decided to create a study group on the medical consequences of the Urals catastrophe and applied for a grant to translate relevant literature on the subject from Soviet journals.

After other talks on ageing, Soviet science and the Urals catastrophe in Nashville, at Argonne National Laboratory, Chicago, Columbus, Madison, and the Gerontological Congress in San Francisco, Medvedev returned to New York on November 26 to find mention of the Urals nuclear disaster on the frontpage of *The Washington Post*. As it turned out, the newspaper, along with antinuclear activist Ralph Nader, had also placed requests under the Freedom of Information Act and received declassified CIA documents, which were heavily censored but did provide an official confirmation for the event Medvedev had first revealed to a Western audience.

The debate over the causes of the accident, however, was not closed yet. The CIA documents mentioned two possible origins: besides the nuclear waste storage failure, the other hypothesis was a failed nuclear weapon test. In August 1978, Zhores Medvedev received a new invitation, from Harold Agnew, director of the Los Alamos National Laboratory, main center of the "Manhattan Project," the US atomic bomb development project. Having heard that Medvedev had planned lectures in Albuquerque in November, Agnew asked him to give a lecture on the Urals nuclear catastrophe and discuss the topic with specialists, including Edward Teller, inventor of the American hydrogen bomb. Medvedev had heard from his contacts at Oak Ridge that experts from Los Alamos disagreed with his explanation of the causes of the accident. In the meantime, Medvedev had done more research on the fate of Soviet liquidators of the accident, thousands of whom had been hospitalized in the Sverdlovsk region, according to the testimony of a recent Soviet émigré in Israel. The CIA documents pointed to the use of tens of thousands of military staff and prisoners from neighboring camps, but the fate of these liquidators remained unknown. In preparation for his lecture at Los Alamos, Medvedev wrote the first draft of a book manuscript on the Urals nuclear catastrophe, the contract for which he signed with W.W. Norton on November 1, 1978.

As always, Medvedev's US tour included conferences in several states on various subjects, from Carter's foreign policy to the Soviet health system, and a Gerontological Congress in Dallas. In Albuquerque, New Mexico, his arrival raised considerable tremor. As he found out, there were several large nuclear waste storage facilities in the state, and Medvedev's arrival had given rise to a harsh debate between proponents and opponents of nuclear weapons in the local press. In Los Alamos, Medvedev had to face hostile questions and remarks from nuclear scientists, who no longer doubted the reality of the accident, but believed that it could have been caused by nuclear tests as far as Novaya Zemlya, a northern Arctic archipelago, or in a closer location. Particularly aggressive was Edward Teller, who accused Medvedev of fearmongering and of being ignorant about physics. Medvedev recalled:

> At first, those present tried to test my knowledge in radiochemistry. I think that I passed it easily... My interlocutors knew radioecology and radiobiology very poorly. They did not understand that the levels of pollution of territories and waters indicated in publications could not be experimental. It was impossible to dispute factual data.

Medvedev left Albuquerque dismayed by the negative local press coverage, which quoted from a statement by the Los Alamos Director accusing him of launching unbuttressed claims to boost the sales of his forthcoming book. Information about the book, which Medvedev had kept secret, had probably been leaked by the publisher. Yet the publication itself was now under threat: W.W. Norton had decided to submit the manuscript to Sir John Hill, chairman of the UK Atomic Energy Authority, to ensure that it did not contain slanderous statements against him. However, the Bertrand Russell Peace Foundation, with whom the Medvedev brothers had friendly relations, arranged the organization of a debate on the Urals Catastrophe with Sir John Hill in the British Parliament in the framework of the commission on Energy.

On March 28, 1979, the Three-Mile-Island nuclear incident in Pennsylvania (level 5 on the INES) radically changed the nature of the debate. Two weeks later, Medvedev's editor called him to announce that the book was being sent to press. In 1979, the scientists of Oak Ridge confirmed Medvedev's findings based on the study of 150 publications from Soviet scientific journals on radioecology. However, in a report commissioned by the Department of Energy, two Los Alamos experts continued to doubt Medvedev's version. "What then did happen at Kyshtym? A disastrous nuclear accident that killed hundreds, injured thousands, and contaminated thousands of square miles of land? Or, a series of relatively minor incidents, embellished by rumor, and severely compounded by a history of sloppy practices associated with the complex? The latter seems more highly probable." The Soviets, they claimed, had begun contaminating the river near Kyshtym in the 1940s through "blatant disregard for their people or their surroundings." There had been no spectacular explosion and no sudden irradiation. "The Kyshtym disaster is just that—a record of the disastrous, long lasting effects man can wreak on his environment if he fails to take adequate steps to protect it."

In the aftermath of the 1973 and 1979 oil shocks, the West was particularly unwilling to recognize that civilian uses of nuclear energy could cause widespread contamination and endanger the life of populations. CIA reports from the catastrophe demonstrated a pattern of dissimulation, which made the revelation of the Kyshtym disaster undesirable even twenty years later.

By 1986, however, the Kyshtym accident had been dwarfed by another nuclear catastrophe on Soviet soil, at the Chernobyl nuclear plant on April 26, 1986. As an internationally recognized expert, Zhores Medvedev was well-placed to analyze the consequences of this accident, and on April 28, the BBC invited him three evenings in a row to comment on the event in Peter Snow's "Newsnight" program. The news had just come out that high levels of radiation had been recorded in Sweden, presumably originating from a Soviet nuclear plant, but Moscow had not released any official statement yet, and the exact location and circumstances of the accident were unknown. The first evening, Medvedev spoke about the Urals nuclear catastrophe, speculating on the origins of the new accident. On the second night, Peter Snow received a TASS press release: the Soviet authorities announced that a reactor of the Chernobyl nuclear plant had been damaged.

Soon, requests for articles and invitations to scientific conferences on the subject started coming in. Medvedev refused all proposals to write "express books" on Chernobyl and preferred to take the time to carefully study the subject he would work upon intensively for several years. He started collecting material from Soviet and foreign sources in late 1987. Since Soviet research on the consequences of the accident was classified, his own research was based mostly on

Western studies. *The Legacy of Chernobyl* came out in February 1990 in English, with translations into German, Spanish and Japanese to follow. This was the first scientific monograph on the subject and clearly not a work of "antinuclear propaganda," in Medvedev's own words. He predicted that the accident would only slow down, but not interrupt the development of nuclear energy, although reactors of the Chernobyl type would no longer be used for energy production. Meanwhile, the failure of the Soviet authorities to dissimulate the Chernobyl catastrophe, coupled with the democratization of Soviet society, allowed for an official acknowledgment of the Urals nuclear disaster and its causes.

By 1989, Zhores Medvedev was well settled in London. Ten years earlier, his five-year contract had been turned into a tenured position, which allowed him to apply for naturalization. With British citizenship, Medvedev could apply for a Soviet visa to attend conferences in the USSR. His hopes to attend the Fourteenth European Biochemical Congress in Moscow in 1984, however, were dashed by the lengthy naturalization process he faced, undoubtedly justified by his status. After he submitted his application in October 1980, British intelligence kept him on a close watch, opening his mail for two months. Finally, in May 1984, Medvedev received his naturalization certificate. By June, he had a British passport, but it was too late to apply for a visa for Moscow.

In January 1989, however, he received an invitation from the Armament and Disarmament Information Unit, a British academic center, to give a lecture on "Nuclear power and global security" at a seminar they were organizing in Moscow in July 1989. After some bureaucratic hurdles, Medvedev eventually received his visa and flew to Moscow in early July with his wife. They were greeted by Roy, Zhores's son Sasha, and Rita's siblings. One may only guess the joy that Zhores experienced as he was reunited with his twin brother and his son for the first time in sixteen years. In Kalinin (Tver'), Medvedev met for the first time his granddaughters Masha and Dasha, who were then eleven and five. His stay in Moscow also gave him the opportunity to reconnect with many former colleagues and friends.

Zhores's impressions of Gorbachev's Glasnost policy were mixed. The lecture he gave on July 17 was limited to a very narrow circle of participants, without any external audience or journalists. Yet, momentous changes were taking place in the Soviet Parliament: on June 30, 1989, the State Committee on Atomic Energy "declassified" the Urals nuclear catastrophe by publishing a short bulletin on the subject, and a group of American congressmen were invited to visit the site of the accident. The Supreme Soviet created a Commission on Ecology with a subcommittee on atomic energy, which organized hearings on the Urals nuclear catastrophe. On July 16, Zhores received a phone call from the subcommittee's secretary, who invited him to participate in the hearings. However, Medvedev's expectations proved overblown. Instead of drafting a bill that would have granted victims of the Urals catastrophe the same status and right to financial compensation as the Chernobyl victims, the subcommittee closed the hearings after just one day, declaring them a "victory of Glasnost."

After the hearings on the Urals nuclear catastrophe, Zhores wrote a critical letter to the organizers, pointing out serious drawbacks in the committee's main report, which underestimated the impact of the accident. He sent a copy to a Cheliabinsk newspaper which had asked for his reaction on the subject. The publication of his letter raised a lot of comments in the local and national press. In January 1990, the Soviet journal *Energiia* started publishing excerpts of Medvedev's book on the catastrophe. In March, the scientist was invited to take part in a closed seminar at the Kurchatov atomic energy institute in Moscow with prominent experts on the subject. The highlight of the trip, however, was an invitation to the site of the accident, where Medvedev visited the Experimental Station created in 1958 near the nuclear plant to study the environmental consequences of the accident and conduct a program of rehabilitation of the contaminated zone.

Zhores Medvedev in Chernobyl, 1990. Courtesy of Zhores Medvedev.

In September 1990, Medvedev also visited Chernobyl for the first time, in the framework of an international conference organized near the nuclear plant. He gave a presentation on the spread of Chernobyl radionuclides in Europe and heard with great interest about the research of Soviet colleagues, who gave him copies of their recently declassified articles on the ecological consequences of the catastrophe. He and other Western participants also used their free time to explore the zone and collect samples of contaminated plants for analysis. After officially retiring in November 1991, Medvedev was invited again to Chernobyl in summer 1992 as a voluntary consultant of a radioecological expedition in the radiated zone. A few months later, when the Ukrainian government organized an international competition to build a sarcophagus over the Chernobyl atomic plant, Medvedev received an invitation to take part in the elaboration of a joint project between a Russian nuclear engineering institute and a laboratory of the Oxford School of Architecture as an expert in radiobiology. The project, which did not win the competition, foresaw not only the construction of a shelter structure, but also a robot-engineered disassembling factory to dismantle the reactor.

Zhores Medvedev's revelation of the Kyshtym nuclear incident was the fortuitous consequence of his numerous speaking engagements on Soviet science in the West, but once the scientist had identified a "blank spot" in international nuclear history, he set out to fill it with the same energy he had once devoted to his history of Lysenko's sway. This time, however, the authorities retaining crucial information were not the Soviet government but the Western nuclear lobby and governmental agencies. The Soviet dissident turned whistleblower thus proved as inconvenient in the West as he had been in the Soviet Union, but his activism was no less significant in revealing the dangers of nuclear energy to the Western public. The irony was that Zhores, by his own admission, was no anti-nuclear activist: his only concern was to uncover truth, and perhaps he was moved by a stubborn desire to prove the veracity of his claims in the face of overwhelming opposition.

Works Cited

Medvedev, Zhores. "Two Decades of Dissidence." *New Scientist*, November 4, 1976, 264–67.
———. "Facts behind the nuclear Disaster." *New Scientist*, June 30, 1977, 761–764.
———. *Nuclear Disaster in the Urals*. New York: Norton, 1979.

———. *Opasnaia professiia*. Moscow: Vremia, 2019.
———. *Soviet Science*. Oxford: Oxford University Press, 1979.
Soran, Diane M., and Danny B. Stillman. "Analysis of the Alleged Kyshtym Disaster." Report. New Mexico: Los Alamos National Laboratory, January 1, 1982.

Further Reading

Akleyev, A. V., L. Yu Krestinina, M. O. Degteva, and E. I. Tolstykh. "Consequences of the Radiation Accident at the Mayak Production Association in 1957 (the 'Kyshtym Accident')." *Journal of Radiological Protection* 37, no. 3 (August 2017): R19–R42.

CHAPTER 15

The Rise and Fall of Gorbachev's Socialist Democracy

Although many dissidents described Roy Medvedev as the last believer in socialist democracy, socialist ideas continued to interest young people into the 1970s and early 1980s. In 1982, the KGB arrested Boris Kagarlitskii, a member of a circle of young socialists who had been editing a samizdat journal. Before his arrest, he had been in contact with Medvedev and had shown him his essay *The Thinking Reed*. The historian found Kagarlitskii's ideas too radical, though, with a "Trotskyist orientation." Their relationship remained unequal: Kagarlitskii was by some accounts Medvedev's research assistant and made translations of English-language literature for him. There were a number of young people who tried to help the famous dissident: Boris Bass was a student majoring in English from a provincial city who admired Medvedev's research on Stalinism and agreed to help him with translations, but after his first meeting with the historian, he was called up for interrogation by the local KGB and gave up. After 1988, Medvedev needed assistance on a more stable basis and his comfortable income allowed him to hire Vladimir Chebotarev, son of his late friend Aleksei Tsybuliatskii, as a personal assistant.

Roy Medvedev, however, did not share the belief of many socialist dissidents that political change could be triggered by grassroots activist groups. He thought that democratization could only come about as a result of reform from above. He thus stood much closer to the convictions and methods of in-system reformers, who wanted to bring about change from within the Soviet apparatus—a belief reinforced by his friendship with consultants from the Central Committee. As Georgii Shakhnazarov, who would become Gorbachev's advisor, stated in his memoirs, Roy Medvedev "was never a 100-percent dissident, long before Perestroika he presented a wholly reasonable concept of reforms which did not infringe on socialist principles of social organization." Gorbachev's ascent to power and his politics of Perestroika (the restructuring of economic and political life) and Glasnost (openness and transparency, a loosening of censorship), starting from 1987, thus represented the realization of Medvedev's longtime political forecast: a reformer from within the apparatus was finally launching the program of democratization of the Soviet system that the dissident had long been calling for. Soon after Gorbachev came to power, with Roy's help, Zhores began work on an "express biography" of the new leader, about whom very little was known. The book came out in February 1986 and was translated into several languages.

Zhores Medvedev, 1987. Courtesy of Zhores Medvedev.

In November 1985, the Medvedev brothers turned sixty. They expected to retire within the next five or six years, and Roy thought about writing memoirs. The Soviet system seemed to be there to stay, if not forever, then at least for the foreseeable future. In 1986, in an essay entitled "How I see the USSR in 2000," Roy Medvedev examined three possible scenarios of development of the Soviet system. Radical reforms or, on the contrary, increased conservatism and a new arms race were possible, but the scenario he judged most likely was moderate reform combined with authoritarian rule. He concluded that no dramatic change was likely to happen until the end of the century. He did not predict that three years later, his books would be published in the Soviet Union, he would be elected to the Soviet Parliament, and his brother would be able to visit him for the first time in sixteen years.

The situation of Soviet dissidents did not improve overnight, however. The police were still stationed on Roy's staircase until May 1985, and he remained under threat of arrest for at least another year. In April, his phone line was suspended and his correspondence with London was partially interrupted for several months. Zhores believed this to be related to his publication of Gorbachev's biography. Another issue of concern was the fact that Rita was repeatedly refused return visas to travel to the USSR. In March 1986, Roy was subjected to a new campaign of anonymous letters. On April 1, after shopping with a Swedish correspondent at a Beriozka shop, he was arrested and interrogated by officials from the criminal investigation police, who wished to clarify the sources and amount of his income. Money transfers from the West remained complicated. Zhores regularly sent him parcels with jeans or hi-tech items, which he could easily sell to friends or through secondhand shops.

On May 9, 1986, Medvedev's phone line was suddenly restored. Changes were happening in the cultural field too. Progressive figures were appointed to key positions: Vladimir Lakshin became deputy editor-in-chief of the journal *Znamia*; another friend of Medvedev's, the writer Vladimir Dudintsev, was preparing the publication of a new novel on the Lysenko affair, *White Robes*. No less exciting was the publication of *Children of the Arbat*, by Anatolii Rybakov, a novel on the Stalin era which Medvedev expected to become "the most important publication of the 1980s," or *Repentance*, Tengiz Abuladze's 1987 film on Stalin-era repression. Excited by these new developments, Roy began to write chronicles in the cultural field for an Italian newspaper, *Rinascita*. By 1987, most previously banned works, from Boris Pasternak's *Doctor Zhivago* to Anna Akhmatova's *Requiem*, were being published. In December 1986, Andrei Sakharov received a phone call from Gorbachev, who informed him that he was free to return to Moscow from the city of Gor'kii where he had been exiled. In February–March 1987, most political prisoners were amnestied and set free. Young people started organizing informal political and discussion clubs. Roy received many invitations to give talks, but he felt too old to participate in these debates. Besides, he had always been more of an individual player.

As a new generation of Soviet leaders was coming to power, the time was finally ripe for Roy's long-planned biography of Brezhnev. This was a period Medvedev knew well, and he was particularly interested in the late 1960s, a period characterized by a political struggle between various party factions, which had strong parallels with the current situation under Gorbachev. The 1970s, with the onset of stagnation, when Brezhnev suffered a stroke and lost much of his ability to exercise power, interested him much less. Medvedev's essay entitled "Galina Brezhneva's diamonds," published in the West and circulating actively in samizdat, contributed to the discreditation of the legacy of "stagnation" and corruption of the Brezhnev era. During his short-lived political career in 1989–1991, Medvedev enjoyed privileged access to archival documents, which allowed him to complete the first part of his biography, published in 1991. However, the fall of the Soviet Union prevented the publication of the second part.

Under Gorbachev, power struggles occurred mostly behind the scenes, but at times they emerged into the open. In April 1988, with the secret support of conservatives within the Politburo, the newspaper *Sovetskaia Rossiia* published the letter of Nina Andreeva, a chemistry teacher, entitled "I cannot forsake my principles," which became a manifesto of pro-Stalinist forces. Shortly thereafter, a *Pravda* editorial officially rebuffed the letter. Gorbachev needed anti-Stalinist allies within the intelligentsia, and Roy Medvedev, with his record of "loyal dissent," could play this role. Starting from March 1987, the dissident had begun to receive publishing proposals from journals, but censorship still precluded such publications. When he received a request for an interview about Stalin-era repression from the youth weekly *Sobesednik*, with a 1.5 million print run, the historian was initially skeptical about its chances of publication, only a year after a similar attempt had failed. However, the Nina Andreeva controversy turned Medvedev into Gorbachev's ally, and the interview in *Sobesednik* unexpectedly came out on April 28. The journalist identified Medvedev not as an opponent of socialism, but as someone who had fought against its distortions, which had led to "stagnation, corruption and a new cult." He concluded "We hope that the Soviet reader can also become acquainted with the works of our unyielding countryman, Roy Medvedev—sharp, polemical, controversial, appealing to the voice of conscience in each of us, surprisingly true and sincere. The times demand these books."

Even as he ceased to be a dissident, Roy Medvedev continued to enjoy the prestigious status of someone who had dared to speak out when others remained silent. Despite the ongoing destalinization campaign, professional historians still stood paralyzed, fearing any bold step. Unlike writers, who had in store works written "for the drawer" or published in tamizdat, historians could not publish overnight on themes that had long been taboo. Writers and publicists enjoyed greater freedom, and it was therefore in the press and in literary journals that the most important anti-Stalinist works appeared. As an independent researcher, Medvedev understood that he enjoyed Gorbachev's support and could use his influence. Invitations to give public lectures started to come in: Medvedev spoke at the Air Force Academy, the Moscow military district Anti-Aircraft warfare quarters, the Ministry of Foreign Affairs and Ministry of Agriculture, at Moscow State University and in theaters, in front of audiences ranging from several hundreds to one thousand five hundred or more. In May 1988, he gave a long interview to Moscow television, ten–twelve minutes of which were broadcast in the popular show *Vzgliad*.

Roundtable with Roy Medvedev at the V.V. Maiakovskii House of the Writer with Daniil Granin and V. Kavtorin, February 19, 1989. Photograph by F. Lur'e. OKhDLSM, F. 333, op. 9, d. 362, l. 1.

A turning point in Medvedev's return to public life was his invitation to a reception with US President Ronald Reagan, in June 1988, at the House of Soviet Writers. Gorbachev had initiated a new détente with the West. After signing the Intermediate Range Nuclear Forces Treaty in Washington in 1987, he had invited Reagan to Moscow. Medvedev was among forty influential intellectuals selected to meet the President, along with the heads of creative unions, famous writers, artists, and poets. Medvedev understood that the authorities' attitude towards him had changed; he had been selected among "the elite of Soviet intelligentsia" because of his status of famous dissident. He believed that the authorities had invited him rather than Sakharov because he was more manageable and "would not say anything provocative." His presence caused a sensation among the guests, who were surprised to see yesterday's dissident in their midst. Journal editors and publishers also understood that the times had changed and came up to him one after another with contract offers. From then on, Medvedev started publishing intensively in the Soviet Union. His works were serialized in journals, and, from 1990 onwards, updated editions of his major books appeared: *Let History Judge* (under the title *On Stalin and Stalinism*), *Khrushchev, All Stalin's Men* ... For the first time his name became widely known beyond the small group of intelligentsia who listened to Western radio broadcasts.

In February 1989, the weekly *Argumenty i Fakty*, with a nine million print run, published Roy Medvedev's answer to the reader's question "How many people were repressed under Stalin?" The historian gave estimates of various categories of victims and came up with an approximative total of forty million persons repressed. Following the publication, Medvedev was flooded with letters, for the most part expressing indignation. But the readers of his journal publications, which raised considerable interest, also helped him correct mistakes and include new information in subsequent editions of his works. The question of Stalinist repression was one of the most widely debated at the time, and public opinion was highly polarized between those who considered that Solzhenitsyn's *Gulag Archipelago* should be published in the USSR and those who, like Nina Andreeva, could not remain silent while their idol, Stalin, was branded a vile criminal. In this context, Roy Medvedev appeared as a compromise figure, radical enough to stand at the vanguard of Gorbachev's de-Stalinization, and yet more moderate than Solzhenitsyn, who remained the regime's number one opponent. This status allowed Medvedev to convert his newly gained influence into political capital on the domestic scene.

In June 1988, Gorbachev announced at the 19th Party Conference a radical democratization of the Soviet political system through the creation of a new parliament, the Congress of People's Deputies, elected for the first time on an alternative basis—that is, with more than one candidate per seat. Whereas the old Supreme Soviet had been a puppet parliament rubber-stamping pre-approved legislation, the Congress now had the power not only to elect representatives to the Supreme Soviet and vote on the bills prepared by this organ, but also to adopt and amend the Constitution, and define the main orientations of domestic and foreign policy. It would be composed of 2,250 deputies, elected partly directly, partly through organizations. Since the electoral law gave local power structures several mechanisms of control over the selection of candidates, it was unclear how democratic the election would be. And yet in many districts the vote proved more competitive than anyone had anticipated.

Roy Medvedev had not planned to run for a parliamentary seat. When he was unexpectedly nominated candidate in three electoral districts in January 1989, he felt certain that only party-backed candidates had any chance of being selected and did not cancel his conference tour in Leningrad to attend the constituency meetings. In one Moscow constituency, he faced the first secretary of the CPSU district committee; in another, a popular doctor nominated by dozens of medical institutions and backed by the party. Little did he know then that belonging to the party apparatus was rather a disadvantage to win the popular vote. Against all odds, his candidacy was approved, along with that of the five other nominees, in the Sixth Voroshilov district in Moscow.

Medvedev began a short but intense electoral campaign. Despite the lack of official endorsement, he led the electoral race on March 25, 1989 with 35 percent of the votes. He faced in the runoff Kseniia Razumova, a professor of the Kurchatov Institute of Atomic Energy who enjoyed Boris Yeltsin's backing. During his campaign, Medvedev had repeatedly criticized Yeltsin, then a rising star of the political opposition to Gorbachev, whom Medvedev accused of populism. The day before the election, curious posters appeared in the district, with absurd slogans: "Vote against Roy Medvedev, he's a millionaire" or "Roy Medvedev is a Jew, and his real last name is Zhores." However, Medvedev's reputation far outweighed his adversary's, and as he noted, "my supporters turned out to be committed people and I think that many of them are my readers." The organization Memorial, founded to commemorate victims of political repression, printed leaflets calling on voters to choose Medvedev, "whose voice will be heard and who has always struggled for perestroika." The historian was elected with 52.33 percent of the votes on April 9.

In his program, which followed the blueprint for reform he had presented in *On Socialist Democracy* in 1972, Medvedev endeavored to support Gorbachev's action and help him unlock the full potential of Glasnost and socialist democracy. He promised to fight to improve "workers' material and spiritual conditions of life," and to vote "for all progressive economic and political reforms and laws." Moreover, as a political theorist, he hoped to contribute to the development of the theory and practice of Perestroika, in particular the ideological evolution which had been called "new thinking." Despite his consensual pro-Perestroika platform, Medvedev played on his image of dissident, insisting on his past political struggle for those very reforms that Gorbachev was now conducting. He promised to remain independent, to continue to "criticize openly" the negative aspects of Soviet life in the new Parliament, to monitor the executive's activity, and never "mechanically vote for any law and decree." Yet by the time the Congress began, in May 1989, Medvedev's membership in the Communist Party had been restored. He did not ask to be reinstated but accepted the offer, on the condition that his confiscated archive would be returned.

Roy Medvedev with insignia of People's Deputy, 1989. Courtesy of Zhores Medvedev.

The election and the First Congress of People's Deputies raised considerable popular interest and even greater expectations. The live public broadcasting of the Congress's sessions offered Soviet citizens an opportunity to witness the work that their elected representatives were conducting, and they followed their activities with passion. Polls showed that 80 percent of Soviet urban adults watched the First Congress's broadcast "constantly." Yet for all parties involved, this constituted a radically new exercise, and all did not go smoothly. Gorbachev seems to have hoped that the Congress would enhance his legitimacy and strengthen his position in the face of the conservative opposition within the Party. However, what Gorbachev had not seen coming was the constitution of a new liberal opposition, led by such charismatic figures as Andrei Sakharov, the historian Iurii Afanasiev, and future Moscow mayor Gavriil Popov. Along with

Gorbachev's number one opponent Boris Yeltsin they created an Interregional Deputies' Group which initially sought to spur Gorbachev to bolder reforms but over time came to constitute an organized opposition to Gorbachev's policies.

At the First Congress, Sakharov's interventions into the debates raised furor among deputies. On the first day, in the name of democracy, he had voiced his opposition to Gorbachev's election to the position of Head of the Supreme Soviet without any alternative candidacy and previous discussion, but his calls had been ignored. On the last day, Sakharov warned about the crisis of confidence of the people towards their leadership and set out to read his "Decree on Power," which called for the abolition of Article 6 of the Constitution, that instituted the Communist Party's monopoly on power. What left a lasting impression on Soviet spectators, however, was not so much the decree's radical content as Sakharov's determination to read his text to the end, even after Gorbachev had repeatedly ordered him to end his speech, and even shut off his microphone. By the time Sakharov suddenly died, during the Second Congress of People's Deputies, in December 1989, he had become a national hero.

Roy Medvedev's political strategy differed from Sakharov's: to further Perestroika, what was needed was not to challenge and thus weaken Gorbachev, but to help him strengthen his power against his conservative political opponents, so that he could show greater boldness in his reforms. The respect of democratic procedures mattered less to him than this paramount political objective. Therefore, at a party meeting ahead of the Congress, Medvedev supported the principle of electing Gorbachev Head of the Supreme Soviet before any discussion. Gorbachev sensed that Medvedev was an ally, and, undoubtedly with his support, the historian was elected to the Supreme Soviet, the legislative body in charge of drafting bills voted by the Congress. Medvedev did not betray the Soviet leader's trust.

At the First Congress, Medvedev spontaneously intervened a few times, stepping in in conflict situations. He would transmit a note to the Congress's Presidium with the summary of his position, and the General Secretary would give him the floor. In a letter to his brother, the historian attributed his election to the Supreme Soviet to "successful interventions during the preparatory and first sessions of the Congress," which helped him win the approval of other deputies, in contrast with the most radical liberal candidates, whose speeches had antagonized the conservative majority. Through his work in the Congress's "redaction commission," in charge of drafting resolutions, he had also made the acquaintance of "half of the Politburo."

When conservative deputies tried to rock the boat during the election of Anatolii Luk'ianov to the position of Deputy President of the Supreme Soviet,

Medvedev defended Luk'ianov, arguing that it was important that the Head and Deputy Head of state lead the "state ship" in the same direction. This would ensure that no ideological shift occurred when Gorbachev was abroad or on vacation, as had been repeatedly the case in the past. The historian revealed that Luk'ianov had known Gorbachev since university, and his loyalty could thus be counted upon.

Although Medvedev did not call for the legalization of an opposition, he still deemed it necessary to have counter-powers within the political system. During the first session of the Supreme Soviet, he spoke against the election of a candidate selected by the party to the head of the Committee of Popular Control, arguing that this organ should be the most independent and "should act in the first instance according to the dictates of conscience, in accordance with state interests and the people's demands." He therefore supported Boris Yeltsin's candidacy to the post.

Medvedev did not systematically vote with the majority of the Congress and his interventions were somehow middle-of-the-road, with a democratic orientation but a pragmatic view on the necessary pace of reforms. He showed more independence within his area of expertise, where he could afford, and was expected, to adopt a principled moral stance. On June 1, the historian intervened into the debate concerning the creation of a commission on the secret protocols of the Molotov-Ribbentrop pact, which had allowed the Soviet Union to occupy the Baltic states. Medvedev had known about the existence of the protocols for a long time and supported this initiative, calling on the Congress to bring the truth to light in this affair. He proposed that Eduard Shevardnadze, the Minister of Foreign Affairs, be designated head of the commission. Gorbachev met this proposal with ambivalence, arguing that no documentary proof of the existence of the protocols had yet been discovered, but proposed to appoint Aleksandr Iakovlev head of the commission.

In private, Medvedev spoke critically about the radical deputies who had united within the Interregional Deputies' Group. He knew some of them and had been invited to attend some of their meetings, but he was perplexed by their pretentions to power and felt ambivalent about the IDG:

> As a recent dissident, I felt close to many of the programmatic demands of the IDG. But I did not agree with the radicality of these demands, the haste with which they were being presented, the methods proposed for their application, the [deputies'] willingness to lead behind them the people and society, which they almost did not know. And these people were very ignorant of the country's and society's real problems.

Medvedev's disagreement with the most radical deputies came to the fore when he was chosen, on Gorbachev's suggestion, to head a parliamentary commission in charge of investigating the politically delicate Gdlian-Ivanov Affair.

Telman Gdlian and his deputy Nikolai Ivanov were heads of a prosecution group appointed in 1983 to fight a vast network of corruption in Central Asia. The so-called "Cotton Affair" led to the arrest and dismissal of prominent political figures from the Uzbek Republic. In June 1988, the two prosecutors published an article in the popular weekly *Ogonek* denouncing the involvement of the central Soviet authorities in the Uzbek corruption scheme during the Brezhnev era. The press hailed the prosecutors as heroes engaged in a selfless struggle to uproot corruption. However, after Gdlian and Ivanov were elected people's deputies in spring 1989, the wind changed abruptly. During their campaign, they launched wholesale accusations against the central party apparatus: they denounced a "Moscow mafia," including Egor Ligachev, a conservative Politburo member, which had allegedly received bribes from the "Uzbek mafia." The affair took on dangerous proportions: the Uzbek authorities denounced Moscow's colonial grip over the Republic, while Gdlian and Ivanov's populist discourse unleashed popular furor against Soviet power.

The authorities responded by a campaign of discreditation: the media revealed that the prosecutors had used illegal methods of investigation. Although such violations were certainly ubiquitous in the Soviet judicial system, witnesses' accounts of how Gdlian's prosecution team had kept suspects in detention without trial for years, and resorted to the arrest of relatives, including wives and children, as a form of blackmail, certainly did not do them honor. A commission composed of respected public figures was established, which published its findings on the eve of the First Congress and confirmed the accusations of violations of legal procedure. In May 1989, the Procuracy of the USSR instituted criminal proceedings against the two prosecutors.

The most urgent task for the Soviet leadership, however, was to restore popular trust. A parliamentary commission was placed in charge of shedding light on this unsavory affair. But its mandate was clearly to confirm the official version, and not to investigate Gdlian and Ivanov's accusations of corruption at the highest level, as some would have it. The two deputies, who were members of the Interregional Deputies' Group, enjoyed broad popular support, particularly in democratic circles, and repeatedly intervened to defend their honor and publicize their accusations. As Anatolii Sobchak, one of the co-chairs of the IDG and later St Petersburg mayor, wrote in his memoirs, he was initially well-disposed toward Gdlian and Ivanov, but their demagogical interventions at the Congress, addressed not to the deputies, but to Soviet voters behind their television screens, disappointed him. They continued to behave "according to the repressive traditions of the 1930s" and if they could launch accusations against Ligachev without bothering to provide any shred of evidence and enjoy the public support of millions based on a mere "class feeling," then not much had changed since the Stalin era.

At the First Congress, the President of the Academy of Sciences of Uzbekistan approached Sakharov to ask him to join the Gdlian Commission, but the dissident declined the offer: he understood that getting involved in this affair could threaten his moral authority. Roy Medvedev, however, accepted this heavy responsibility at Luk'ianov's request and was designated chair of the commission, composed of fifteen other deputies. Uzbek deputies protested his designation, believing him to be on Gdlian and Ivanov's side by virtue of his dissident credentials. To alleviate the pressure, the commission eventually designated two other co-chairs: Nikolai Strukov, a lawyer and investigator from Kursk, and Veniamin Iarin, a metallurgy worker from Nizhnii Tagil.

Medvedev was prepared to invest months of work to conduct the careful investigation necessary to shed light on the events, but his mission was far from easy. Commission members had to face considerable public pressure and direct intimidation attempts from the Uzbek authorities and the committees in defense of Gdlian and Ivanov. On October 7, 1989, sixty thousand people formed a "living chain" from Zelenograd to the Manezh square near the Kremlin in support of Gdlian and Ivanov and against corruption. As Roy Medvedev complained, Gdlian and his supporters also harassed him and other members of the commission through insults, pestering phone calls at home and at the commission.

In the fall of 1989, the commission held daily meetings and witnesses' hearings. Initially, members of the commission refrained from any comments to the press about the affair, but as public pressure mounted, they allowed the press and deputies of the Supreme Soviet to attend their meetings. Despite his invitations to these "open door" sessions, Medvedev complained that Gdlian and Ivanov had declined to attend and preferred to attack him. In an interview, Medvedev pleaded for the public to help the commission, instead of expressing impatience and exercising pressure.

> If Gdlian and Ivanov often needed four years to demonstrate (and unfortunately, not always rightly), that a given person was corrupt, how can people expect us to solve a question linked with thousands of volumes of criminal cases, with the work of a commission which was composed of around 200 people. And in

addition, with Gdlian and Ivanov's accusations against 18 staffers of the Central Committee of the CPSU, the Politburo, the Procuracy of the USSR, the Supreme Court of the USSR.

The commission presented its preliminary conclusions at the Second Congress in December 1989, and a final report in front of the Supreme Soviet on April 17, 1990. The latter, presented in front of a very large audience composed of deputies, judicial officials, journalists, and members of the Politburo and government, pointed to violations of Soviet legality committed by Gdlian and Ivanov, but also to serious issues in the functioning of the Procuracy, especially concerning its monitoring of lower instances. On April 18, 1990, the Supreme Soviet issued a decree repealing Gdlian's and Ivanov's deputy immunity due to the destabilization that their unverified accusations had caused, authorizing their dismissal from the Procuracy, but also that of their hierarchical superiors. Gdlian and Ivanov, however, did not attend the hearings. They had fled to Armenia, where they were soon elected to the Armenian parliament and continued to claim their innocence.

Roy Medvedev's image suffered from his involvement in the affair, and he earned in democratic circles the reputation of a compliant politician. In his own electoral district, he faced opposition and a petition to demote him. His critics complained about his support of the party apparatus, his discreditation of Gdlian's investigation group and progressive people's deputies. They claimed to have "voted for a progressive and independent democrat," who had promised to struggle for the cancellation of Article 6 of the USSR Constitution about the CPSU's monopoly on power. However, when the question had been put to a vote, he had abstained (in fact he was absent that day). Nor had he solved the ecological problems he had promised to address during his campaign. The petitioners quoted Solzhenitsyn's critique of Medvedev to underline that the historian had never been a dissident. Medvedev and his assistants rebuffed these attacks in the local press, underlining that, unlike his critics who had remained silent until Perestroika, he had actually been a dissident since the late 1960s.

With Perestroika, Roy Medvedev had finally had a chance to participate in those democratic reforms he had been calling for since the 1960s. Given his belief that political change could only come from above, Medvedev showed his loyalty to the Soviet leader who had heralded these reforms and used his popularity to buttress Gorbachev's legitimacy. Medvedev's involvement with the Gdlian and Ivanov commission also obeyed the same logic: the priority was to restore the Soviet people's confidence in its leadership, and discredit those who launched unverified accusations of corruption against the Kremlin leaders.

However, no political figure disappointed Roy more than Gorbachev did, and by 1991, Medvedev had lost any illusion concerning the Soviet leader's ability to conduct the necessary reforms and maintain stability.

For Zhores Medvedev as well Perestroika was a time of change. In December 1987, his name appeared in print in the USSR for the first time since his emigration. The zoologist Iurii Polianskii, who had been on the commission that had recommended Medvedev's book for publication in 1966, declared that the publication of a history of the Lysenko phenomenon was long overdue. Following Roy Medvedev's "legalization" the two brothers published their memoirs about their parents in June 1988. In February 1989, the literary journal *Knizhnoe Obozrenie* published a long excerpt of Zhores Medvedev's manuscript *History of the Biological Discussion in the USSR*. Roy informed his brother that a Soviet editorial house was interested in publishing his book. *The Rise and Fall of T.D. Lysenko* eventually came out in Russia in 1993.

Zhores Medvedev, London, 1987. OKhDLSM, F. 333, op. 14, d. 39, l. 3.

Zhores, however, remained in emigration, *persona non grata* in his own Fatherland. In January 1989, in an article entitled "Our Strangers," Soviet writer Daniil Granin mentioned Zhores Medvedev in a call to the authorities to restore the Soviet citizenship of those intellectuals who had been sent into exile. "These people did not commit any crimes, stripping them of their citizenship was a violation of their basic human rights," he argued. Various artistic unions, scientific organizations, and individual intellectuals started petitioning the authorities on behalf of exiled scientists and artists. Zhores had heard from his friend Nikolai Vorontsov, a zoologist, that the All-Union Society of Geneticists and Breeders had sent such a petition on his behalf on January 24, 1989, followed by further petitions by scientific institutions. In July 1989, Vorontsov, soon to be appointed Minister of Ecology, initiated another petition for Medvedev's rehabilitation on behalf of the Supreme Soviet Committee on Science, Education and Culture, which he headed. However, Gorbachev still feared the return of the regime's boldest critics from exile and had misgivings about taking such a decision. It was one thing to restore the citizenship of such harmless cultural figures as theater director Iurii Liubimov or composer Mstislav Rostropovich, but behind them loomed the threatening shadow of Solzhenitsyn, on whose behalf the Soviet intelligentsia increasingly petitioned the Soviet government.

On June 30, 1990, Roy called his brother to inform him that the evening news broadcast had announced the restoration of the Soviet citizenship of Zhores Medvedev, Vladimir Maksimov, and Aleksandr Zinov'ev. Although the Soviet public was expecting a symbolic gesture towards Solzhenitsyn, the first decree included only these three names of second-rank dissidents, and a vague mention that the rehabilitation process would be continued. On August 15, a new decree with twenty-one new names, including Solzhenitsyn's, was issued.

Zhores Medvedev's new Soviet passport opened the possibility for him to get a Soviet retirement pension. In October 1991, he and Rita travelled to the USSR to solve this issue and to collect material on Soviet science for Medvedev's retirement lecture at the London Medical Institute. However, two months after the August putsch attempt and ban of the Communist Party, the country was in a state of political disarray which had dire consequences not only for the "science cities" that he visited but also for the whole Soviet people. The Soviet regime was crumbling before his eyes.

Works Cited

"Iz reki po imeni fakt." *Sobesednik*, no. 18 (April 1988): 12.
Medvedev, Roy. *Sovetskii Soiuz. Poslednie gody zhizni*. Moscow: Vremia, 2015.
Medvedev, Zhores. *Opasnaia professiia*. Moscow: Vremia, 2019.
"Roi Medvedev: 'Budem rabotat' bez speshki'," *Rezonans*, no. 1, November 1989, 3.
Sobčak, Anatolij. *Chronique d'une chute annoncée*. Paris: Flammarion, 1991.

Further Reading

Cucciolla, Riccardo Mario, "Legitimation Through Self-Victimization: The Uzbek cotton affair and its repression narrative (1989–1991)," *Cahiers du monde russe* 58/4 (2017), 639–668.
Davies, R.W. "Soviet History in the Gorbachev Revolution: The First Phase." *The Socialist Register* 24 (1988): 37–78.
Sauvé, Guillaume, *Subir la victoire. Essor et chute de l'intelligentsia libérale en Russie (1987–1993)*. Presses de l'Université de Montréal, 2019.
Shane, Scott. *Dismantling Utopia: How Information Ended the Soviet Union*. Chicago: I.R. Dee, 1995.
Taubman, William. *Gorbachev His Life and Times*. New York: WW Norton & Company, 2017.

CHAPTER 16

The End of the Soviet Order

In August 1991, Roy Medvedev was vacationing in a luxurious sanatorium in Kislovodsk in the North Caucasus along with other deputies. A year earlier, in July 1990, he had been unexpectedly appointed a member of the Central Committee of the CPSU, apparently at Gorbachev's initiative. However, the Party's ruling organs were steadily losing power in the face of mounting protests. Medvedev increasingly felt the weakness of Gorbachev's leadership and had lost confidence in his ability to reform the Soviet Union. On the morning of August 19, the deputies gathered in the sanatorium's hall to discuss the concerning news from Moscow. What Roy had long dreaded had finally happened: on August 17, a group of conservative figures, who opposed Gorbachev's plan of signing a new Union treaty reforming the Soviet Union's political structure, had placed the Soviet leader under house arrest in his vacation residence in Crimea and had formed a "State Committee on the State of Emergency" (GKChP). The coup attempt was led by KGB Chairman Vladimir Kriuchkov. In the months leading up to the coup, several of its protagonists had sought advice from Roy Medvedev. Kriuchkov was concerned with Gorbachev behaving "badly," and Marshal Akhromeev had shown Medvedev a letter to Gorbachev of two hundred generals expressing discontent with the situation in the army. Akhromeev did not dare show it to the General Secretary and eventually committed suicide after the putsch. Medvedev shared their feeling of helplessness but had no solution.

In Kislovodsk, the deputies were required not to return to Moscow or give any interviews. It seemed like they had been intentionally sent off from the capital while the coup was being prepared. They followed the events with anguish but obeyed orders from the Supreme Soviet and stayed put. After two days, the putsch attempt was halted. Yeltsin emerged victorious from this confrontation: images of his speech standing on a tank symbolized the triumph of democracy over sheer force. Yet the coup had dealt a fatal blow to the Soviet regime. As Soviet republics declared their independence one after another in late August and September 1991, Gorbachev resigned from his position of General Secretary of the CPSU. From then on, real power was transferred into Yeltsin's hands.

The crumbling of Soviet power was heartbreaking for Roy Medvedev. In the two years leading up to the coup, he had unsuccessfully attempted to use his influence to steer events in what he deemed the right direction. Gorbachev faced opposition both from the conservative wing of the party, which opposed democratic reforms, and from democratic deputies led by the charismatic Yeltsin, who demanded more radical measures. However, Medvedev's short exchanges with Gorbachev had been frustrating: the Soviet leader seemed more inclined to speak than to listen to advice or criticism from outside. One telling episode was the consultation Anatolii Luk'ianov conducted with Medvedev in February 1990, concerning Gorbachev's plan to reform the Constitution, introducing a post of "President of the USSR," elected not directly, but by the Congress. Medvedev opposed these reforms: Gorbachev's popularity was dwindling, and a direct election would have been too risky, but an indirect one would expose his unwillingness to submit to the popular vote and further undermine his legitimacy. The best solution was to maintain the status quo. However, Gorbachev ignored his advice and went on with his plan. When the object was put to a vote in the Congress, Medvedev voted in favor of it.

Indeed, despite his concerns, Medvedev refused to further rock the boat of Perestroika. He still believed in supporting Gorbachev as the leader of the progressive wing of the party, to allow him to conduct the necessary reforms and to avoid a conservative coup. Medvedev could not understand why Gorbachev had not moved more decisively against Yeltsin and instead allowed him to turn into his main challenger. Yeltsin's popularity had soared in 1990 and he had been elected Head of the Supreme Soviet of the Russian Soviet Federative Socialist Republic (RSFSR). Medvedev knew that Gorbachev possessed compromising information he could have used against Yeltsin to eliminate him politically. Before Yeltsin's election, Gorbachev had shown Medvedev his opponent's medical records, which documented a suicide attempt, alcoholism, and mental health issues. The Soviet leader apparently expected Medvedev to use these documents against Yeltsin in the Soviet parliament, but the historian felt he had no legitimacy to do so. Only Gorbachev had the political authority necessary to reveal this information to the public, yet he did not act.

Gorbachev's closest advisors also felt helpless, as they watched the General Secretary make one mistake after another, and they eventually lost his ear. By the time Medvedev was elected member of the Central Committee, this ruling organ had lost much of its power and control over the situation. After Article 6 of the Constitution establishing the CPSU's monopoly on power was repealed, the Soviet republics held their first free parliamentary elections, which saw the triumph of nationalist candidates who no longer accepted subordination to Moscow. Several parliaments issued declarations of sovereignty. To halt this movement, Gorbachev tried to reform and consolidate the Soviet Union. In April 1991, he opened negotiations at Novo-Ogarevo with the heads of nine Soviet Republics to conclude a new Union treaty, which would have transformed the USSR into a loose confederation of republics. The General Secretary had consulted Medvedev on his plan for a new treaty. Medvedev did not approve of Gorbachev's decision to negotiate over Soviet citizens' heads and considered that a new Union treaty could only be concluded after summoning a Congress of Soviets, as had been done when the USSR was founded in 1922. But once more Gorbachev was not so much asking for advice as approval. These encounters testified to a deep misunderstanding: while Gorbachev saw Medvedev as a loyal supporter, the historian had hoped to be a political advisor, whose proven analytical skills, he thought, could have saved Gorbachev some mistakes.

In early 1991, in a message transmitted through Luk'ianov, Medvedev advised Gorbachev to progressively leave power and start by resigning from the position of General Secretary. "I considered that Gorbachev as a reformer and political actor had already exhausted himself; he had already done what he could do. And in January–February 1991 I made attempts to negotiate with him, asked a few times to meet him, but Gorbachev eluded any discussion, and the meeting did not take place."

When he returned to Moscow after the putsch, Roy Medvedev participated in an Extraordinary Session of the Supreme Soviet on August 26, 1991. He remembered:

> Many of us experienced feelings of perplexity and confusion, but many deputies were in a very belligerent and even aggressive mood, not in relation to the arrested members of the GKChP, but to the whole CPSU . . . Gorbachev appeared a few times in the conference hall. But his short speeches did not contain any new information or proposals. The sessions went on without any clear agenda. There were many Soviet and foreign correspondents, but most questions could be summed up as: "Will the Soviet Union survive?"

In reaction to the putsch, the Supreme Soviet pronounced the dissolution of the CPSU. Roy Medvedev was one of the few deputies to oppose it and to speak up against the transfer of authority from the Soviet Union to the Russian Republic. On September 3, he spoke in front of the 5th Congress of the People's Deputies to defend the CPSU's right to political existence. The peaceful competition between various political and social currents was an indispensable feature of civil society in a democratic state. Just as the CPSU's monopoly on power and elimination of political opposition had been illegal and criminal, "the current attempt to eliminate *de facto* the Communist Party, stopping its activity, depriving it of material means is illegal and arbitrary." Medvedev pleaded for the democrats to "overcome their divisions and create one or two strong political parties" but without depriving their opponents of the right "to work quietly, without overstepping the boundaries of law and the Constitution." However, Medvedev knew that his words had no bearing on the events. The Congress was dissolved soon thereafter, and by the end of the year the USSR had ceased to exist.

The fall of the Soviet Union came as a shock to the Medvedev brothers. Despite his usually accurate prognoses, Roy had proved too optimistic about the survival chances of the Soviet regime. In 1995, he confessed in an interview:

> What I did not expect was that the Communist Party of the CPSU would fall apart and turn out to be such a weak, impotent organism, that it would not be able to polemicize with anyone: as an ideological rival it turned out to be absolutely invalid, devoid of immunity to criticism. It stood only thanks to the monopoly of this false conception which was "hammered" into the heads of Soviet people. Even more surprising for me was the fall of the Soviet Union.

Nevertheless, the historian was among those who sought to use the new opportunities offered by democracy to push through his socialist democratic ideas. When the Communist Party was banned in October 1991, millions of former party members found themselves in a state of stupor, and the army of party workers who had stood in its ranks suddenly remained unemployed. Numerous surrogate communist parties began sprouting up throughout the country, catering to various fringes of the electorate. Valentin Kuptsov, a recent Politburo member with whom Medvedev was on friendly terms, invited him to join an initiative for the creation of a new socialist party. Medvedev eagerly jumped into the boat. Soon he spoke up in favor of openly breaking with Gorbachev, but the party's co-founders were more cautious on this point.

The creation of a new party of Marxist orientation was announced in early October 1991 in the press through a declaration calling on "Russian left-wing forces of socialist orientation" to unite. The bitter realization that the CPSU had "exhausted itself, lost trust and *de facto* ceased to exist" constituted a "tragedy for millions of communists," but it paled in comparison with the upheavals and sufferings that Russia was enduring. "Precisely in these dramatic days, but full of new hopes, we call on all those who are still politically active and capable of action to unite in the name of civil peace, of a peaceful, constitutional withdrawal of the country from chaos and disintegration, of a deep renewal of the axes of our life." The declaration was signed by seven people's deputies and local politicians, four of whom were recent members of the CPSU's Central Committee, and two workers. The initiative was also backed by Valentin Kuptsov and Liudmila Vartazarova, until recently Secretary of the Moscow City Committee of the CPSU.

Immediately after the publication, the initiative group of what would become the Socialist Workers' Party was flooded with phone calls from communists throughout the country. In London, Ken Coates, by then elected deputy of the European Parliament for the Labor Party, collected money on behalf of the SWP, which the party used to rent a small office in Moscow. The Founding Congress of the SWP, in which 315 delegates from sixty-eight regions took part, representing about five thousand members, took place on October 26, 1991, in a factory club in Moscow. By mid-November, the party had officially been registered, and on December 20–21, the First Congress of the SWP opened. The bulk of the 298 delegates were from the intelligentsia, 85 of them were people's deputies, and only 23 percent were workers and peasants. Adopting a model of collective leadership, the Congress elected seven co-chairs: Liudmila Vartazarova, Anatolii Denisov, Mikhail Lapshin, Aleksandr Mal'tsev, Roy Medvedev, Ivan Rybkin, and Gennadii Skliar. The decision to call the new formation "Socialist Workers' Party" rather than "communist" was a necessary distancing from the CPSU's legacy, which the SWP was not afraid to criticize. Yet many communists refused to forsake this historical legacy and shunned the SWP's lukewarm platform. In his speech at the congress, Medvedev inscribed the SWP's action within a long tradition of socialist thought, while recognizing the loss of authority of the CPSU and its past leaders among the population; the SWP's goal was therefore "to restore the attractive power of the ideas and practices of socialism." This would be done, the SWP's chairs believed, by combining the ideals of equality and fraternity with freedom, which the CPSU had neglected.

Roy Medvedev at the Congress of the SWP, December 1991. OKhDLSM, F. 333, op. 14, d. 39, l. 8.

In the following year, the SWP significantly increased its membership, up to two hundred thousand and established relations with left-wing parties in Western and Eastern Europe, the post-Soviet space and Asia. At the Fourth Congress of the SWP in February 1994, the party adopted a program, which insisted on the need to build a society in which the evils of both capitalism and the previous model of "state socialism" would be overcome. This program significantly departed from the CPSU's legacy: it recognized the need for a "socially oriented and regulated" market economy and called for pluralism in the political and economic realms. In relation to the legacy of Stalinism, the SWP recognized past accomplishments—identified as the people's—but also condemned Stalin's crimes. Finally, the SWP rejected the CPSU's authoritarian legacy and the dogma of the dictatorship of the proletariat: the state's role was to be limited to establishing the rule of law, without seeking to control civil society.

Roy Medvedev was also a member of the editorial committee of the SWP's bimonthly newspaper *Levaia Gazeta*, in which he (and occasionally Zhores) published articles. Initially, Roy contributed some of his honoraria to help fund the publication, but by 1993 the print run had reached one hundred thousand copies and the newspaper did not need any additional funding.

However, the party's influence remained limited, in part due to the lack of a charismatic figure at its head, but also because of the intense political competition between different left-wing parties with similar platforms. In 1993, after the Communist Party of the Russian Federation (CPRF) was founded, most of the SWP's members left for what is today the second party in Russia, and the SWP's membership fell to fifteen thousand members. Two of the SWP's most influential chairmen, Rybkin and Lapshin, were elected to the executive committee of the CPRF and participated in the creation of the "Agrarian Party of Russia" in February 1993. After retaining several affiliations for some time, they eventually left the SWP. Medvedev did not feel close to the CPRF's platform, in particular its glorification of Stalin, but he did have good relationships with CPRF leader Gennadii Ziuganov, about whom he wrote a sympathetic essay. The SWP also participated in the CPRF's first two Congresses, to which it sent delegates, but there was no extensive collaboration between the two parties.

Roy and Zhores Medvedev at a demonstration under the SWP banner, 1992.
OKhDLSM, F. 333, op. 14, d. 39, l. 5.

Although the SWP tried to occupy a middle ground in the increasingly polarized political system, the constitutional crisis of October 1993 forced its members to take sides. Faced with increasing opposition to his reforms from a united communist-patriotic front in the Supreme Soviet, President Yeltsin attempted to dissolve the Parliament. His opponents reacted by trying to impeach him and organized demonstrations in Moscow. When demonstrators moved to storm the Moscow mayor's offices and the Ostankino television tower, Yeltsin declared a state of emergency. The army shelled the Duma building and arrested the culprits. In this crisis, the SWP stood firmly on the Parliament's side. Several SWP members were deputies elected to the Supreme Soviet and belonged to the Communists' fraction. Yet Ivan Rybkin, one of the party's co-chairs at the time, abandoned the Duma building before the storming and entered into a compromise with Yeltsin. He was rewarded with the position of Speaker of the Parliament after the October 1993 elections. Roy Medvedev, who was at the time in Bonn on an invitation from German social-democratic deputies, recalled telling his audience: "What would you say, if here in Bonn, the President or the Chancellor unexpectedly dissolved the Bundestag, announced the cancellation of the Constitution of the GFR and called for the creation of new organs of power?"—"Russia is not Germany," replied one of the deputies. "He has obviously forgotten how quickly the Germans submitted to Hitler in 1933" commented Roy in a letter to this brother.

After 1993, the SWP remained too weak to exercise any significant influence on the political scene and could only present candidates within larger electoral coalitions. In the 1995 parliamentary elections, the SWP entered the coalition "Congress of Russian Communities" headed by General Aleksandr Lebed', but the coalition failed to reach the 5 percent threshold. Only three of the SWP's members, running under other banners, were elected to the Duma and Federation Council. At the 1995 presidential election, the SWP supported neither Yeltsin, nor Ziuganov. The lack of funding was another issue plaguing this largely volunteer-based political formation. Medvedev himself invested part of his income in the party, contributing between one hundred and one hundred fifty dollars a month to the publication of its newspaper *Levaia Gazeta* and occasionally paying the salary of board members of the party leadership. However, the lack of any big sponsor was a hindrance on the SWP's growth: according to Medvedev, the only large donation they received was from the Chinese Communist Party when he travelled to China in 1992.

As a member of the Socialist Workers' Party and a former member of the Central Committee, Roy Medvedev was also invited to take part in the constitutional hearings of the so-called trial of the CPSU in 1992. This did not constitute an equivalent of the Nuremberg trial. The Constitutional Court was tasked with examining an appeal by deputies of the Supreme Soviet concerning the constitutionality of Boris Yeltsin's decrees, issued in the aftermath of the August 1991 putsch, banning the CPSU and its Russian branch and nationalizing its property. Beyond the question of property, the trial was also an opportunity for Yeltsin's opponents to rewrite the history of the Communist Party, emphasizing the difference between the CPSU in Stalin's time and under Gorbachev. Roy Medvedev's testimony, condemning Stalinism but defending the Communist Party's right to existence, certainly held weight. In a TV interview on September 7, 1992, he insisted on the state of disarray of Russian society after the dissolution of the Soviet Union.

The court eventually confirmed the constitutionality of the ban on the CPSU's commanding structures and the confiscation of property with state or municipal ownership. Since the party itself had ceased to exist, the court could not judge the constitutionality of the party itself, but the dissolution of local party cells and seizure of the party's property were declared unconstitutional. This judgement opened the door to the foundation of the CPRF. Medvedev judged this compromise fair: what was condemned was not the communist idea but the political practice of the CPSU and Stalinism. It was also a victory for Yeltsin since it largely confirmed the validity of his decrees. The Russian President was himself a former "apparatchik" and had no interest in conducting a policy of lustration of former Communist cadres—a policy Medvedev judged impossible in the conditions of the time.

During the trial of the CPSU, Medvedev was shown archival documents about the Khrushchev and Brezhnev eras and about his own case, which Yeltsin had selected to try to influence his opponents and prove the CPSU's criminal record. Another participant in the trial, the dissident Vladimir Bukovskii, went further and scanned some of these documents, which he made public. The process of declassification of archival documents, however, was a long one, which would radically change the work of historians of the Soviet system. Although Medvedev continued to base most of his research on published sources, he also started using archival document in his historical works.

The 1990s were a period of great hardships for the vast majority of Russians: with the closure of unprofitable factories and the rise of unemployment, inflation combined with stagnation of salaries brought many people to the brink of starvation. Compared with the average Russian, Roy Medvedev enjoyed a privileged material situation. In addition to his regular collaboration with up to thirty Western and Russian newspapers, he occasionally received large honoraria in foreign currencies, for instance as a consultant for films. In addition to his Moscow apartment, which he eventually sold, he had bought a modest country house on the Western outskirts of Moscow. He faced difficulties of a different kind, however: with the rise of criminality, he did not feel safe and carried around a handgun bought by friends in Germany. After his house was burglarized, he had bars installed on his windows.

The economic shock of the 1990s also indirectly hit Zhores's family. After 1991, he began to travel every year to Russia, where he could access the libraries and archives necessary to his research and see his son's family. In 1994, he was granted an apartment in Obninsk in compensation for the loss of his flat in 1973. Zhores and Rita had always been absentee parents, but the years of separation with their elder son Sasha had not passed unnoticed. In later years, Zhores was inclined to believe that his son was a victim of the regime's repressive policies, a "hostage," just like Sakharov's stepchildren, who had to emigrate to the United States. Sasha had a troubled teenagerhood, and it is likely that the regime used this circumstance to pressure his father. "It wasn't anything particularly serious, anybody else would have gotten a slap on the wrist but he got locked up for seven years for hooliganism," remembered his brother Dima. The exile of his parents and brother when he was just twenty certainly did not help his rehabilitation process after prison, although Roy and Rita's family did their best to support him financially. In 1990 and 1993, Sasha visited his parents in London. He worked part time and depended on his parents' financial help to feed his family. But by 1994, he had lost his job and his health had deteriorated so much that he was hospitalized with pneumonia. In July 1996, he died of a stroke, leaving two daughters, aged eighteen and twelve. In his memoirs, Zhores preferred not to discuss his son's death in detail but explained it in the context of the general sanitary catastrophe which hit Russia in the Yeltsin era, following the economic crisis caused by "shock therapy" and the liberalization of vodka sales. Male life expectancy, in particular, plummeted due to the rise of alcoholism and suicide.

The fall of the Soviet Union also meant a change of status for Roy and Zhores Medvedev, who ceased to be Soviet dissidents and had to reinvent themselves as public figures. Initially, Roy had difficulties finding new themes of research. The deep changes his country was experiencing, the fall of the Soviet regime, the transition to democracy and capitalism were overwhelming for the majority of citizens in the post-Soviet space. But they were also disorienting for a historian and political analyst who had specialized in the study of the Soviet system. During the 1990s, Medvedev wrote a series of "political portraits": besides Stalin's close collaborators and other historical figures of the Soviet era, about whom new archival documents were becoming available, he published biographical essays on prominent politicians of the Yeltsin era.

As book sales dropped and invitations for paid lectures ceased in the 1990s, Zhores also had to reorient his activities. He turned to political analysis, writing newspaper articles for honoraria to supplement his small pension. The fall of the Soviet Union, which coincided with his retirement, gave a new impulse to his journalistic activities, and his first articles were published in over thirty newspapers around the world. In the following years, he also received numerous requests for comments on Yeltsin's economic and agrarian reforms, but his articles, which were highly critical of the Russian "shock therapy," were already at odds with the liberal consensus in the West. After Yeltsin's confrontation with the Russian Parliament in 1993, the pro-Yeltsin consensus in the Western media caused the Medvedev brothers to reorient their activities towards a Russian readership. Zhores flew to Moscow in mid-October 1993 to write articles for several European left-wing journals, which also appeared in Russia. In later years, his expertise continued to be in demand on a broad range of topics, from the consequences of the Chernobyl catastrophe to the wars in Chechnya or in Yugoslavia.

By 2005, Zhores had stopped publishing articles on political themes, which Roy, living in Russia, was better placed to write. But when Roy started writing the biography of Moscow mayor Iurii Luzhkov, whom he clearly admired, Zhores helped him place Luzhkov's management of Moscow in perspective, by comparing the Russian capital with London. He cautioned him: "You have to be moderate in your evaluations. Moscow is a bad, uncomfortable, unhealthy city." The poisoning of former FSB agent Aleksandr Litvinenko in Britain in 2006 also aroused Zhores's interest: he wrote a series of articles and a book on the case, questioning the official version about Russia's involvement in the assassination and drawing attention to Litvinenko's blackmailing of a Russian oligarch.

After retiring, Zhores started devoting a lot of his time to gardening. He and Rita had two vegetable plots in a neighboring cooperative. Millions of impoverished Russians had taken up this hobby in the 1990s to grow their own food in times of crisis, and Medvedev's essay "Six acres in London," published in the Russian newspaper *Your Six Acres*, had a lot of success. In 1999, the retired scientist started writing popularization articles on questions of health and longevity for the Russian press. In 2012, he published a book on the subject, entitled *Nutrition and Longevity*.

By the late 1990s, Roy had also found a new impulse, and resumed work at full speed, mostly on biographies of post-Soviet political actors. He no longer wrote for a Western audience, but concentrated on a Russian readership, although some of his books were still translated into Chinese, Japanese, or Serbian. He had a good sense of where the wind was blowing, politically speaking, and his accessible, highly readable publicistic works enjoyed success with the Russian public. Despite initially modest print runs, from one thousand to five thousand copies, he reached a larger audience by publishing several successively updated and enlarged editions of each title.

Roy and Zhores Medvedev in London, 2004. OKhDLSM, F. 333, Op. 14, d. 39, l. 9.

In 1998, he published an analysis of Russia's transition to market economy under the title *Post-Soviet Russia. A Journey Through the Eltsin Era* (in Russian: *Capitalism in Russia*). It examined Russia's transition to a market economy from 1991 to 1995. His appraisal of Yeltsin's rule was critical, and he chronicled popular disenchantment towards the new capitalist and political elites. In 2011, he published an equally critical biography of Boris Yeltsin, which started with the following admission:

> The political movement I participated in in the 1990s was in political opposition to Boris Yeltsin, and already for this reason I cannot consider myself a fully objective observer. And still, as a specialist of the history of the USSR and Russia I have no right to avoid either the times or the figure of Boris Yeltsin. The end of the twentieth century was not just a difficult time for Russia, it was a decade of chaos and decline, and absolutely not a period of blossoming of democracy… However, a historian cannot choose only the "best pages" for his work. One should also write about difficult, and even in some ways shameful times and deeds.

Roy Medvedev's appraisal of the 1990s, like the majority of his compatriots', was utterly negative. The end of Soviet rule had brought Russia neither democracy nor prosperity, and Yeltsin had squandered Russia's political capital, turning the country into a second- or third-rate power. After the failure of his political project, the Socialist Workers' Party, Medvedev gave up on political activities, concentrating instead on political and historical analysis. Ironically, his disappointment with political rulers of reformist orientation led him to stake instead on those rulers of the post-Soviet space who successfully restored their states' political and economic status on the international stage—even if this meant praising the same kind of authoritarian rule he had once combated.

Works Cited

"Delo KPSS - Byl li upushchen shans." *Radio Svoboda*, July 11, 2014. https://www.svoboda.org/a/25452052.html.

Medvedev, Roy. *Sovetskii Soiuz. Poslednie gody zhizni*. Moscow: Vremia, 2015.

———. "Vospominaniia. Poslednie dni Sovetskogo Parlamenta. Iz lichnykh vpechatlenii." *Novaia i noveishaia istoriia*, no. 2 (2003): 165–71.

Medvedev, Zhores. *Opasnaia professiia*. Moscow: Vremia, 2019.

"Zapis' besedy R.A. Medvedeva i S. Koena (Iiun' 1995 goda)." *Novaia i noveishaia istoriia*, no. 2 (2006): 94–101.

Further Reading

Bender, David L., Bruno Leone, and Bonnie Szumski. *The Collapse of the Soviet Union*. Paul A. San Diego: Greenhaven Press, 1999.

Smith, Jeremy. *The Fall of Soviet Communism*. London: Palgrave Macmillan, 2005.

CHAPTER 17

Praising the Strong Rulers

During his two-and-a-half years as a deputy of the Supreme Soviet, and as the head of a parliamentary commission, Roy Medvedev received access to a range of archival documents from the Supreme Court, the Procuracy, and the Central Committee that he could only have dreamed of in previous decades.

> For instance, I would come to the Supreme Court and tell the president, Smolentsev, that I needed the judicial protocols of the Galina Brezhneva affair. They gave me a separate office and brought me 14 or 15 volumes of interrogation protocols of Brezhnev's daughter and people around her. I could look at any criminal file that had gone through the Supreme Court. I had the right to access secret archives of the Central Committee of the CPSU... Gorbachev authorized me. But it was forbidden by special regulations to take any notes. I sat in the semi-basement where the archivist brought me documents, I read, memorized, and wrote down at home. There were more names, events, facts than I could grasp in one or two monthly visits... but I managed to conserve the most important facts and then made them public.

Based on these documents, he published first his biography of Brezhnev and then another of Andropov. Roy's interest in Andropov dated back to the 1960s, when the Soviet leader was still a Central Committee Secretary. Several of his acquaintances and university friends were then consultants in Andropov's team. As Medvedev remembered, "My friends often talked with great respect about Andropov, who, in terms of knowledge, intellect, and workstyle, was absolutely unlike any other Central Committee secretary." Medvedev's belief that Andropov had protected him from arrest also influenced his perception of the Soviet leader, which was largely positive.

Using his political position, Medvedev had shown his manuscript to those who had personally known Andropov: in the introduction, he listed no less than fifteen people among Andropov's former consultants, his Politburo and Central Committee Secretariat colleagues and KGB generals, whose testimonies he had used, including Bovin and Shakhnazarov, but also Gorbachev, Luk'ianov, Ryzhkov, and KGB head Kriuchkov. This insider perspective made it a unique biography. In December 1991, Medvedev published a series of articles on Andropov in *Sovetskaia Rossiia*, and a first version of the book came out in 1992 under the title *The General Secretary from the Lubianka*.

As usual, material gathered after the first publication, such as newly published memoirs, allowed Medvedev to prepare an expanded version of his work, with the assistance of Andropov's son Igor'. Yet, he faced difficulties in publishing his book: Russian publishers required publication at the author's own expense, and he had no offers from Western publishers. Unexpectedly, however, when Medvedev complained about the difficulties he faced during a visit to Japan in 1998, a friendly businessman offered to pay the ten thousand dollars demanded by the publisher to cover the editorial costs. *The Unknown Andropov* thus came out in 1999.

This publication coincided with a wave of sympathy for Iurii Andropov and, more broadly, the KGB and its post-Soviet heir, the FSB, which would lead to the election of Vladimir Putin to the Russian Presidency in 2000. In 1998, Andropov was the thirteenth most popular figures of the twentieth century among Russians. Medvedev's book, published in seven editions, contributed to the popularization of this figure. Andropov offered a positive counterpoint to Brezhnev's corrupt leadership and a "milder" instance of authoritarian rule than Stalin. As popular resentment mounted against the oligarchs, who had appropriated lucrative national assets at the expenses of simple folks, Russians looked back to Andropov's energetic campaign against corruption with approval. As the historian recognized in his introduction, Andropov's short career as General Secretary had revealed that a large segment of Soviet society longed for "order" and a "strong leader," concerned less with his own privileges than with the people's welfare. The same tendency could be observed within Russian society after a decade of chaotic political and economic reforms, which had led to the fall of the people's standard of living, a rise of criminality and national, and social conflicts.

Roy Medvedev's work on Andropov's biography led him into closer contact with the Russian secret services. Upon hearing about Medvedev's research, General-Lieutenant I.V. Rozanov, who had worked with Andropov in the KGB, offered to give the author important documents. When he died, shortly thereafter, a file entitled "For Roy Medvedev" was found in his office, and Deputy Director of the FSB Colonel-General Valerii Timofeev personally transmitted it to the historian. When the book came out in 1999, Medvedev sent a copy to Timofeev, who decided to offer it to then FSB Director Vladimir Putin. Soon, Medvedev received an invitation to give a talk at the FSB headquarters for the celebrations of Andropov's eighty-fifth birth anniversary on June 15, 1999. Medvedev was intrigued by this invitation—wasn't he, a former dissident, an unlikely guest to celebrate the birthday of a KGB head?—but he accepted it.

This somewhat coincidental chain of events had unexpected consequences for Roy Medvedev. Just as his 1964 encounter with Andropov may have sealed his fate, Medvedev's 1999 meeting with the man who would rule Russia for the next several decades was a turning point in his career. Medvedev believed that Putin had singled out his biography of Andropov because it was written most sympathetically. The celebrations were part of Putin's strategy to rebrand the FSB to break with the legacy of the Stalin era. They included laying wreaths at Andropov's bust at the FSB headquarters on Lubianka square and at his grave on Red Square. Putin greeted Medvedev at his arrival to the FSB headquarters and told him he had read parts of his book and liked it. Sixty-six generals of the FSB, including former directors, had been invited to the celebrations and attended Medvedev's forty-minute talk. No questions were asked. Medvedev was favorably impressed by the honors he received and by Putin's friendly offer to help him, which he would remember in times of need. The historian was also invited to give a talk at the FSB Academy and was interviewed in several films about Andropov broadcast for the celebrations. In 2007, Medvedev received the FSB's First Prize for his biography of Andropov. The ideological transformation of the former dissident turned biographer of a KGB head was complete. Those who had always denounced Medvedev as a KGB agent did not need any other evidence, but when he also turned into Putin's main hagiographer, he lost his last dissident credentials.

As soon as Putin was elected President of the Russian Federation, Roy Medvedev set out to analyze his political action, starting with *The Putin Enigma* (2000), the first of a long series of books on the Russian leader. He expressed the hope that Putin would live up to the expectations of Russian citizens who had elected him. "In the end we do not have much of a choice: either order or the continuation of unrest and chaos." Although little was yet known of Putin's moral qualities, Medvedev found this aspect secondary, for leaders with high moral standards, such as Yeltsin or Gorbachev, had tended to evade difficult decisions, letting others take responsibility to keep their own hands clean. Answering criticism about Putin's career in the KGB, Medvedev argued that the

President had not been involved in political repression but worked in the prestigious intelligence services. Comparing Putin with Andropov, Medvedev noted that the latter had raised many hopes, but had immediately resorted to strict measures to restore order, including against dissidents. "Russia today is also in dire need of order and stability. But maybe Putin will be able to combine order and legality in Russia with real liberalism and reasonable democracy."

As he explained in interviews, Medvedev had grown fond of Putin while working on his books, and this was reflected in his analysis. However, he emphasized that he was not driven by the kind of naïve admiration widespread among Russians. He was not blind to Putin's complexity and contradictions, and recognized his occasional mistakes, although he praised his honesty and his pragmatism. Still, he recognized in 2011:

> I will not hide that I write about Putin to some extent with the aim of supporting him. I wrote all my books about Putin with an element of sympathy, but I tried to be as objective as possible. I saw in his action a chance for Russia. I, as a citizen, am not indifferent to the fate of my country . . . At the moment, I am happy with this fate, with the way power is exercised. In these works, I spoke not as a historian but rather as a political analyst, a participant in events, which are happening around us.

After Putin's first term, Medvedev published *Vladimir Putin: Four years in the Kremlin*. It was followed in 2006 by *Vladimir Putin: a second term* (an enlarged edition of which appeared a year later under the title *Vladimir Putin: no third term?*). In these books, Medvedev provided a sympathetic overview of Putin's first years in power, a period during which, according to the author, "Russia has made important progress in almost all fields." Based on Putin's declaration that he would not seek a third term—a possibility ruled out by the Constitution—Medvedev concluded that Moscow mayor Iurii Luzhkov was the best candidate to succeed Putin as President. However, to avoid sliding into dictatorial rule it was crucial to transfer some of the President's excessive powers by strengthening the role of the government and political parties, especially the ruling party "United Russia." This, in Medvedev's view, could be best accomplished by nominating Putin Prime Minister.

In 2010, Medvedev published *Vladimir Putin. To be continued*. In the preface, he wrote that this book would end the series he had started on Putin as a president. It gave an appraisal of his first eight years in power, underlining that the eighth year had been "the most successful for [Putin] and for Russian society.

Russia is healing and healing fast. But we are not talking about a return to the past. Russia is developing as a country in line with the demands and challenges of the twenty-first century." Following the chaos engendered by the fall of Tsarism in 1917 and the fall of the Soviet Union in 1991, Putin had focused on the main priority: "the strengthening of the new Russian statehood." This did not mean reinforcing the President's personal power but required a broadening of his power base by increasing the responsibility and independence of office holders. When Dmitrii Medvedev was elected President in 2008, the historian released two books about his namesake: *Dmitrii Medvedev: President of the Russian Federation* (2008) and *Dmitrii Medvedev: The Double Stability of Power* (2010).

Arguably his most significant work on Putin, however, was a full-scale biography published in 2007 by "Molodaia Gvardiia" in the series "Life of Remarkable People," traditionally devoted to heroes of the past. According to Medvedev, Putin initially opposed the project but after reading Medvedev's manuscript, he approved of the publication. In the interests of objectivity, however, there were no consultations prior to writing the book, Medvedev insisted. This did not prevent his critics from calling the book a hagiography and accusing the author of "groveling" before Putin. They were only split on the matter of whether the book had been ordered by the Kremlin or was Medvedev's own initiative. Slanderous accusations of Medvedev's alleged collaboration with the KGB surfaced as a possible explanation for his praise of the former KGB agent Putin. Needless to say, these works did not meet the acclaim of the Western public. Medvedev's first book on Putin was translated by the US State Department and edited for internal use only but did not interest any American publisher. The winds had changed, and the West was no longer interested in a sympathetic view of Russia and Putin.

Medvedev did write about Putin of his own initiative, yet one cannot say that he did not draw any personal benefit from the situation. In 2007, as he faced health issues, he sent the President a new year card, reminding him of their first encounter and Putin's offer to help him. Putin's reaction was prompt. Two weeks later, the historian received a call from the President's Main Medical Administration with an offer to check into their hospital for treatment. Overall, he received treatment four times in the Kremlin hospital and was successfully restored to health.

In 2010, on Medvedev's eighty-fifth birthday, Putin, who was then Prime Minister, invited Roy Medvedev to his residency in Novo-Ogarevo to hand him an honorary certificate. Medvedev brought several of his books as presents for Putin and his family, and he observed during the conversation that the Russian leader was familiar with his work. In the end, Putin asked him if there was any problem that he could help him solve. "At the moment I am in good health," replied Medvedev, "but I would like to publish my collected works." Putin picked up his phone and arranged for the publication of sixteen volumes of collected works of the Medvedev brothers. They were released with the financial support of the Federal Agency of Press and Mass communications by the publisher "Vremia," which had edited Andrei Sakharov's and Aleksandr Solzhenitsyn's collected works.

Although Roy Medvedev recognized that he never wrote critically of leaders in power, his positive opinion of Putin remained constant, even after the beginning of the 2022 war on Ukraine. He had been working with his coauthor Dmitrii Andreev, a historian from Moscow State University, on a new edition of his Putin biography, initially planned to be published for the leader's seventieth birthday in October 2022. However, as events were unfolding on the Ukrainian front, the historian had to postpone this publication and decided to work instead on a book to be entitled *Vladimir Putin in 2022*. Yet the Putin administration still counted on him for the jubilee: in September 2022, Rafael Guseinov, who had published several volumes of interviews with Medvedev in the past, released another one under the title *Putin's Path*, richly illustrated by seventy color photographs of the President. According to Medvedev, the publication had been ordered by Putin's press secretary Dmitrii Peskov and it was subjected to extensive post-editing, with whole paragraphs being attributed post factum to Medvedev, including a critique of the organization Memorial, dissolved in December 2021 by orders of the Russian Supreme Court. Yet it makes no doubt that Medvedev's words of appraisal of the President's "special operation" in Ukraine, recorded in April 2022, were heartfelt: he praised both the President's role as Supreme Commander and the Russian armed forces, and duly condemned Ukrainian "nationalism."

Roy Medvedev's enthusiastic support for Putin was not an isolated incident in his political biography. It coincided with his generally positive appraisal of those (generally authoritarian) post-Soviet leaders who had managed to maintain or restore order in their fiefdoms. In the early 2000s, the historian had plans to write a large study on the post-Soviet republics. Although this project remained unpublished, he did dedicate several works to individual states and their leaders, especially those for whom he harbored sympathies. In the late Soviet period, as he was a member of the Supreme Soviet, and then of the Central Committee of the Party, he made the acquaintance of several leaders of Soviet republics who remained in power into the post-Soviet era. In the framework of his work as head of the Gdlian and Ivanov commission, Medvedev met Islam Karimov,

Uzbekistan's supreme leader from 1990 to 2016. He gained Karimov's sympathy by largely whitewashing the Uzbek leadership regarding Gdlian and Ivanov's accusations of corruption. The commission did uncover instances of bribe-taking but shied away from inquiring further into a system that existed on similar levels in many Soviet republics, and which involved a vast network of actors, with potentially explosive interethnic ramifications.

Medvedev had also followed with attention the career of two Caucasian leaders who conducted energetic anti-corruption campaigns in their respective republics: Eduard Shevardnadze and Heydar Aliyev. He had more sympathy for the latter than the former, and when Aliyev became a Politburo member and First Deputy Premier of the USSR in 1982, Medvedev published an enthusiastic article about him in the Western press. Medvedev believed that the Azerbaijani leader read the article and liked it, and although the two men never met, the historian later received repeated invitations to Azerbaijan and requests for interviews about Aliyev. Medvedev, however, turned down a request to write the biography of Ilham Aliyev, Heydar's son and successor.

The figure Medvedev found most enticing in the post-Soviet space was Nursultan Nazarbayev, president of Kazakhstan from 1990 to 2019. Medvedev remembered that at every Central Committee plenum that he attended, the Kazakh leader, a Politburo member since 1990, spoke not only eloquently but with "a clear intellectual superiority in his understanding of political and economic problems." Medvedev's first encounter with Nazarbayev confirmed his positive impression: he found him a "strong, calm, very talented person." They met again in 1992, when Medvedev travelled to Kazakhstan. In the turmoil of the last Soviet years, Medvedev and his colleagues hoped for a figure of authority such as Nazarbayev to be elected Prime Minister, and to make up for Gorbachev's indecisiveness. When Gorbachev created the position of President of the USSR for himself, he considered offering the position of Vice-President to Nazarbayev. However, Gorbachev was probably unwilling to have a potential strong competitor at his side. Nor was Nazarbayev inclined to accept a purely honorific position without any real power. In retrospect, Medvedev believed that Nazarbayev's appointment as Prime Minister could have saved the USSR from dissolution, instead of which Gorbachev staked on two "weak" politicians to fill the top positions—a choice he later regretted.

When Medvedev began to work on a study of post-Soviet states in 2005–2006, he visited the embassies of countries to obtain information. The Kazakh ambassador immediately seized the potential of this visit and invited the historian to write a book on their national leader. Medvedev accepted, on the condition that documentary material would be made available to him and that he would be invited to visit the country. Nazarbayev, who still remembered Medvedev, penned the official invitation himself. The historian was treated as a guest of honor during his whole stay and granted access to archives. During the writing process, Medvedev sent chapters for review to Imangali Tasmaganbetov, one of Nazarbayev's closest collaborators, and the President himself read and annotated the manuscript. In 2008, Nazarbayev's daughter organized a reception at the embassy to celebrate the publication. Medvedev's overwhelmingly positive assessment of Nazarbayev's regime could not but please the Kazakh leadership, and *Kazakhstanskaia Pravda*, the main government-backed newspaper, published excerpts of the biography.

Medvedev's enthusiastic introduction showed that he identified post-Soviet Kazakhstan as a counter-model to the failed democratic experiment in Russia.

> How, without resorting to violence and repression, avoiding chaos, civil wars and acute interethnic conflicts, without shooting at one's parliament and without overthrowing previous leaders, without subjecting one's country to the will of other states and without entering into conflict with any of them, but with the force of the intellect, will, convictions, by way of skillful diplomacy and with the support of the overwhelming majority of the people, did the leadership of Kazakhstan manage to maintain continuity in the country's governance and walk the difficult path of radical reform in the economic and political system, the social system and all other spheres of national and state construction?

Although Medvedev stated in his introduction that he had asked to read opposition publications, he clearly did not sympathize with Nazarbayev's opponents, who, in his view, "continue to put on a show of mayhem and internal division, while calling on the population to join mass actions of civil disobedience" intended to "weaken the position of the head of state."

Medvedev's flattering study of Kazakhstan was a tempting propaganda stunt for another dictator whom Medvedev held in good esteem: Aleksandr Lukashenko, President of Belarus. Longest-serving head of state in the post-Soviet space, often called "Europe's last dictator," Lukashenko has been in power since 1994 and has resisted more than one popular revolt, including a serious revolutionary situation in 2020. When Medvedev received a request from the Belarusian administration to write a book about Lukashenko, he replied that he was ready to fulfil the order, provided the necessary material was placed at his disposal: newspaper archives, including from the oppositional press, official documents, and books. Sometime later, a whole pouch was delivered on Medvedev's doorstep, containing the documents he had requested.

After working over this material for a year and writing the first chapters, the historian decided to visit Belarus on a trip funded and organized through the Belarusian Embassy. However, when Medvedev found out that the official program of his visit only included a press conference, a visit of Minsk, and an exhibition of his works at a library, without any lectures, he refused to abide by the planned schedule. His hosts, who had certainly hoped to limit Medvedev's contacts with civil society to the bare minimum, were embarrassed when he adamantly demanded to speak with university students and professors and meet oppositional figures and scholars he had singled out. They advised him to raise the issue directly with the President.

The next day, during his meeting with Lukashenko, Medvedev volunteered his expertise to both entertain and please his host, offering to tell him what Russians thought about him. Lukashenko apparently appreciated Medvedev's informative analysis and frankness. Finally, at the end of the conversation, Medvedev raised the question of his program of visits and the length of his stay, which the Administration wanted to limit to a few days. Lukashenko replied: "Roy Aleksandrovich, what are you talking about! You're our guest and you can go wherever you want and do whatever you like!" Medvedev's meetings with oppositional figures, however, did not alter his altogether very positive impression of the Lukashenko regime. He considered that the opposition held "wrong views" on Belarus's history and was not in a position to rule. When I interviewed him in late 2020, Medvedev conceded that the regime was authoritarian and that Lukashenko should have stepped down, yet he still considered his record to be overwhelmingly positive. What he praised was Lukashenko's loyalty to the Soviet heritage, his choice to retain many of the Soviet economic and social structures, and the country's industrial base, his close partnership with Russia and rejection of the nationalist path adopted by Ukraine. The book pleased Lukashenko and was published twice in Belarus and once in Russia.

Through the Belarusian and Kazakhstani models, Medvedev was looking for positive alternative paths of economic development, which he judged preferable to the Russian shock therapy of the Yeltsin era. In the backdrop of his praise of the stable political order of these countries, one could sense which countermodel he constantly had in mind: Ukraine. His study of Russia's close neighbor, published in 2007, focused on Ukrainian politics, economy, and identity issues. The title *Divided Ukraine* reflected the author's critical stance towards a country, which, three years after the "Orange Revolution," appeared deeply divided between a nationalist, Ukrainian-speaking West and a Russophile, Russian-speaking East. Like many of his fellow countrymen, Medvedev considered Ukraine an instance of political and national failure: the country was economically inefficient, suffered from a range of political, linguistic and national divisions, and was politically instable. The historian contrasted this situation with that of Kazakhstan, which, under the energetic leadership of Nursultan Nazarbayev, had overcome its divisions by focusing on economic development first. He considered that instead of eternally looking backwards to the Soviet past, Ukraine should look into the future. Only after catering to its population's most pressing economic problems would the choice of a political orientation, whether eastward or westward, make sense.

While Roy Medvedev had become famous in the 1970s for his publications in the West criticizing Soviet authoritarianism, by the 2000s he had made a fundamental U-turn and fully reoriented his research towards a Russian and post-Soviet readership, but also a Chinese audience.

During his student years, Medvedev had read with enthusiasm translations by fellow students and professors of texts by Mao, Liu Shaoqi, Zhou Enlai and other Chinese communist leaders, and written his diploma thesis on the "Specificities of the Chinese Revolution." In the 1980s, many of Medvedev's books were published in China for scholarly use only. In 1986, he published *China and the Superpowers*, which was followed by a series of articles about this country.

After the fall of the Soviet Union, Medvedev received an official invitation to visit China from the Chinese Academy of Social Sciences. During his twenty-day stay he met with high-ranking party officials who recorded a four-hour interview with him concerning the reasons for the fall of the Soviet Union. He spoke in front of young members of the administration and at Chinese universities. In 2002, he visited the country for the second time. Ten years later, he published *China's Rise*, a book giving a sympathetic view on the Chinese economic and political model, without much afterthought for the lack of democracy in the country. Although Medvedev noted the problem of corruption, he added that the Chinese authorities had vigorously combated this phenomenon. Medvedev's collaboration with Chinese publishers and journals has remained strong: his books sold well in the country, and in 2020–2021 he released two successive versions of a book coauthored with Dmitrii Andreev, a Russian China expert, comparing the leadership of Vladimir Putin and Xi Jinping, written on order from a Chinese publisher.

Roy Medvedev in his home office, Nemchinovka, 2002. OKhDLSM, F. 333, Op. 3, d. 16, l. 1.

The Medvedev brothers' interest in the figure of Stalin never waned. Throughout the post-Soviet years, Stalin's popularity has been steadily rising from 1989 to 2017, the proportion of Russians who considered him the most brilliant person in history had risen from 12 to 38 percent, and since 2012, Stalin has been ranking first in all popularity polls in Russia. The Medvedev brothers, who lived under Stalin's rule the first twenty-eight years of their lives, wanted to offer what they considered to be an "objective" view on Stalin as a political and military leader, and as a person. They disagreed both with works rehabilitating the Soviet leader and with those presenting the Stalin era in an exclusively negative light. With the opening of archives, new possibilities arose to study this fascinating and at once repulsive figure. They were keen to find out what happened to Stalin's archive, which seemed to have disappeared. Other topics interesting them were the relations between Stalin and Lysenko, but also the history of the "atomic Gulag," where thousands of prisoners and internal exiles extracted uranium in appalling conditions or worked on the Soviet atomic project during the Stalin era.

In 1998, the Medvedev brothers decided to collect these various essays under one cover. Their book *The Unknown Stalin*, five editions of which came out between 2001 and 2011, with translations into twelve languages, had little in common with *Let History Judge*. If the book served a political purpose, it was to back Vladimir Putin's attempt to give a "balanced" evaluation of the Soviet leader. It was a compilation of previously published sources focusing on various key aspects of Stalin's leadership and legacy, with occasional personal remembrances or testimonies of witnesses. As non-professional historians, the Medvedev brothers did not have the institutional support and funding necessary to undertake large-scale archival research. But they had experience working with memoirs and oral testimonies, which could help answer historical enquiries for which no archival documents existed. Some chapters shed light on unsolved mysteries or little-known questions, such as the enigma surrounding Stalin's death, which had raised rumors of an assassination. More unexpected was the chapter "What did Stalin read?" describing not only Stalin's personal literary tastes, but also his censorship of literature. Stalin's repressive actions were central to chapters on his Jewish politics or the execution of Stalin's political opponent Nikolai Bukharin in 1938 and his negative role in Soviet science was examined based on the examples of history, biology, linguistics, and military science. The format of the book allowed the authors to publish several expanded editions, based on new material. It was translated into Japanese, English, Serbian, Czech, Slovak, Greek, Italian, Spanish and Brazilian Portuguese. The book was acknowledged as an original work and received positive reviews, although the Medvedevs' attempt to make Stalin appear more "human" also raised some criticism.

An essay on Stalin and the Jewish question, which Zhores had initially prepared for an enlarged Russian edition of *The Unknown Stalin*, was finally published as a separate book in 2003. Although Robert Tucker, one of the most prominent experts on Stalin, praised the manuscript for its good coverage of the subject and readability, it was not translated into English. Medvedev believed that his book raised eyebrows in the West because it denied that the goal of the 1953 "Doctors' Plot" was to justify a large-scale deportation of Jews to the far-eastern Jewish Republic of Birobidzhan. Solzhenitsyn's book *Two Hundred Years Together*, published in 2001–2002, adopted the same perspective on the question, but the author's overall framework was judged antisemitic by many reviewers.

Roy Medvedev's gallery of flattering portraits of authoritarian rulers, although little known in the West, certainly sheds a different light on the man once hailed as a Soviet dissident. His reconversion, however, mirrored the political evolution of the Russian people, who enthusiastically greeted the return of law and order in the 2000s after a decade of upheaval and scarcity.

Works Cited

Medvedev, Roi, and Rafael' Guseinov. *Medvedev o Putine*. Moscow: Izdatel'skii dom "Tribuna," 2012.

Medvedev, Roi. *Aleksandr Lukashenko. Kontury belorusskoi modeli*. Moscow: ZAO "BBPG," 2010.

———. *Nursultan Nazarbaev. Kazakhstanskii proryv i evraziiskii proekt*. Moscow: ZAO "BBPG," 2008.

———. *Raskolotaia Ukraina*. Moscow: INES MAIB, 2007.

———. *Zagadka Putina*. Moscow: Izdatel'stvo "Prava Cheloveka," 2000.

Rykovtseva, Elena. "'Vladimir Putin' Roia Medvedeva: Pochemu izdatel'stvo pozvoliaet avtoram obozhat' svoikh vlastnykh geroev." Radio Svoboda, January 29, 2008. https://www.svoboda.org/a/432522.html.

"Vydaiushchiesia liudi," *Levada-Tsentr*, June 26, 2017, https://www.levada.ru/2017/06/26/vydayushhiesya-lyudi/

Further Reading

Smith, Kathleen E. *Mythmaking in the New Russia*. Politics and Memory in the Eltsin Era. Cornell University Press, 2018.

Conclusion

Roy and Zhores Medvedev's questionable political record certainly explains why, despite their historical role in the denunciation of Stalin's crimes, they have attracted much less academic attention than Solzhenitsyn or Sakharov. In April 2021, Radio Liberty devoted two of its broadcasts to these "strange dissidents." The presenter Ivan Tolstoi and his guest Andrei Gavrilov both recalled the strong impression that the Medvedevs' works had produced on them when they first read them in samizdat and tamizdat. Yet the Medvedevs' later declarations—or rather these statements as reflected through the distorting lens of other dissidents' memoirs—cast a shadow on their previous activities. Long before Roy Medvedev received the FSB's Prize for his Andropov biography and his book on Putin was called hagiographical, the harsh words of Solzhenitsyn, Sakharov, and Bukovskii had seriously tarnished his and his brother's reputation. In the early 1980s, Western newspapers still closely followed Roy Medvedev's fate, but many journalists called him a "non-conformist" rather than a dissident historian.

It has not been my goal to prove or disprove the applicability of the label of "dissident" in relation to the Medvedev brothers. Roy Medvedev was certainly not a dissident when he started writing *Let History Judge* in 1962, nor was he one when he was elected People's Deputy and reinstated into the party in 1989. Zhores Medvedev did not perceive himself as a dissident when he wrote his history of Lysenko's sway over Soviet biology. One may easily argue that the West created dissidents for its own propaganda needs and picked the figures who matched the role at a given time. Zhores Medvedev's highly publicized incarceration in a psychiatric ward made him an ideal candidate for the role of a martyr for truth at the hands of the Soviet regime. But in the end, the Medvedevs did not quite fit the bill: they never turned anti-communist and always retained some degree of loyalty, if not to the regime in its current incarnation, then at least to its ideology and founding elements.

The Medvedev brothers continued to occupy the Western media stage throughout the 1970s and 1980s primarily because they were prolific and well-informed authors with indubitable publicistic talent, whose independent analyses about the Soviet system still had the aura of "dissent." While Roy smartly navigated the stormy waters of KGB surveillance, Zhores no less skillfully negotiated publishing contracts and toured Western universities. What distinguished them from other dissidents was certainly their pragmatism, a quality at odds with the idealism of their peers, which allowed them not only to remain afloat throughout the Soviet era but also to make the dangerous leap into the post-Soviet years and find success in an entirely new political context. Whether or not one approves of the turn taken by their publishing activities after the fall of the Soviet Union, it remains a fact that they continued to occupy the media stage and to find readers, this time predominantly in their homeland.

Ironically, the Medvedev brothers proved most influential politically not as dissidents but as loyal supporters of political leaders whose actions they found constructive for their country, from Khrushchev to Putin. It was to support the Communist party's de-Stalinization policy that Roy Medvedev undertook his research *Let History Judge* and published *On Socialist Democracy*. Zhores was more independent politically, but he shared Roy's optimistic view that détente would bring about a democratization of the Soviet system. Constructive criticism was their hallmark, and some Soviet politicians perceived the difference between this loyal dissent and Solzhenitsyn's anti-communist opposition.

Moreover, the Medvedevs were prepared to moderate their criticism of negative aspects of Soviet or post-Soviet reality if they considered that a certain policy or leader should be supported. Perhaps Roy Medvedev's tragedy was an excess of faith in rulers who proved not quite up to the task and who ended up disappointing him. Khrushchev was inconsistent in his anti-Stalinist policies and was overthrown. Gorbachev, who came to power to realize Medvedev's ideal of socialist democracy, ended up witnessing, powerless, the fall of the Soviet Union. These disappointments may in part explain why the historian welcomed Putin's stable and predictable rule, even though it was neither socialist, nor democratic.

Some may say that the Medvedev brothers suffered from an excessive longevity: had they retired after the fall of the Soviet Union, they would certainly have gone down in history as Soviet dissidents. The history of their post-Soviet careers was murkier and ceased to interest Western audiences. When NATO bombed Kosovo in 1999, both Roy and Zhores wrote op-eds criticizing Western intervention, which were published in the Western press. These would be Roy Medvedev's last publications in the Western media: as he complained at the end of his life, his position had become unpalatable to a Western audience. Despite offers made to several publishers, his books on Putin were not published in the West. Western Russophobia was not a fundamentally new factor, but the Medvedev brothers' evolution from dissidents into supporters of Putin's regime certainly affected their reception in the West. Roy's friendship with Stephen

Cohen, who suffered from similar ostracism, continued until the American historian's death in 2020.

Both Roy and Zhores remained intellectually fit and prodigiously productive until the end of their lives. Zhores managed to write extensive memoirs, first serialized in a Ukrainian weekly and then partly published posthumously under the title *A Dangerous Profession*. The two brothers also published memoirs about famous intellectuals they had known (*Solzhenitsyn and Sakharov: Two Prophets* [2002]; *Selected Memoirs* [2010]). The two brothers remained in close contact: Zhores travelled every year to Obninsk in September to collect his Russian pension and meet his granddaughters. From 2002 to 2006, Roy also visited Zhores in London every summer. A picture from his first trip shows him and Zhores standing next to Karl Marx's grave. Zhores passed away on November 15, 2018, the day after his and Rita's birthday.

Roy and Zhores Medvedev in front of Marx's grave, London, 2003.
OKhDLSM, F. 333, Op. 14, d. 39, l. 6.

When I first visited Roy Medvedev in 2012, he had already left Moscow to settle in the Moscow suburbs with his son's family. He was proud of his twin granddaughters Galina and Larisa, born in 2001, both of whom have become European Taekwondo champions. Despite surviving his wife's passing in 2016 and Zhores's death in 2018, he continued unperturbed to complete one research project after another. Just as he remained the last prominent dissident out of prison in the 1980s, he seems intent on surviving all his dissident peers and remains one of the last witnesses to this bygone era.

Works Cited

Medvedev, Roy, and Zhores Medvedev. *Neizvestnyi Stalin*. Moskva: Vremia, 2007.

Tolstoi, Ivan, and Andrei Gavrilov. "Sotsializm forever. Strannyi dissident Roi Medvedev," *Radio Svoboda*, May 30, 2021, https://www.svoboda.org/a/31280092.html.

Tolstoi, Ivan, and Andrei Gavrilov. "Strannyi dissident Zhores Medvedev," *Radio Svoboda*, April 21, 2021, https://www.svoboda.org/a/31221136.html.

Index

Abovin-Egides, Petr, 134–37, 138, 146
Abramov, Ivan, 161–62
Abuladze, Tengiz, 181
Afanasiev, Iurii, 186
Afghanistan, 159
Aftenposten, 123
Agapova, Liudmila, 156, 158
Agitprop, 123
Agnew, Harold, 172
Akhmatova, Anna, 181
Akhromeev, Sergei, 195
Al'tshuler, Semion, 80
Albania, 33
Albion, 113
Albuquerque, 172–73
Aliyev, Heydar, 214
Aliyev, Ilham, 214
America. *See* United States
Amsterdam, 92
Andreev, Dmitrii, 213, 217
Andreeva, Nina, 182, 184
Andreyeva Carlisle, Olga, 64
Andropov, Iurii, 51–52, 68–69, 81, 85, 87, 92, 94, 153–55, 159–65, 208–211, 221
APN, press agency, 126, 133
Arbatov, Georgii, 52, 160
Argentina, 104
Argonne National laboratory, 113, 171–72
Argumenty i Fakty, newspaper, 184
Armenia, 32, 49, 191
Arzamas, 66, 69
Astaurov, Boris, 25, 29–30, 66, 80

Astrachan, Anthony, 91–92
Astrakhan, 5
Auerbach, Stanley, 171–72
Austria, 87, 162
Avtorkhanov, Abdurrakhman, 141–42
Azerbaijan, 49, 214
Azov, 13

Baital'skii, Mikhail, 130, 133
Bakhteev, Fatikh, 25
Baku, 6, 14
Baltic region, 1, 81, 188
Baltimore, 72, 113
Baranov, Vadim, 156–58
Barghoorn, Frederick, 108
Bass, Boris, 179
BBC, 67, 101, 174
Belarus, 7, 215–16
Benn, Tony, 166
Beria, Lavrentii, 39, 49
Berlin, 27
Birobidzhan, Jewish Republic of, 219
Black Sea, 1, 8, 13, 80, 94
Bliss, Chester, 23
Bloomington, 169
Bobkov, Fipip, 144
Böll, Heinrich, 145
Bolsheviks, 48, 52–53, 57, 59, 80, 86, 90, 96, 124–25, 139, 141
Bonn, 202
Bonner, Elena, 117, 141
Borovsk, 82, 97, 99, 102
Boston, 113
Bovin, Aleksandr, 26, 51, 81, 160, 209
Brandt, Willy, 162

Brezhnev, Leonid, 1, 29, 51–52, 59–60, 81, 84, 88, 109, 116, 137, 142, 147, 149, 154, 159–61, 164–65, 182, 189, 203, 208–9
Brezhneva, Galina, 208
Bristol, 77
Britain, 23, 45, 205
Brno, 74
Brodskii, Iosif, 78
Brooke, Gerald, 168
Brumberg, Abraham, 168
Buffalo, 115
Bukharin, Nikolai, 9, 11, 53, 55, 145, 151, 219
Bukovskii, Vladimir, 97, 203, 221
Bulgaria, 33, 46
Bundestag, 202
Burg, David, 120
Burgen, Arnold, 103
Burlatskii, Fedor, 26, 52, 160
Burlington, 168
Buzina (Medvedeva), Margarita, 4, 20, 27, 76, 79, 101, 104, 106, 149, 166, 175, 181, 193, 204–5, 223
Byelorussia. *See* Belarus

Carter, Jimmy, 135, 173
Caspian Sea, 5, 20
Caucasus, 6, 32, 36, 43, 49, 195
CBS, 159
Central Asia, 26, 189, 200
Chagin, Boris, 41–42
Chalidze, Valerii, 80, 91, 100, 113
Chebotarev, Vladimir, 179
Chebrikov, Viktor, 163
Chechnya, 205
Cheliabinsk, 170–71, 176
Chernenko, Konstantin, 153, 164–65
Chernobyl, 169, 174–77, 205
Chicago, 113, 172
Chiesa, Giulietto, 145, 152–53, 164, 166
Children of the Arbat, 181

China, 33–34, 36, 38, 52, 122, 145, 202, 217
Christian Science Monitor, The, newspaper, 115
Chukhrai, Grigorii, 59
Chukovskaia, Lidiia, 116–17
Churganov, Anatolii, 158–59
CIA, 68, 72, 102, 154, 171–74
Ciba Foundation, 72–73
CIS, 214
Civil War, 5–6, 9, 38–39, 48–49, 107, 145
Cleveland, 115
Coates, Ken, 108, 118, 162–63, 166, 199
Cohen, Stephen, 151, 223
Columbia University, 75–76
Columbus, 172
Comfort, Alex, 99, 113
Connecticut, 168
Cornell, 115
Corriere della Sera, newspaper, 152
CPRF, 201, 203
CPSU, 24, 26, 73, 85, 90, 140, 154, 157–58, 185, 191, 195–200, 202–3, 208
Crick, Francis, 21
Crimea, 20, 28, 62, 195
Cronkite, Walter, 159
Cullen, Robert, 164–65
Czechoslovakia, 33, 61, 69, 74, 87, 118, 137, 159

Daily Telegraph, newspaper, 92, 123
Dallas, 173
Daniel, Iulii, 60, 92, 138
Danilov, Viktor, 93, 95
Darwin, Charles, 129
Darwinism, 17–18
Delbrück, Max, 113
Deliusin, Lev, 52
Denisov, Anatolii, 199
Dershowitz, Alan, 97
Dobzhansky, Theodosius, 75, 113

Doctors Plot, 219
Dolinin, Viacheslav, 4
Dudintsev, Vladimir, 59, 181
Duma, 202
Dvadtsatyi vek, journal, 126, 129–30, 133–36, 143, 145

Ecuador, 104
Edinburgh, 23
Efroimson, Vladimir, 20, 24–25
Egorychev, Nikolai, 28
Ehrenburg, Il'ia, 47, 55, 59
Ekaterinburg, 36, 170
Engelgardt, Vladimir, 25, 28, 30, 73
Engels, Friedrich, 32, 129
England, 45, 73, 133, 140, 169
Esenin-Vol'pin, Aleksandr, 60, 156
Estonia, 94
Europe, 27, 36, 171, 177, 200
Evanston, 113, 168
Ezhov, Nikolai, 11

Fedorov, Evgenii, 169
Feifer, George, 120
Finland, Gulf of, 43
Fireglow, 55
Ford, Gerald, 115–16
France, 87–88, 117, 133, 140
Frolov, Evgenii, 58
FSB, 205, 209–210, 221
Fukushima, 169
Fulbright, William, 115–16, 125, 168

Gaevets, Mikhail, 159
Gaidina, Galina, 43–45, 104, 148–49
Gavrilov, Ivan, 12, 39, 48, 221
Gazarian, Suren, 49, 59, 94
Gdlian, Telman, 189–91, 213–14
Georgia, 32, 49
Gerdt, Zinovii, 94
Germany, 12, 27, 90, 109, 121, 125, 141, 202–3

Gershon, David, 98–99
GFR, 202. *See also* Germany
Gibbs, Peter, 169
Ginzburg, Aleksandr, 67, 138–39, 141
Ginzburg, Evgeniia, 54–55
GKChP, 195, 197
Gladnev, I. F, 85
Gorbachev, Mikhail, 166, 175, 179–89, 191–93, 195–97, 199, 203, 208–210, 214, 222
Gorbanevskaia, Natal'ia, 97
Gorkii, 143
Granin, Daniil, 192
Grigorenko, Piotr, 97, 141–42
Grossman, Vasilii, 55
Guardian, newspaper, 116–17
Gulag, 11, 21, 25, 27, 39, 41–42, 48–49, 52, 54–55, 63, 65, 67, 87, 110, 120, 124–27, 129, 138, 184, 218
Guseinov, Rafael, 213
Gustafsson, Ake Karl, 75
Gwertzman, Bernard, 91–92

Hanford, 169
Harriman, Averell, 115
Harvard, 101, 113, 115
Haupt, Georges, 87, 92
Hayflick, Leonard, 98–99, 113
Heeb, Fritz, 120
Hegel, Georg Friedrich, 32, 36
Hegge, Per, 65
Helsinki Accords, 147
Helsinki group, 141, 147
Henri, Ernst, 66–67
Hill, John, 170, 173
Hitler, Adolf, 125, 129, 202
Holliday, Robin, 101
Holocaust, 55

Iakir-Krasin trial, 109
Iakir, Piotr, 64, 88, 100, 108, 140
Iakovlev, Aleksandr, 188

Iakubovich, Mikhail, 53, 125–27, 129
Iampol'skii, Boris, 129
Iarin, Veniamin, 190
Il'ichev, Leonid, 28, 51, 86
India, 33
Iron Curtain, 23, 58, 75, 87, 106, 109, 116, 132
Israel, 98, 100, 107, 170, 173
Italy, 23, 87, 121
Ivanov, Nikolai, 189–91, 213–14
Izvestiia, newspaper, 42–43

Jackson-Vanik amendment, 110–11, 113, 115
Jackson, Henry, 109–110, 114–15, 132, 135
Japan, 209
Jaurès, Jean, 7
Jerusalem, 168
Jews, 35, 55, 110, 185, 219
Joravsky, David, 113

Kagarlitskii, Boris, 179
Kaiser, Robert, 65, 120
Kalinin, 43, 164, 175 43, 175. *See also* Tver
Kaluga, 74, 79–80, 82, 139
Kamenev, Lev, 5, 9, 53
Kansas City, 113
Kant, Immanuel, 32
Kapitsa, Piotr, 80
Karaganda, 127
Karelia, 43
Kariakin, Iurii, 160
Karimov, Islam, 213–14
Karmal, Babrak, 159
Karpinskii, Len, 26
Kazakhstan, 52, 127, 214–15, 217
Kazakhstanskaia Pravda, newspaper, 215
Keldysh, Mstislav, 30
Kennan, George, 115

KGB, 1, 27, 52, 59, 63–64, 66, 68, 72, 75, 78–79, 81–82, 85, 87, 90, 92–95, 99–100, 102, 109–110, 117, 120, 130–32, 135–36, 138, 140–45, 147–52, 154–55, 159–62, 164, 166–67, 179, 195, 209–210, 212, 221
Khabarovsk, 26
Khimki, 20–21
Khovrino, 148
Khrushchev, Nikita, 1, 21, 24, 26–30, 34, 40, 47–54, 57, 59, 63, 66, 72, 89, 145, 154, 165–66, 169, 184, 203, 222
Kiriushin, Y, 79
Kirov, Sergei, 5, 8–9
Kirpichnikov, Valentin, 25, 28
Kislovodsk, 195
Kissinger, Henry, 113, 115
Klechkovskii, Vsevolod, 19, 27, 169
Kliuchevoe, 43
Knizhnoe Obozrenie, journal, 192
Knopf, Alfred, 87
Kolyma, 11–12, 49
Komintern, 96
Kommunist, journal, 58, 88, 90
Komsomol, 33–35, 38
Komsomol'skaia Pravda, newspaper, 25–26
Kontinent, journal, 128, 132, 141–42
Kopelev, Lev, 116–17, 129, 141, 150
Koplenig, Johann, 87
Kopylov, S. N, 75–76
Kosovo, 222
Krasin, Iurii, 51, 81, 160
Krasin, Viktor, 108
Krasnaia Pakhra, 55
Krasnodar, 13–14, 159
Krasnyi Ural, 36
Kreisky, Bruno, 162–63
Kremlin, 10, 122, 142, 190–91, 211–12
Kriuchkov, Vladimir, 195, 209

Kuniants, Ivan, 59
Kuptsov, Valentin, 198–99
Kurchatov Institute, 176, 185
Kurgan, 171
Kursk, 190
Kutaisi, 13
Kuzovkin, Gennadii, 4
Kyiv, 26, 97–98
Kyshtym, 169, 171, 174, 177

L'Unita, newspaper, 152
Lakshin, Vladimir, 93, 95, 132–33, 147–48, 181
Lamarck, Jean-Baptiste, 16
Lapshin, Mikhail, 199, 201
Larin, Iurii, 151
Leaf, Alexander, 104
Lebed, Aleksandr, 202
Lebedev, Daniil, 29
Lenin, Vladimir, 5, 7–9, 39, 41, 48–49, 53, 89, 93, 125, 129, 147
Leningrad, 1, 5, 8, 11, 14, 25, 33, 35–36, 38, 40–41, 43–44, 51, 84–86, 94, 185
Leontovich, Mikhail, 29, 80
Lepeshinskaia, Ol'ga, 19
Lerner, Michael, 74–75, 87, 113
Lert, Raisa, 95, 130–32, 134–38, 141
Levaia Gazeta, newspaper, 200, 202
Levin, Bernard, 92
Liberty, Radio, 58, 68, 90, 102, 117, 123, 147, 154, 221
Ligachev, Egor, 189–90
Lithuania, 158
Litvinenko, Aleksandr, 205
Liu Shaoqi, 217
Liubimov, Iurii, 193
Liubishchev, Aleksandr, 24–25
Liverpool, 101
London, 2–3, 45, 65, 72, 100–101, 104, 106, 116, 123, 131, 133, 145, 164, 166, 168, 175, 181, 193, 199, 204–5, 223

Los Alamos, 172–74
Los Angeles, 113, 152, 164
Lubianka, 209–210
Luk'ianov, Anatolii, 187–88, 190, 196–97, 209
Lukashenko, Aleksandr, 215–16
Luzhkov, Iurii, 205, 211
Lysenko, Trofim, 16–26, 28–30, 48, 53, 63, 66, 74–76, 79, 87, 170, 177, 181, 192, 218, 221

Maclean, Donald, 96, 144
Madison, 172
Maiakovskii, Vladimir, 8
Maisurian, Nikolai, 25
Makarov, F. F, 85–86
Maksimov, Vladimir, 112, 116, 123, 128–29, 132, 136, 193
Mal'tsev, Aleksandr, 199
Mandel'shtam, Nadezhda, 55
Mao Zedong, 34, 217
Markstein, Elisabeth, 87
Marx, Karl, 32, 84, 129, 223
Marxism, 85, 124, 132
Marxism-Leninism, 49, 61, 85–86, 89, 122, 148
Meany, George, 115
Medunov, Sergei, 159
Medvedev, Aleksandr (Roy and Zhores's father), 1, 5-12
Medvedev, Aleksandr (Roy's son), 148
Medvedev Aleksandr (Zhores's son), 20, 78, 117, 175, 204
Medvedev, Dmitrii (president), 212
Medvedev, Dmitrii (Zhores's son), 27, 100–101, 104, 106, 204
Memorial, 185, 213
Mendel, Gregor, 17, 74
Menshevik, 52–53, 125–26
Mexico, 81
Michurin, Ivan, 17
Mill Hill, 101, 106

Minneapolis, 113
Minsk, 216
Mironov, Philip, 145
Molotov-Ribbentrop pact, 188
Molotov, Viacheslav, 39
Morgan, Thomas Hunt, 17–18
Morozov, Georgii, 80

Nader, Ralph, 172
Nashville, 171–72
National Frontiers, 72, 77
NATO, 61, 222
Nazarbayev, Nursultan, 214–15, 217
Nekrich, Aleksandr, 30, 84
Neva, journal, 25, 28
New York, 65, 74, 91–92, 97, 113, 120, 122, 147, 151, 168–70, 172
Newsweek, weelky, 68
Nikolaev, Igor, 84–85
Nixon, Richard, 109, 115
Nizhnii Tagil, 36, 190
NKVD, 1, 10–11, 41, 48–49, 151
Nobel Prize, 23, 28, 55, 78, 101, 103, 110–111, 121, 123–24, 129, 168
Novaya Zemlya, 173
Novo-Ogarevo, 197, 212
Novosibirsk, 26
Novyi mir, journal, 25, 48, 53–55, 63, 132
NTS, 90, 123, 147, 170
Nuremberg, 202
Nuzhdin, Nikolai, 28, 66

Oak Ridge, 132, 171–72, 174
Obninsk, 27–28, 63–65, 73–76, 78–79, 95, 104, 204, 223
Odessa, 94
Ogonek, weekly, 189
Ogorodnitskaia, Evgeniia, 144
Ol'shanskii, M. A, 28, 62, 66
Old Believers, 37
Oslo, 123

Ossetia, 43
Ostellino, Piero, 145, 152

Paris, 22–23, 104, 110, 120, 128, 142, 168
Pasternak, Boris, 23, 181
Pavlinchuk, Valerii, 59, 64
Pel'she, Arvid, 86
Pennsylvania, 173
Perestroika, 51, 179–80, 185, 187, 191–92, 196
Peron, Juan, 104
Perova, Galina, 88–89
Peskov, Dmitrii, 213
Petrovskii, Boris, 80
Pliushch, Leonid, 97
Poiski, journal, 136, 138
Poland, 38
Polianskii, Iurii, 192
Politburo, 85, 89, 91, 162–63, 182, 187, 189, 191, 198, 209, 214
Ponomarev, Boris, 51–52
Popov, Gavriil, 186
Portland, 115
Posev, journal, 88, 90–91
Prague, 61, 67, 92, 107
Pravda, newspaper, 9, 18, 28, 43, 88, 182
Prezent, Izaak, 17
Princeton, 168, 171
Pruchanskii, 41
Putin, Vladimir, 2–3, 209–213, 217, 219, 221–22

Rabinowitch, Alexander, 169
Rapoport, Iosif, 29
Razumova, Kseniia, 185
Reagan, Ronald, 183–84
Red Army, 6, 13, 27, 108
Reed, 179
Reiman, Iuliia Isaakovna, 6, 13, 40
Rekunkov, Aleksandr, 163
Reshetovskaia, Nalal'ia, 63–64
Reve, Karel van het, 92

Revolution, 7, 34, 48–49, 53, 91–92, 108, 124, 129, 133, 145, 159, 217
Riazan, 63–64
Riga, 26
Rinascita, newspaper, 181
Rome, 7
Romm, Mikhail, 61
Rostov-on-the-Don, 11–14
Rostropovich, Mstislav, 193
Roy, Manabendra, 7
Rozanov, I. V, 209
RSFSR, 79, 196
Russell, Bertrand, 118, 162, 173
Russia, 11, 57, 92, 122, 132, 139, 145, 168, 192, 199, 201, 204–7, 210–212, 215–16, 218
Rybakov, Anatolii, 181
Rybkin, Ivan, 199, 201–2
Ryzhkov, Vladimir, 209

Sakharov, Andrei, 2, 28–29, 46, 62, 65–69, 77–78, 80, 87, 91, 93, 101, 107, 109–113, 117–18, 121–23, 137, 143, 146, 152, 154–56, 159, 162, 166, 168, 170, 181, 184, 186–87, 190, 204, 213, 221, 223
Salt Lake City, 169
Samizdat, 23–24, 26, 54–55, 57–62, 64, 67, 69, 79, 84–85, 87–88, 90–93, 108, 116, 120, 126–31, 133, 135–36, 141–42, 145, 160, 179, 182, 221
San Francisco, 23, 102–3, 171–72
Santa Barbara, 113
Sargeant, Howland, 68
Sel'skaia Zhizn', 28–29, 62, 66
Sergeev, Vsevolod, 4
Shafarevich, Igor, 128, 132
Shakhnazarov, Georgii, 51–52, 160, 179, 209
Shalamov, Varlam, 67
Shatunovskaia, Ol'ga, 49

Shauro, Vasilii, 87
Sheffield, 73–74
Shemiakin, Mikhail, 73
Shevardnadze, Eduard, 188, 214
Shipler, David, 151
Sholokhov, Mikhail, 129–30, 145
Siberia, 26, 122, 171
Simongulian, Roland, 32, 149
Simonian
Simonov, Konstantin, 54–55, 59
Siniavskii, Andrei, 60, 92, 138
Skliar, Gennadii, 199
Smena, newspaper, 8
Smith, Hedrick, 65, 120, 146
Smith, Kathleen, 4
Smolentsev, Evgenii, 208
Snegov, Aleksei, 49
Snezhnevskii, Andrei, 78, 80
Snow, Peter, 174
Sobchak, Anatolii, 189
Sobesednik, weekly, 182
Sochi, 158
Socialism, 54, 67–68, 89, 113, 122, 124, 129, 132, 134–37, 145, 182, 199
Solzhenitsyn, Aleksandr, 2, 48, 54, 62–65, 68, 72, 80–81, 93, 101, 107, 109–113, 118, 120–29, 132–38, 141, 143, 146, 155, 161–62, 170, 184, 191, 193, 213, 219, 221–23
Sovetskaia Rossiia, newspaper, 182, 209
Soviet Union, 1–3, 12, 17, 22–23, 26, 28, 30, 45, 50–53, 60, 64–65, 68, 74–75, 78, 84, 92–93, 96–97, 99–100, 102–3, 107, 115–16, 123, 133, 135, 144, 146, 149, 156, 161, 163, 177, 181–82, 184, 188, 195, 197–98, 203–4, 212, 217, 222. *See also* USSR
Soyfer, Valery, 19
Spiegel, Der, journal, 122

Stalin, Joseph, 1, 5, 8–9, 11–12, 15–17, 20–22, 24–25, 30, 34–36, 38–41, 46–55, 57–60, 63, 66–68, 76, 84, 86, 88–89, 107–8, 112–13, 124, 145, 151, 181–82, 184, 190, 200–201, 203–4, 209–210, 218–19, 221
Stalingrad, 13, 24
Stalinism, 1, 19, 24, 28, 30, 40, 42, 47, 49–50, 53, 58, 66–68, 75, 84, 89, 121, 124, 145, 179, 184, 200, 203
Stampa, newspaper, 152
Stanford, 113
Starikov, Sergei, 145
Stepakov, Vladimir, 86–87
Stockholm, 124
Stoliarova, Natal'ia, 55
Stone, Jeremy, 113–14
Strehler, Bernhard, 72–73, 99, 113
Strukov, Nikolai, 190
Supreme Court, 39, 191, 208, 213
Suslov, Mikhail, 85–86, 88
Sverdlovsk, 26–27, 36, 38, 156, 158, 170, 172
Svetlana, 43
Sweden, 174
Switzerland, 121
Sychev, Vladimir, 156–58
Synge, Richard, 23

Taman peninsula, 13
Tamm, Igor, 28–29, 80
Tashkent, 26
Tasmaganbetov, Imangali, 215
TASS, 103, 109, 174
Tbilisi, 13–14, 32, 40, 43
Teller, Edward, 172–73
Tennessee, 171
Teplov, General, 82, 161
Ter-Akopian, Norair, 32, 148–49
Texas, 171
Thaw, the, 27, 47–48, 53, 55, 57
Tiflis, 6

Timakov, Vladimir, 76
Timiriazev Academy, 14, 16–20, 23, 25, 27
Timofeev-Resovskii, Nikolai, 27, 63, 65, 74–75, 77, 169–70
Timofeev, Valerii, 210
Tökes, Rudolf, 168
Tolmachev, Nikolai, 9, 11
Tolstoi, Ivan, 132, 221
Toronto, 113
Trapeznikov, 87
Trifonov, Iurii, 55
Trotskii, Lev, 53, 121, 161
Tsaritsyn, 38
Tsybuliatskii, Aleksei, 144, 179
Tuck, Robert L., 68
Tucker, Robert, 151, 219
Tukhachevskii, Mikhail, Marshal, 9
Tumerman, Lev, 170
Turchin, Valentin, 59, 91, 154
Tvardovskii, Aleksandr, 53–55, 59, 129, 132
Tver, 43, 175. *See also* Kalinin

Ufa, 26
Ukraine, 213, 216–17
UNESCO, 22, 103
United Kingdom, 170
United States, 18, 72–73, 75, 100, 102, 109–110, 113–14, 148, 168, 172–73, 188, 204, 207, 213–15
Urals, 26–27, 36–37, 42, 169–76
USA. *See* United States
USSR, 2, 10, 13, 20, 22, 26, 30, 33, 39, 42, 49, 56, 58–59, 61–63, 75, 77–82, 84, 87, 89, 92, 94, 96–97, 102–103, 106, 108–9, 111, 114–16, 118, 120–23, 125, 128–29, 134, 136–37, 142, 144, 146, 148, 152, 154, 159–63, 166, 168–69, 175, 181, 184, 189, 191–93, 196–98, 206, 214. *See also* Soviet Union
Ustinov, Oleg, 4
Uzbekistan, 190, 214

Vanik, Charles, 110
Vartazarova, Liudmila, 199
Vasiukov, 41
VASKhNIL, 17–19, 21, 28, 62
Vavilov, Nikolai, 17, 25–26, 75
Vekhi, 128
Vienna, 71, 87, 162
Vitkovskii, Dmitrii, 129
Vladikavkaz, 43
Vladimov, Georgii, 139–41, 150
Volgograd, 24
Vorontsov, Nikolai, 193
Voznesenskii, Aleksandr, 36
Vyborg, 43
Vzgliad, show, 183

Washington Post, newspaper, 65, 91–92, 120, 154, 172
Watergate scandal, 115
Watson, James Dewey, 21
Windscale, 169
Wolstenholme, 73

Xi Jinping, 217

Yale, 113
Yalta, 19
Yeltsin, Boris, 185, 187–88, 195–96, 201–7, 210, 216
Yugoslavia, 33, 205

Zeit, Die, newspaper, 111
Zelenograd, 190
Zhebrak, Anton, 18, 25
Zhoravsky, David, 87
Zhou Enlai, 217
Zhukovskii, Piotr, 17–20, 25
Ziman, John, 77
Zinov'ev, Aleksandr, 193
Zinoviev, Grigorii, 5, 9, 53
Ziuganov, Gennadii, 201–2
Znamia, journal, 181
Zorina, Dora, 94
Zuckerman, Boris, 77
Zurich, 121

www.ingramcontent.com/pod-product-compliance
Lightning Source LLC
Chambersburg PA
CBHW072042160426
43197CB00014B/2592